American Trails Series
XI

ONATE'S MARCH INTO THE NEW MEXICAN COUNTRY
By Charles M. Russell. Courtesy Amon Carter Museum, Ft. Worth, Texas

THE ROAD TO CALIFORNIA

The Search for a
Southern Overland Route
1540-1848

by
HARLAN HAGUE

THE ARTHUR H. CLARK COMPANY
Glendale, California 1978

To Carol

Contents

Illustrations

Preface

Among the most exciting stories about western America are the histories of trails and the journals of trailmakers. Particularly absorbing are the narratives of the earliest expeditions to Oregon and California, the stuff of adventure and empire and the great American obsession with being first. Yet, nowhere in all this literature is the complete story told of the first overland route to the Pacific Ocean coast of what is now the United States. The first non-Indian to reach the coast by a land route was neither English nor American; he was Spanish. The year was 1774. The trail ran not beside the Platte River through the central plains, but along the Gila River through the southwestern deserts. There were many variations of the latter trail, the last not established until 1848. It is that story, the beginnings of the southern overland route to California, that this book tells.

Unlike northern trails, the southern route was never a single, well-defined path connecting two points. Anza's route originated in Sonora. The Old Spanish Trail crossed southern Colorado, Utah and Nevada. The trappers' trail that ran beside the Gila River from western New Mexico to the Colorado River subsequently was followed by General Kearny's Army of the West. The wagon road pioneered by Lieutenant-Colonel Philip St. George Cooke and the Mormon Battalion dipped southward into present-day Mexico before turning back toward Tucson and the Gila. Though Cooke's road eventually became the most-heavily traveled route through the Southwest, thereby symbolizing an end in the search for a trail to California, it was never used to the complete exclusion of alternative paths.

Certainly, there was no "Gila Trail," as the term is commonly used in western literature. The title is misleading. It has fostered the myth that the southern route to California was a solitary trail, running along the Gila River.[1] The route of the Army of the West might qualify as a "Gila Trail," but Kearny's route never became popular. Cooke's road followed the river only a fraction of that trail's length. Anza's routes touched the Gila even less often. The Old Spanish Trail touched it not at all. Argonauts of 1849 and the 1850s who traveled the variations of the southern route did not call them the Gila Trail, so far as we know. Some spoke of "Cook's route," "Major Graham's trail," "Cook's trail,"

[1] The myth of a single southern route to California called the "Gila Trail" persists. That no such single "Gila Trail" existed can be illustrated with a few examples. The examples indicate the confusion as well as the myth. Rufus Kay Wyllys believed that the trapper's trail along the Gila, later followed by Kearny, was the "Gila Trail" and wrote optimistically that it "provided a fairly good route clear across the country." *Arizona: The History of a Frontier State* (Phoenix, 1950), 75, 95, 268. George Ruhlen's "Gila Trail" is the same as Kearny's route, all the way from Santa Fé to San Diego! *See* Ruhlen's "Kearny's Route from the Rio Grande to the Gila River," *N.M. Hist. Rev.,* XXXII (July 1957), 215-17. The title of Benjamin Butler Harris' reminiscence, edited by Richard H. Dillon, is *The Gila Trail: The Texas Argonauts and the California Gold Rush* (Norman, 1960). A glance at a map on pages 26-27, titled "The Gila Trail" in the list of illustrations (xv) shows how little of Harris's route followed the Gila River. Odie B. Faulk considers "Cooke's Wagon Road" and "The Gila Trail" one and the same. *See* his *Land of Many Frontiers: A History of the American Southwest* (New York, 1968), 136, and *Tombstone: Myth and Reality* (New York, 1972), 9, and *Destiny Road: The Gila Trail and the Opening of the Southwest* (New York, 1973), 60. Ferol Egan is more accurate when he differentiates between "Cooke's Wagon Road" and the "Gila Trail," the latter referring only to that portion of the route that actually paralleled the river. *See* Egan's *The El Dorado Trail: The Story of the Gold Rush Routes Across Mexico* (New York, 1971), 60, 111, 135, 157, 160. Most writers who use the term, however, equate Gila Trail with Cooke's route. (Full citations of any sources listed in the footnotes may be found in the Bibliography at the end of this volume.)

"Cook's road," "Colonel Cooke's trail," and also "Cook's wagon route." Others gave no particular name to the paths they followed. The term, Gila Trail, has become popular only in recent years when some historians appeared to need a solid title for the southern route. The selection of "Gila Trail" to fill that need was unfortunate.

Until now, the story of the southern route has been scattered in bits and pieces throughout the literature of the period. The closest attempt thus far to treat the southern route as an integrated topic is Jack D. Forbes's "The Development of the Yuma Route before 1846." [2] Due to its briefness and limited scope, however, the article falls short of a complete analysis of the southern route. As the title indicates, Dr. Forbes confined his study to the trails that converged and crossed the Colorado River at Yuma, thereby excluding the attempts to open a direct connection between New Mexico and California, a trail which would have crossed the river north of Yuma. Yet, the stories of Escalante, Armijo, Wolfskill and the northern travels of Garcés are essential to an understanding of the history of the southern route. Ending his study at 1846, furthermore, Dr. Forbes did not include the marches of Kearny's Army of the West, Cooke's Mormon Battalion or Graham's command. But the story of the development of the southern route is not complete without these three marches.

Attempting to fill an empty space in western literature, this book then is concerned with the search for and use of the southern overland route to California from the earliest Spanish penetration into the present United States Southwest to 1849, just before the country was inundated, comparatively speaking, by California-bound argonauts. Spe-

---

[2] *Calif. Hist. Soc. Qtly.*,XLIII (June 1964), 99-118.

cifically, it is perhaps easier to state what the study is not
than to say what it is. It is not a history of the Spanish
Borderlands, though there is much history of the southwestern United States and northern Mexico here.[3] Neither
is the Santa Fé Trail given thorough treatment, though the
fabled road constituted a vital link in the trail between the
United States and California.[4] Instead, the story is confined
largely to the development of the trails in the present states
of New Mexico and Arizona and to a lesser extent in
California and northern Mexico.

The study often notes, but does not dwell on, hardship,
though travelers suffered extreme hardships. Every diarist
tells of thirst, hunger, rough country, heat, discomfort,
fatigue and the unending search for water and grass. But
once stated, it can be assumed that all travelers experienced
the same hardships, and a repetition in the narrative is
unnecessary, indeed tedious, unless repeating adds somehow
to the story. On the other hand, a lack of suffering, being the
exception, is worthy of mention.

The story of the southern route is high drama. It is filled
with examples of courage, endurance, fulfillment and not
a little tragedy and failure. It is a story about people. This
book constitutes both an attempt to make a coherent whole
of the experiences of those generations of path-followers and
bystanders and an introduction to a fascinating era.

The debts accumulated in the preparation of the book run
back too far and too long to detail here. I must nevertheless

[3] For a rather exhaustive bibliography on the Spanish Borderlands before the
Mexican Revolution, *see* John Francis Bannon, *The Spanish Borderlands Frontier,
1513-1821* (New York, 1970). A shorter list of titles is in *Journal of the West,* VIII
(Jan. 1969).

[4] For a bibliography of Santa Fé Trail literature, *see* John K. Rittenhouse, *The
Santa Fé Trail: A Historical Bibliography* (Albuquerque, 1971).

express by gratitude specifically to Russell R. Elliott for his scholarship, R. Coke Wood for his inspiration, and, for so many kindnesses, the good people of Chastleton in England's north Cotswold Hills where the first draft of the manuscript was written. For generous assistance, I wish to thank the personnel at the Pacific Center for Western Studies at University of The Pacific, the Bancroft Library, the Huntington Library, the Bodleian Library and the British Museum. Special thanks go to Robert A. Clark of The Arthur H. Clark Company who was determined to produce a high quality book in spite of the author's impatience.

HARLAN HAGUE
Stockton, California

CHAPTER I

An Ancient Land

The Southwest was the first "known" region of what is now the United States, and the southwestern trails certainly were older than the other western trails, at least from the viewpoint of use by white people.[1] It would be meaningless to say that the trails to California that ran through northern Mexico and the southwestern part of the present United States were unique. Most phenomena are unique in some way or another. Perhaps it would be safer to say simply that the southwestern trails were different from the other trails to the far reaches of the American West. The climate and terrain of the arid Southwest[2] presented hardships to a degree not experienced by most travelers of the northern trails. On the other hand, while Indians along northern trails

---

[1] Europeans were reading about the region as early as the sixteenth century in published works. Cabeza de Vaca told about his travels in his *Naufragios,* an edition of which appeared in 1542 at Zamora and another in 1555 at Valladolid. A history of New Mexico in the form of a book-length epic poem, Gaspar de Villagra's *Historia de la Nueva Mexico,* was published at Alcalá in 1610, just three years after the landing of the first English colonists at Jamestown and ten years before the Pilgrims stepped ashore at Plymouth. Eusebio Francisco Kino, s.j., *Kino's Historical Memoir,* trans. and ed. by Herbert Eugene Bolton (Berkeley, 1948), I, 27. Villagra was with the Oñate expedition to New Mexico. *Also see* Hubert Howe Bancroft, *History of Arizona and New Mexico, 1530-1888,* Vol. XVII of *The Works of Hubert Howe Bancroft* (San Francisco, 1889), 112.

[2] There is no single term suitable to delimit the region covered by this study. The "Spanish Borderlands" designation is not appropriate because Texas and Florida are not included. According to twentieth-century boundaries, the study encompasses the United States Southwest and northern Chihuahua and Sonora. In the context of the period studied, the best term is simply "northern Mexico." Various geographical designations are used in the text, such as Arizona, New Mexico, northern Mexico, American Southwest, and the reader should not be confused.

were largely hostile or indifferent to white travelers, Indians of the Southwest, with some notable exceptions, welcomed whites.

The land was and is one of contrasts. The elevation ranges from sea level at the mouth of the Colorado River and nearby deserts to highlands in the north of 8,000 feet, with many peaks in the central and northern parts of the region rising above 10,000 feet. The face of the land varies from the arid and semi-arid country that dominates the landscape to forested mountains in the north. The climate runs the gamut from blistering desert sun to the chilling snows of the high mountains.

Though the contrasts are quite visible, aridity is the dominant characteristic.[3] It is in this land of little rain that the story of the search for a southern route to California largely takes place. The average annual precipitation of the southwestern region is around twelve inches, with six to eight inches in the deserts. Yuma receives less than five inches. Throughout most of the area, there is too little rain to support the growing of crops without irrigation, but usually enough to support grazing. The threat of drouth, however, is ever-present, and more than once cattle and sheep have suffered when the rains have failed to come. At other times, the scanty annual rainfall has come all at once, causing the often-destructive flash floods common to the region. In spite of the extremes, precipitation over the years has been sufficient to prevent the land from becoming a sterile desert of shifting sands, but not so much that its predominantly tropical nature has been altered.

Life in the arid country has shown an amazing capability for adaptation. Plant life has come to terms with the desert

---

[3] Ross Calvin's *Sky Determines* (Albuquerque, 1965) is an interesting discussion of southwestern climate as the decisive factor in the development of the region.

by becoming drouth-resistant and water-storing or by developing a cycle of life keyed to the infrequent, short rains. As if jolted to life by the moisture, desert plants experience a rapid growth, mature quickly, produce seeds, then die. Also adapting to the peculiar demands of the land and climate of the Southwest were the various animal species, not the least of which was man himself.

Man is known to have inhabited the American Southwest for 15,000 years and perhaps 20,000 years. These nomadic ice-age hunters eventually gave way to settled communities that set the pattern for aboriginal life in the region. The introduction of corn probably made the difference.[4] By the first century A.D., it was being grown in southeastern Arizona by the already long-established Cochise people and a short time later by the Anasazi, or Basketmakers, in the four-corners country where the states of Arizona, New Mexico, Colorado and Utah meet.

The Hohokam, descendants of the Cochise people, were farmers in the area of the confluence of the Salt and Gila rivers. A peace-loving, democratic society, the Hohokam practiced extensive irrigation. By 700 A.D., their water works included hundreds of miles of intricate canal systems. Some of the waterways were as wide as twenty-five feet and as deep as fifteen feet. A single complex paralleling the Salt River contained 150 miles of canals. The accomplishments of these contemporaries of Mayas were not limited to agriculture. The Hohokam, for example, developed an etching process around the year 1000 A.D., hundreds of years before chemical etching was first known in Europe.

---

[4] Lesley Byrd Simpson makes a fascinating and convincing case for corn as the first and greatest agent for reducing nomadic peoples to a state of "civilized immobility." See *Many Mexicos* (Berkeley, 1967), chapter 2. *See also* Alan Linn, "Corn, the New World's Secret Weapon and the Builder of its Civilizations," *Smithsonian*, IV (Aug. 1973), 58-65.

Descended from the Hohokam are the Papagos who live in the deserts of southern Arizona and the Pimas who live farther north, notably along the Gila River where generations of Spaniards, Mexicans and Americans found them. The word, "Hohokam," in fact, is a Pima word meaning "Those who have gone." Also probably descended from the Hohokam are the Yumas and related tribes who live principally on the Colorado River.

The culture of the previously-mentioned Anasazi was marked by skills in basketmaking and architecture. They built huge multi-storied pueblos of stone in villages of several thousand inhabitants. The largest of these great structures, Pueblo Bonito in northwestern New Mexico's Chaco Canyon, was five stories high and had over 800 rooms. It could have housed well over 1000 people. Pueblo Bonito was the largest multiple-family dwelling in the United States until 1882 when a larger one was built in New York City. The Indians completed their apartment building about 900 years earlier.

The Anasazi, or Pueblos as they might more properly be called by the thirteenth century, gradually moved southward from their homes in the four corners country. Doubtless, they were driven by years of drouth, but perhaps also by incursions from the north by marauding Apaches and Navajos. One Pueblo group migrated southwestward to live peacefully among the Hohokam, later to drift eastward. Other groups settled in the northeastern corner of Arizona and in the Rio Grande country in northern New Mexico.

Navajos and Apaches also found lives in the Southwest. Though the Navajos did not give up their pillaging completely, they gradually assumed a more settled existence with herds of cattle and sheep. The Apaches, originally hunters, turned parasitic, living on the spoils of their raids against the Pueblos.

It was the descendants of these same Pueblos whom
Spaniards would visit later at Zuñi, Santa Fé and Oraibe.
And it was these same Apaches and Navajos, who came
first to the Southwest as invaders, that would provide the
strongest resistance to the successive waves of white-skinned
conquistadores.[5]

White people, even the earliest Spaniards, opened few
new trails as they moved into and through the Southwest.
There is ample evidence to show that trails in the region
were extensive and well-traveled long before the appearance
of Europeans. There seems to have been a regular trade
among Indians of the interior, even as far east as New
Mexico and beyond, and California coastal tribes. Probably the most sought-after commodity by the inland tribes
were sea shells from the Pacific coast and Gulf of California.
The desire for the treasured shells, indeed, appears to have
been the prime factor in the development of the inter-
tribal trade. Shells have been found at archaeological sites
throughout the region, as far removed from the coast as
Utah and New Mexico. Pacific coastal and mountain Indians contributed other products to the commerce: steatite,
asphaltum, acorns and deerskins. From the interior of Mexico came live macaw birds and from southern Arizona,
pottery. Indians of New Mexico offered blankets, a trade
good that was still valued by Californians as late as the
second quarter of the nineteenth century.[6] Spaniards who

[5] The rather narrow topic of this study precludes any substantial treatment of a
clash-of-cultures theme, however interesting. On that subject, *see* Edward H. Spicer,
Cycles of Conquest, 1533-1960 (Tucson, 1962), and Elizabeth A. H. John, *Storms
Brewed in Other Men's Worlds: The Confrontation of Indians, Spanish, and French
in the Southwest, 1540-1795* (College Station, Texas, 1975). Unfortunately, John's
Southwest includes only New Mexico and Texas.

[6] For an overview of Indian trade in the Southwest from pre-history to the early
seventeenth century, *see* Forbes, "Yuma Route," 99-102, from which the brief account
here is largely extracted.

later ventured into this "unknown" land benefited immeasurably from the knowledge of these native merchants who were hired to guide the explorers over the well-known trade routes.

The earliest explorations northward from settlements in New Spain were motivated by a search for a water route through the American land mass and a continuing thirst for riches. Columbus's failure to find a water passage and the subsequent failure to locate the link in the region of New Spain did not diminish the expectation of finding it. Indeed, the existence of the rumored Strait of Anian gradually became generally accepted as fact rather than speculation. As interest in the north grew, all sorts of rumors about that mysterious country were rife in the Spanish settlements. When one begins to appreciate the Spaniards' total ignorance of the geography of the north, coupled with the hope of discovering rich cities and the fabled strait, it becomes easier to understand how explorers could believe the fantastic tales they heard of that country.[7]

Chief among the rumor-mongers was Alvar Nuñez Cabeza de Vaca. The only known survivors of Pánfilo de Narvaez's disastrous expedition to Florida in 1528, Nuñez and his three companions arrived in Culiacan in 1536 after wandering for eight years along the Caribbean coast and in northern Mexico. Whether their route led them into present New Mexico and Arizona is still a matter of debate. Some observers place their wanderings south of today's international boundary; others credit the castaways with being the first non-Indians to see the United States Southwest.[8]

---

[7] For a thorough treatment of the Northern Mystery, *see* Hubert Howe Bancroft, *History of the Northwest Coast, 1543-1800*, vol. XXVII of *Works* (1884), chapters I-III.

[8] Until the nineteenth century, it was widely held that Nuñez's party had entered the Southwest. Later historians disagreed. Bancroft, for example, does not grant

Nuñez's own account of the Spaniards' ordeal throws little light on the route they followed. His narrative is at best puzzling, and at worst virtually incoherent.[9]

One interesting, indisputable fact emerges from this otherwise confusing journal. Nuñez and his party did not wander aimlessly in a wilderness. Nuñez was no pathfinder. The trails were already there. In his narrative, Nuñez directly mentions trails or roads seventeen times and implies travel over a defined path in many other passages. The little party probably had Indian guides and escorts throughout. Furthermore, the trails must have been well known to the Indians. Only once in his narrative does Nuñez mention that water was carried along. And he adds that their Indian companions on that occasion objected strenuously to taking that particular trail. This could only mean that potable water was found daily on all other occasions.[10] In the dry

them this honor, believing their route to have been south of the international boundary. *See Arizona and New Mexico,* 15. Adolph and Fanny Bandelier agree with Bancroft, though with less certainty. *See* Alvar Nuñez Cabeza de Vaca, *The Journey of Alvar Nuñez Cabeza de Vaca and his Companions from Florida to the Pacific, 1528-1536,* trans. by Fanny Bandelier, ed. by A. F. Bandelier (New York, 1905), xix. (Subsequent reference to this document is to "Nuñez.")

Herbert Eugene Bolton changed his opinion on the issue. In a 1925 publication, Bolton appears to have accepted the view that Nuñez did not enter New Mexico or Arizona, essentially agreeing with the route described by the Bandeliers. *See* the map facing the title page in Bolton's *Spanish Exploration in the Southwest, 1542-1706* (New York, 1925). In 1949, however, Bolton placed Nuñez's westward route farther north and concluded that these "four castaways were the real European pioneers of the great Southwest. First to see New Mexico and Arizona." *Coronado on the Turquoise Trail: Knight of Pueblos and Plains* (Albuquerque, 1949), 10. Bolton may well be correct in tracing Nuñez's route, but he errs in one respect. One of the party, Estevanico, was not a European; he was a black African.

Perhaps the strongest case for Nuñez as the discoverer of the United States Southwest is made by Cleve Hallenbeck who has the Spaniards following the Gila River in Arizona before turning southward toward the Spanish settlements. *The Journey and Route of Alvar Nuñez, Cabeza de Vaca* (Glendale, 1940), 222, 226.

9 It seemed that Nuñez, as Bandelier commented, "in consequence of long isolation and constant intercourse with people of another speech, had lost touch with his native tongue." Nuñez, *Journey of Alvar Nuñez,* xxii.

10 Hallenbeck, *Journey and Route of Alvar Nuñez,* 107-8.

season, only certain trails would satisfy this requirement;
therefore, the Indians must have known enough trails to
discriminate among those that had water and those that did
not.

The significance of the castaways' wanderings lies not in
their route, but in their stories of rich cities and unknown
lands beyond the northern frontier. Nuñez and his companions volunteered that they had never actually seen the
cities, but had received all their information secondhand
from Indians. That fine point was of no importance to the
eager conquistadores who had been looking in all directions
for new sources of treasure and adventure since the subjugation of the Aztec empire.

Among those who were intrigued by Nuñez's tales was
Don Antonio de Mendoza, the viceroy of New Spain. The
enthusiastic Mendoza shortly sent out a small expedition to
confirm the stories. The party was led by Fray Marcos de
Niza, a Franciscan who had served God and King with
Pizarro in Peru and in Nicaragua before coming to Mexico. Marcos was accompanied by the black slave, Estevanico,
who had been with Nuñez during his wanderings.

Traveling northward in the spring of 1539, Marcos and
his companions found the Indians friendly and eager to tell
the strangers about far-off peoples who lived in magnificent
cities. Estevanico was sent ahead to scout the way and apparently was welcomed everywhere he went. Word eventually
reached Marcos, however, that the black man had been
killed upon reaching the fabulous, rich city of Cibola. Fearing to enter the town lest he not survive to tell what he
had seen, the padre viewed Cibola from a distant hilltop.
Satisfying himself from this vantage point that everything
he had heard about the richness of the land was true, Marcos
formally took possession of the country, which he named

El Nueva Reyno de San Francisco, and departed. Thus
Marcos described his journey.

Controversy continues to swirl about the pretensions of
Fray Marcos, as it did during his own time. The debate
centers not so much on his route as on the northernmost
extent of his penetration and whether he really saw what he
said he saw. As in Nuñez's case, the controversy eventually
comes around to the question of whether Fray Marcos and
Estevanico should be credited with the discovery [11] of New
Mexico and Arizona, a question which has been amply
argued elsewhere.[12] The evidence indicates that Marcos
believed the wonderful tales Indians told him and that he
had verified them to his satisfaction from his hilltop viewpoint. If this were not so, he would not have been so im-
prudent to accompany the subsequent Coronado expedition
as its guide, thereby risking the wrath of a whole army.
Patently, he expected Coronado to confirm his reports.

---

[11] Pimas, Apaches, Navajos and numerous other tribes that inhabited northern
Mexico would not agree that Nuñez, Marcos, Coronado or any other Spaniard "discovered" their lands. The term as used here simply means the first viewing by a
non-Indian.

[12] Some of Fray Marcos' detractors hold that he never got north of the present
international boundary, others that he did not have time to cover all the ground that
he says he covered. It has been suggested that those who received his report inter-
preted it too liberally or that the viceroy, already determined to explore northward,
simply wanted Marcos to furnish the "proof" necessary to justify a large expedition.
See Warren A. Beck, *New Mexico: A History of Four Centuries* (Norman, 1962),
44.

In defense of Fray Marcos, Adolph F. Bandelier points out that the friar's critics
often do not distinguish between what Marcos says he saw and what he says he was
told. *Contributions to the History of the Southwestern Portion of the United States*
(Cambridge, 1890), 106-8. Bancroft believed that Marcos did indeed enter Arizona
and reached the region of Zuñi in west-central New Mexico. He attributes Marcos'
exaggerations to his zeal for spiritual conquest of the new land and an accompanying fear that the field might be abandoned. *Arizona and New Mexico,* 34. If the
friar, in fact, had lied about his experiences, it would seem that he would have been
punished by the Order of Saint Francis, which was then at its peak of moral and
intellectual growth in New Spain. There is no record of any punishment or reprimand of any sort. Bandelier, *Contributions,* 106-8.

Whatever the truth of the matter, Viceroy Mendoza was satisfied and directed the governor of Nueva Galicia, Francisco Vasquez de Coronado, to prepare a major expedition to exploit Marcos' findings. Believing Cibola to be near the sea, the viceroy fitted out a fleet to co-operate with the land force, with orders to touch the gulf coast as often as possible to provision the army.[13] Commanded by Hernando de Alarcón, the fleet eventually did reach the mouth of the Colorado River, which Alarcón named the Buena Guia. Boats sent up the Colorado in late summer 1539 might have reached the confluence with the Gila, though this has not been confirmed. Hearing no word of the army's advance, the commander left letters at the head of the gulf and departed. The letters actually were found later by a party sent out by Coronado.[14] Alarcón's ships never did make direct contact with the land column, therefore figure no more in the story of Coronado's expedition.

Meanwhile, the land expedition got underway. A scout-

[13] George P. Hammond and Agapito Rey, *Narratives of the Coronado Expedition, 1540-1542* (Albuquerque, 1940), 9: Instructions to Alarcón, 117-23.

[14] With a force of twenty-five men, Melchoir Díaz in 1540 marched from northern Sonora to the Gulf of California and on to the mouth of the Gila River. The Spaniards named the river the Tizón or Firebrand River after observing the generally friendly Indians carrying firebrands to warm themselves. Hammond and Rey, *Coronado Expedition*, 20-21. Bancroft disagrees, saying that the name, Rio del Tizón, was given to the Colorado River and that the party probably did not reach the Gila though it might have passed the present international boundary. *Arizona and New Mexico*, 39. Father Zárate Salmerón, writing about Oñate's journey to the Colorado in 1604, noted that the Colorado at its mouth was called the Rio del Tizón. *Relaciones,* trans. by Alicia Ronstadt Milich (Albuquerque, 1966), 66.

Probably with the help of Indians who had seen Alarcón, Díaz found the letters. From that moment, bad luck plagued the Spaniards. After some difficulty with the Yumas, the soldiers crossed the Colorado River on rafts and started down the Lower California peninsula. Encountering lava beds, they were forced to turn back to try to return to Sonora as they had come. Díaz never made it. He died of a wound that was accidentally self-inflicted while trying to spear a dog that was harrying the expedition's sheep. Hammond and Rey, *Coronado Expedition*, 21: Castañeda, 210-12, 231-32.

ing party of fifteen men under Melchoir Diaz and Juan de Zaldivar late in 1539 probably reached the valley of the Gila River before turning back. Coronado himself set out in April 1540 with a small advance force of seventy-five horsemen, twenty-five foot soldiers and some Indians.[15] The ponderous main body of approximately 300 Spaniards and 1,300 Indian allies was ordered to follow at a more leisurely pace.[16]

The advance force, guided by Fray Marcos, soon learned the truth of Cibola. Exhausted and near starvation by the time they reached the Gila River, the Spaniards turned eastward and found Cibola, probably the village called Hawikuh, located a few miles southwest of the present-day Zuñi pueblo. Within a few days, the soldiers subdued Cibola and other nearby pueblos. Surveying the heralded Seven Cities, of which they were now the masters, the Spaniards were stunned. There were no riches to be seen. They found instead a collection of small villages inhabited by poor farmers. The disappointed soldiers fell on Fray Marcos whom they felt was responsible for all their suffering. The disgraced padre soon left the expedition and returned to Mexico.

[15] Hammond and Rey, *Coronado Expedition,* 15: Castañeda, 206; Letter of Coronado to Mendoza, Aug. 3, 1540, 162-63; Traslado de las Nuevas, 179; Jaramillo's Narrative, 295. Bancroft, *Arizona and New Mexico,* 37-39.

[16] For more detail on the composition of the force and descriptions of clothing and weapons, *see* Hammond and Rey, *Coronado Expedition,* 7-8. It is interesting that the muster rolls show the horses that each person took along. The listing makes a distinction between horses (caballos), usually stallions at this time, and mares (yeguas). Only two mares are noted. It is not recorded whether the two mares returned to New Spain at the conclusion of the expedition, but even if they had not, it would still have been biologically impossible for the western plains to have been stocked with the strays from the Coronado expedition, a romantic notion that still survives. *See* Bolton, *Coronado on the Turquoise Trail,* 68. More likely, the wild horse herds owe their beginnings to strays from later Spanish settlements on the northern frontier. "Strays" often were numerous when Indian raiders were not able to consolidate their booty in time to prevent loss of some of the stampeded animals.

From Cibola, Coronado dispatched exploring parties to try to locate the rich cities that he still believed existed somewhere in the vicinity of the pueblos. Don Pedro de Tovar was sent to the Hopi villages in northeastern Arizona. Soon after, Lopez de Cárdenas was ordered westward to locate a great river that the Hopis had described to Tovar. Cárdenas and his twelve companions became the first Europeans to see the awesome Grand Canyon of the Colorado River. Neither Tovar nor Cárdenas found any treasure, but their journeys can be seen as unconscious probes in the later search for a trail from New Mexico to California.

Coronado sent another party eastward under Hernando de Alvarado to investigate the tales he had heard about a region called Cicuye. En route, the Spaniards visited the mesa-top pueblo of Acoma, which Alvarado called one of the strongest pueblos he had ever seen. Arriving at the Rio Grande, the Spanish found a broad valley dotted with towns. The inhabitants were friendly, and Alvarado sent word back to Coronado at Cibola, recommending the valley, called Tiguex, as the site for their winter quarters. The region was pleasant indeed and eventually would become the center of Spanish settlement in New Mexico. Completing his journey to Cicuye, probably located in northeastern New Mexico at the edge of the plains, Alvarado saw great herds of buffalo. He was more intrigued with the stories told him about an even more distant country called Quivira where there were rich cities and great stores of gold and silver. With this promising report, Alvarado's party returned to Tiguex where Coronado, following Alvarado's suggestion, had set up winter quarters for the expedition.

The Spaniards spent two unhappy, unproductive winters in Tiguex. The Indians at first welcomed the strangers to their villages, but the soldiers soon became overbearing. The Spaniards made unreasonable demands of their hosts, requisitioning lodgings, blankets, food and clothing that the poor Indians could not spare. The exasperated natives finally rebelled, for which they were brutally chastised by the soldiers. From that time, the Indians became virtual captives in their own towns and the pattern of encroachment on the rights and lands of Indians by Europeans began to take shape in New Mexico.

The Spaniards were no more successful in their search for treasure. A full-scale expedition to Quivira found only the populous, but poor, province of the Wichita Indians, probably in present Kansas. The whole story, in fact, had been a hoax. On behalf of the people of Cicuye, the expedition's guide, an Indian the soldiers called "the Turk," was to have led the Spaniards astray on the plains where they would exhaust themselves and their supplies and thus fall easy prey to the pueblo Indians on their return. The Turk was promptly put to death, and the disillusioned army turned back.

In the spring of 1542, all the tales of riches having proven false, Coronado terminated the expedition and the army departed Tiguex for New Spain. At the Gila River, the Spaniards met reinforcements and a supply train. This prompted a number of gentlemen adventurers to petition the commander for a return to the northern explorations, but the great body of the army would listen to no suggestions for arresting their speedy journey to the south. By this time, Coronado had almost lost control of the force and would have been powerless to reverse the retreat even if he had wished to do so. Reaching Culiacan in June 1542, the once proud army melted away gradually until the remnants, about 100 men, arrived in Mexico with Coronado in mid-summer.[17]

---

[17] Bancroft, *Arizona and New Mexico*, 68.

It is understandable that fame did not come immediately to Coronado. The expedition had set out in search of treasure; it found none. Therefore, it was a disappointment, and the general was severely criticized for his conduct of the enterprise. Viceroy Mendoza remained his friend, however, and never failed to defend him.[18] The immediate result of the expedition was that it laid to rest, for a time at least, the widely-held belief and hope that there were riches to be found in the northern lands. The expedition gained instead valuable knowledge of the geography and inhabitants of the country, treasure that was put to no use.

For the next half century, Spanish penetration into the upper frontier regions was sporadic and, with the exception of the expedition led by Don Antonio Espejo, of little consequence in the development of trails to California. A small party of friars and soldiers under Fray Augustin Rodríguez and Sanchez Chamuscado probably reached the pueblos of Tiguex in 1581 in a search for a reported superior Indian civilization. Soon after the soldiers left the padres to return to New Spain, rumors circulated in the settlements that they had been killed.[19]

To investigate the fate of their brothers, Franciscan authorities dispatched an expedition of about fourteen soldiers and some Indian servants under the leadership of Padre Bernardino Beltran and Espejo, an adventurous, rich citizen who had offered to finance the undertaking and to serve as the military leader.[20]

Reaching Tiguex in the fall of 1582, the nature of the expedition soon changed. During the course of explorations and visits to pueblos, Espejo learned that the padres indeed

18 Hammond and Rey, *Coronado Expedition*, 28-31.
19 Bancroft, *Arizona and New Mexico*, 75-79.   20 *Ibid.*, 80-81.

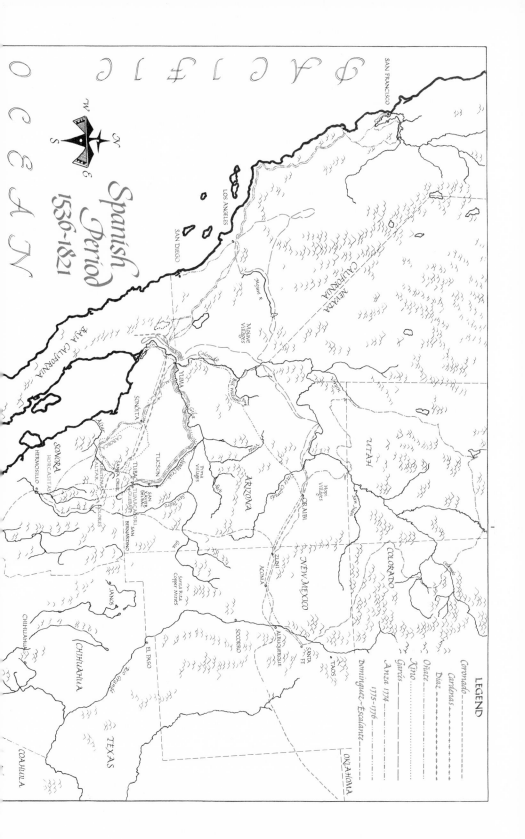

PACIFIC OCEAN

N
W · E
S

Spanish Period 1536-1821

BAJA CALIFORNIA

SAN FRANCISCO

LOS ANGELES

SAN DIEGO

Mojave R.

Mojave Villages

Colorado

NEVADA

CALIFORNIA

Virgin

UTAH

San Juan

Colorado

COLORADO

Hopi Villages

ORAIBI

ZUNI

ACOMA

NEW MEXICO

TAOS

SANTA FE

ALBUQUERQUE

SOCORRO

EL PASO

Rio Grande

TEXAS

COAHUILA

CHIHUAHUA

CHIHUAHUA

JANOS

Santa Rita Copper Mines

SONORA

HERMOSILLO

HORCASITAS

SONOITA

ARIVACA

CABORCA

SARIC

TUMACACORI

CALABAZAS

SANTA CRUZ

GUEVAVI

SAN BERNARDINO

ALTAR

DOLORES

TUBAC

TUCSON

SAN XAVIER DEL BAC

Pima Villages

YUMA

Gila

Salt

Colorado

Bill Williams

ARIZONA

LEGEND

Coronado ————
Cárdenas ·-·-·-·-
Díaz ++++++++
Kino ~~~~~~~~
Oñate ————
Garcés ————
Anza 1774 ————
1775-1776 ————
Domínguez-Escalante ————

OKLAHOMA

had been killed. He also was told about Coronado's visits and, in fact, found at Zuñi three Christian Indians who had accompanied the Coronado expedition and had remained when the army departed. The Indians told Espejo about a great lake to the west whose bank was well-populated by people who had great amounts of gold. Though Father Beltran objected that their mission was not to seek treasure, Espejo with nine soldiers, the Christian Indians and 150 local Indians set out to locate the great lake. The padres remained, determined to return to Nueva Vizcaya.[21]

Espejo's party met with mixed success. Led eventually by Hopi guides, through whose land the early-day argonauts passed, the Spaniards actually found mines in the mountainous region north of present Prescott, Arizona. Here they also heard of a great river to the west, undoubtedly the Colorado, but they did not visit it. Espejo returned to Zuñi just before Father Beltran and his companions set out for the south. Espejo stayed to explore further in northern New Mexico.

As the explorations progressed, the Indians' resistance, or the Spaniards' brutality, or both, hardened. The Indians increasingly refused the Spaniards' demands for food. The soldiers responded by "punishing" the Indians. Homes and maize fields were burned, but the Indians remained uncowed. On one occasion, angry Indians attacked the Spaniards so vigorously that a member of the expedition begged God to "preserve us for His holy service and keep us under His protection, for we are really in distress." The Spaniards decided that they would have to set an example. The next time they were refused food, they shot and garroted sixteen Indians and burned alive others who had hidden themselves

[21] *Ibid.,* 87.

in a building.[22] When hostility continued to grow, Espejo returned to Mexico in late summer, 1583.

Interest in the conquest and settlement of the northern frontier country increased. The reports of Espejo and Father Beltran encouraged those who saw great prospects for mineral wealth and colonizing ventures there. The mysterious and rich settlements to be found on the great lake and river in the west had to be investigated. The expectations of locating Quivira and the Strait of Anian were undiminished. To the faithful, the real challenge of the northern country was still the multitude of lost souls to be saved.

The heightened interest in the north resulted in a rush to secure a commission to reduce the area of New Mexico to Spanish dominion. When bureaucracy and hostile officials stymied all applicants, not excluding Espejo himself, some decided to forego the applications. Gaspar Castaño de Sosa, the lieutenant-governor of Nueva Leon, in 1590 dispatched an expedition of over 170 persons which eventually established a settlement in the vicinity of the Pecos pueblo. The venture ended abruptly in 1592 when Captain Juan Morlete with a force of fifty men arrested Castaño for exploring without official permission. Another illegal penetration of New Mexico was made around 1595 by one Captain Francisco Leiva Bonilla. Little is known of his journey since no written record was kept by any of the participants.[23]

The story of the development of the southern route to

[22] Diego Pérez de Luxán, *Expedition Into New Mexico by Antonio de Espejo, 1582-1583,* trans. and ed. by George Peter Hammond and Agapito Rey (Los Angeles, 1929), 108-12, 115-16. Bancroft paints a different picture of Espejo's relations with Indians. According to Bancroft, Espejo was able to wander peacefully from province to province and compared him favorably with Coronado who had been guilty of "barbarous oppression of unoffending natives." *Arizona and New Mexico,* 90.

[23] For more detail on the exploration of the north during the interim period between the Espejo and Oñate expeditions, *see* Bancroft, *Arizona and New Mexico,* chapter v.

California comes into focus again with the journeys of Juan
de Oñate. A leading citizen of Nueva Galicia, it was Oñate
who eventually received the appointment to lead the conquest of the north. The Oñate name was well-known in
New Spain. His family had played a prominent part in the
original conquest, and his father had participated in the
subjugation of Nueva Galicia. Oñate's wife was a grand-
daughter of the Aztec chief, Montezuma.[24] Added to these
qualifications of family lineage, Oñate was wealthy and
would bear the major burden of financing the expedition.

The force that left Santa Barbara in January 1598 under
Oñate consisted of at least 100 soldiers with their families
who intended to settle in New Mexico. The total count of
expeditionary members has been estimated as high as 400
or more. A group of eight or ten Franciscan fathers under
Padre Alonso Martínez joined the column shortly after its
departure. In the train were eighty-three wagons and 7,000
head of cattle.[25]

The conquest of the north country proceeded as planned.
Striking the Rio Grande near the site of present-day El
Paso, Oñate formally took possession of New Mexico for
God, the King of Spain – and himself. The Spaniards
marched north along the Rio Grande, in July reaching the
San Juan pueblo at the junction of the Rio Grande and the
Rio Chama. Here Oñate established his headquarters. Dur-
ing the following months, the Spaniards explored in the Rio
Grande valley in northern and central New Mexico, prob-
ably venturing as far east as the Texas panhandle. In the
course of explorations, many pueblos were visited and
homage received from the inhabitants.

In October 1598, Oñate determined to lead an expedition

---

24 Bolton, *Spanish Exploration*, 201.
25 Bancroft, *Arizona and New Mexico*, 124-25.

to the South Sea. The Spaniards were still after riches, pearls this time. Marching westward, they visited Acoma, pausing long enough to receive that pueblo's submission, Zuñi and finally reached the Hopi towns which also submitted peacefully to the soldiers. Deciding to remain there for a time, Oñate sent a small party under Captain Marcos Farfán to look for mines in the same region previously visited by Espejo. Minerals were found on the Bill Williams Fork, and Farfán hurried back to report to his commander.

Before Farfán's discovery could be investigated, Oñate was forced to abandon the western expedition. He received word that a party under Juan Zaldívar had been attacked by Acomans and most of the Spaniards, including their leader, had been killed. The soldiers had been bound for Hopi country to reinforce the expedition for the intended march to the South Sea. Oñate returned to San Juan to make new plans.

A force under Vicente de Zaldívar, brother of the deceased Juan, was sent to subdue the Acomans, now branded rebels. The Spaniards accomplished their purpose. The diary of the punitive expedition reads simply: "Most of . . . [the Acomans] . . . were killed and punished by fire and bloodshed, and the pueblo was completely laid waste and burned." [26] From a population estimated between 3,000 and 6,000, a remnant of 600 survived the slaughter and were permitted to surrender and settle on the plain. [27]

It was 1604 before Oñate could revive his ambition to reach the South Sea. During the years since his previous abortive attempt, a party of twenty-five under Vicente de Zaldívar had reached a point on a westward trek which was,

[26] Quoted in Bolton, *Spanish Exploration*, 204.
[27] Bancroft, *Arizona and New Mexico*, 145.

they were told by Indians, but three days' march from the sea. Oñate's latest South Sea expedition included thirty soldiers and Father Francisco de Escobar who kept a detailed journal of the journey.

Departing in October, the Spaniards passed peacefully through the Zuñi and Hopi regions. Traveling southwestward from the Hopi towns, they crossed the Little Colorado River and probably the two branches of the Verde River north of modern Prescott. Escobar noted that in this area Spaniards had taken copper ores from mines discovered originally by Espejo.[28] Ascending the Verde to its source, Oñate then struck westward until they came to another river, the Santa Maria or Bill Williams Fork.

Moving down the Bill Williams, the expedition arrived at the junction with the Colorado River, which the Spaniards named the Rio de Buena Esperanza, because "we reached it on the day of the expectation or hope of the most happy parturition of the Virgin Mary, our Lady." [29] Oñate knew he was near his destination and set out down the River of Good Hope.

---

[28] In the same region, the Spaniards met Indians they called "cruzados" from their custom of wearing small crosses of cane on their foreheads. Escobar did not comment on the origin of the curious custom, except to guess that it could be traced somehow to Christianity. Francisco de Escobar, "Father Escobar's Relation of the Oñate Expedition to California," ed. by Herbert Eugene Bolton, *The Catholic Hist. Rev.,* v (April 1919), 27. Father Zárate Salmerón, who was not a member of the expedition, but who did use accounts of members, wrote twenty years later that: ". . . it has become known that many years ago, a religious of my father Saint Francis was traveling through that land, and he told them that if at some time they should see bearded white men, in order that they might not offend or harm them, they should place on themselves those crosses, which are something that they esteem." Salmerón, *Relaciones,* 66. If Salmerón's account is true, no record survives to give this mysterious Franciscan some of the glory showered on the memories of other missionary explorers.

[29] Escobar, "Relation," 28. This practice of naming a geographical feature after the holy day on which the feature was first seen was quite common among the Spanish explorers.

The Spaniards found both banks of the river heavily populated all the way to its mouth.[30] The Indians generally were friendly and furnished the expedition with food from their often meager stores. Indeed, the Spaniards perhaps at times regretted the cordiality of the Indians. On some days, more than 300 of the curious natives followed the Spanish party.[31]

Escobar's description of the Colorado River Indians, the first detailed account we have, is worth noting:

> The people of . . . this river are very fine looking and of good disposition, tall in stature, and well made. The custom among all the people who live along this river in regard to clothing is to wear none, but to go naked from the sole of the foot to the top of the head, the women merely covering their loins with two handfuls of grass or with twists of grass ready to hand, without taking the trouble to cover any other part of the body. All wear their hair loose, and reaching only to the shoulders. This shelterless costume is possible because the country is not cold, for we did not feel cold during the whole time we were there, which was during the heart of winter. The language appeared to me easy, with no difficulties of pronunciation.[32]

Indeed the language was easy, for Escobar at least. In the course of the journey, the padre learned no less than ten different Indian languages! On the return trip to New Mexico, he was able to converse with these same tribes.[33]

---

[30] Salmerón's account differs substantially at this point. He noted that shortly after arriving at the mouth of the Bill Williams Fork, Oñate sent Captain Gerónimo Márquez up the Esperanza (Colorado) to look for the land of the Amacavas (Mojaves), about whom they had heard. In the course of this journey, they met Indians who told them of a lake called Copalla, the shores of which were densely populated by a rich people who wore trinkets of gold on their wrists and arms and in their ears. The Indians told the Spaniards that they were then but fourteen days' journey away from the lake. The narrative abruptly drops the subject of Copalla and Márquez's trek, and we are not told why no effort was made to reach the lake. Salmerón, *Relaciones,* 67. Escobar mentions neither Copalla nor Márquez. If the captain did indeed make the detour, he was the first European to see the stretch of the Colorado north of the mouth of the Bill Williams Fork.

[31] Escobar, "Relation," 33-34.   [32] *Ibid.,* 29-30.

[33] Bancroft, *Arizona and New Mexico,* 156.

Continuing down the Colorado, the expedition arrived at the confluence with another river, smaller than the Colorado, which the Spaniards named the Nombre de Jesús. This was the Gila River which from this moment figures heavily in the story of the search for a route to California. Eventually reaching the mouth of the Colorado and viewing at last the spectacle of the Gulf of California, some seamen in the party proclaimed it the finest bay they had ever seen. The port, for it was assumed that it would be so one day, was duly named the Port of the Conversion since it was first seen on the day of the Conversion of the Glorious Apostle St. Paul. Turning from the gulf, Oñate led his party on the path homeward to New Mexico.

Oñate, like his predecessors, Nuñez, Coronado, Espejo and others, however brave and resourceful, pioneered few trails through virgin country during his explorations. For the most part, the paths he followed were well-worn and well-known by the Indians who generally either guided the Spaniards or advised them which trails to take. Oñate did show, nevertheless, that Spaniards could travel from New Mexico to the Colorado River and without undue hardship. He lost not a single man on his journey to the South Sea.

The expeditions of Oñate are of undeniable significance in the opening of the Southwest and as a step toward California. By 1605, he and his lieutenants had explored again almost all the ground covered by Coronado and Espejo and had traveled trails not seen by them. Oñate's western expedition was particuliarly important in stimulating interest in the Colorado River area. He explored a considerable stretch of the river and reached the mouth where it was expected a great port would be established. The Colorado was assumed to be navigable, thereby opening up the interior to exploration. New interest was kindled in the question of whether California was an island, now that Indians had convinced some of the expedition's members that the head of the gulf curled westward from the mouth of the Colorado, then toward the north. Indeed, the Spaniards had not been able to locate anyone who knew where the head of the gulf lay. Indians on the Colorado had told of large pearls from the gulf and metals, assumed to be gold, silver and perhaps tin and copper, that came from mines to the west. The Spaniards also heard tales about wonderful and monstrous nations that lay just a short trek away. All the mysteries of this fruitful march would have to be solved, and this indicated further exploration.

Yet, the knowledge gained by Oñate's expedition was not used. It had been the same with those who had explored the northern country before him. Accounts of journeys, often recorded in minute detail by members of expeditions, typically were ignored or temporarily lost, to be recovered from dusty archives in the nineteenth or twentieth centuries. Following the safe return of Oñate to New Mexico from his journey to the Gulf of California, the region below the Gila River was not visited by Spaniards for almost 100 years. It would be almost two centuries before central Arizona would be seen again by the Spanish.

CHAPTER II

Spanish Expeditions

By the time Spaniards once again entered present-day Arizona, the thrust for exploration in the region had shifted from New Mexico to Sonora. New Mexico by then was taking on the air of a settled province. Its progress was not smooth, being violently interrupted by the successful pueblo revolt of 1680 and, following the reconquest in 1692 by Diego de Vargas, again in 1696. The struggle to maintain, then expand, the settlements so occupied the minds of Spaniards in the northern outpost that they had little time to devote to further exploration of the west country.

There was, of course, no such province as "Arizona," nor were the regions of the Grand Canyon, the Gila and Colorado rivers known collectively by any other name. It was not part of California or New Mexico, though the Hopi region, now part of the state of Arizona, often was considered part of New Mexico because Spaniards from that province regularly visited the Hopi towns. Actually, California was never thought to extend east of the Colorado, and the western boundary of New Mexico, with the exception of the Hopi lands, was generally agreed to be at Zuñi. The country lying between New Mexico and California was increasingly thought of as the upper frontier of Sonora. It was in this area that the next phase of exploration was to be carried out by Father Eusebio Francisco Kino, the first of the great missionary explorers.

Born in the Austrian province of Tyrol, Kino was one of the many non-Spanish fathers who served God and the King of Spain in the new world. He had hoped to follow the footsteps as well as the example of Saint Francis Xavier, who was his inspiration, to the Far East. In 1678, he was sent to New Spain instead. He accepted the post and the challenge willingly.

Father Kino's first missionary assignment in America did not go well. He was sent to Lower California where his order, the Jesuits, were responsible for the spiritual part of a new attempt to colonize the peninsula. This was the latest attempt in a conquest of that land which had continued fitfully for over 250 years. Combined military and ecclesiastical expeditions were launched, and settlements were founded. All failed, due mostly to financial problems and Indian hostility, though the Indians had appeared friendly at first. Of course, there are no Indian accounts to explain the reasons for that hostility. In 1685, the California enterprise was put aside.[1]

When it became a certainty that the conquest of Baja California was to be abandoned, Father Kino expressed a wish to work with Indians on the west coast of New Spain. His request was granted in substance, though he was sent not to minister to the Guaymas, as he had hoped, but to the Pimería Alta. This broad northern frontier of Sonora stretched from the Altar River in Sonora to the Gila River on the north and from the Colorado River eastward to the San Pedro River. The northern and western limits were artificial, distance alone preventing further penetration by Spaniards. The eastern boundary was real. Beyond the San Pedro lay Apacheria, the home of the Apaches.

Kino's achievements rest on his successes as both missionary and explorer.[2] In the course of his journeys from the

---

[1] It was a temporary reversal. The project was renewed in 1697 by Kino, then stationed in Sonora, and Father Juan Maria de Salvatierra.

frontier mission of Dolores where he served from 1687 to
1711, he baptized thousands of Indians and preached to
tens of thousands throughout the Pimería Alta. He built
churches on both sides of the present international boundary,
principally along the Altar and Magdalena rivers west of
Dolores and a chain of missions northward from Dolores.
Notable for this study were the three northernmost missions
in this chain: San Gabriel de Guebavi, San Cayetano de
Tumacácori and San Xavier del Bac, all located north of
the present Sonora-Arizona border.³ Kino did not need four
walls to preach, however. He took the word of God to
Indians wherever and whenever he found willing ears. At
most Indian villages during his explorations, no matter how
tired he might be from the day's journey, he had the energy
and the time to preach.

² Happily for the student of the American Southwest, Kino was a meticulous
diarist. Like many other invaluable historical documents, the diary was known and
used briefly after Kino's death, then was "lost." After lying unknown for over a
century and a half in Mexico City archives, it was discovered early in the twentieth
century and published in 1919. In addition to the *Historical Memoir,* there are other
notable publications on Kino. Herbert Eugene Bolton's *Rim of Christendom* (New
York, 1936) is an outstanding biography of Kino. Another useful volume is Eusebio
Francisco Kino, *Father Kino in Arizona* (Phoenix, 1966), ed. by Fay Jackson Smith,
John L. Kessell and Francis J. Fox. The book includes the daily account written by
Kino in 1698 during the first extended overland expedition to locate the mouth of
the Gila River. Both of the last-named publications contain excellent bibliographies
on Kino.
It should be pointed out that some of the travel narratives in the present book are
based on accounts written by the sole diarists of expeditions. This is particularly
true in the cases of Kino and other missionary fathers who often traveled with few
companions. Yet, though contemporaries seldom verified the padres' veracity, the
fact that so many of the exploring fathers, living in different time periods, wrote
similar accounts of their experiences, notably their relationships with Indians,
indicates that each was telling the truth. This view is more impressive when one
considers that the fathers appear generally not to have read the diaries of their
forerunners.
³ Bancroft claimed that Kino did not establish any missions north of the present
international boundary. *Arizona and New Mexico,* 373. But Bancroft's history was
published in 1889 without access to Kino's diary which was not discovered until
almost twenty years later.

Kino's contribution as explorer equals and perhaps exceeds his accomplishments as missionary. During his twenty-four years in Pimería Alta, this stout padre made more than fifty journeys, crossing and criss-crossing the region. At least fourteen of the trips were into present-day Arizona. On six of these he reached the Gila River [4] over five different routes from Dolores. Two of the fourteen expeditions found him on the Colorado. On one of these, he crossed the river into California and reached the mouth,[5] thereby completing the first leg of the first overland trail to California.

Of all the pioneers who trekked the southwestern trails from the sixteenth century through the nineteenth, Kino is probably most deserving of the title of pathfinder. He seldom had any military scort. If any, there were only a few soldiers. On some expeditions, he had little companionship save that of his Indian servants. It should be emphasized that they usually were servants, not guides. It is obvious, however, that Kino often traveled on Indian trails. In his diary, he made revealing references, for example, to a "very level road" and again to a "very good Road." [6] In the same sense, it would

---

[4] Every reader of exploration narratives will admit to confusion at the different names given by different explorers to the same places. It is natural that each explorer entering a strange land should assign an identifying name to each prominent river and land feature. As time passes, the puzzle continues to be compounded until a particular name "sticks." For example, names given by Spaniards to the Colorado River include Rio del Tizón, Buena Guia, and Rio Grande de Buena Esperanza. The Gila was early named the Rio del Nombre de Jesus. Father Kino added to the confusion by naming the Colorado the Rio de los Martires (Garcés later gave the same name to the present Mojave River) and the Gila the Rio de los Apostoles. He also referred to the Gila as the Rio Grande de Gila. By Kino's day, the name Gila apparently was beginning to stick. The first formal use of the name was in a report of 1630 which referred to a province of New Mexico located at the source of the Gila River just east of the present Arizona-New Mexico state boundary. Bancroft, *Arizona and New Mexico*, 35, 39, 155-56; Kino, *Historical Memoir*, I, pp. 312, 339.

[5] Kino, *Historical Memoir*, I, pp. 22, 54. Also see the foldout map in the same volume. The map of Pimería Alta illustrates the principal expeditions of Kino and his companions during the years 1687-1711. [6] *Ibid.*, I, pp. 248, 251.

be ridiculous to suggest that Kino did not listen to advice given by Indians who lived in or near the country through which he was traveling, but more often than not, Kino was his own guide.

Most of the trails the padre traveled either had never been seen by Europeans or had been completely forgotten. Kino encountered and befriended Indians who had never before seen whites. He crossed and recrossed desert paths that as late as the mid-nineteenth century during the gold rush to California were considered virtually impassable. The bones of travelers deposited in later years along the desert road called Camino del Diablo, or Devil's Highway, from San Marcelo de Sonóita to the Gila River, which Kino traveled at will, testify to the friar's skill and stamina.

Until 1700, Kino devoted his energies to building missions and otherwise extending the influence of the church within the boundaries of present-day Sonora. Though he did not cease in his quest for souls, the friar from that year occupied himself most fervently in the search for a land route to California. California had long been thought by many people to be an island; others considered it a peninsula. Kino had arrived in America with the belief that it was a peninsula, but he soon had come to accept the island theory, which was then the most popular opinion.

It was during his expedition to the Gila in 1699 that he changed his view again, once more to consider California a peninsula. Near the mouth of the Gila, Kino was given some blue shells that were similar to some that he had seen on the Pacific side of Baja California in 1685. He had never seen the blue shells any other place. He deduced that the shells he saw in the Pimería must have come to the Yumas from the South Sea. If that were so, then there would have to be a land connection between the country of the Yumas and the Pacific Ocean. The following year at San Xavier del Bac, when Kino talked at length with Indians from hundreds of miles around, he became convinced that the blue shells indeed had come overland from the South Sea.[7]

Father Kino believed that an overland route to California would be immeasurably valuable to the Spanish. He speculated that it would serve immediately as an alternative supply route for the Lower California missions. Father Salvatierra at Loreto agreed. He thought such a road an absolute necessity, just in case supply of the missions by sea should fail. Indeed, Salvatierra went to Dolores to accompany Kino on an expedition in 1701, the precise purpose of which was to find a land route to California.

Kino added that extending the road to the Pacific coast would facilitate provisioning the Manila Galleon from Pimería Alta. The lives of many sailors who every year sickened and died on the Galleon would be saved. The overland route, furthermore, would permit the Pimería Alta to participate in trade with the Galleon.[8] Kino believed that the Pimería thereby would prosper and the Spanish hold on the region would be strengthened. Trade between the Pimería and the interior of Mexico then could be expanded and the once active commerce between the Pimería and New Mexico could be reopened.[9] That done, the Pimería then could trade via New Mexico with New France. This direct route would cut the distance of the long and circuitous journey via Mexico City and Vera Cruz in half.[10]

---

[7] *Ibid.,* I, pp. 55, 230-31, 234-37.   [8] *Ibid.,* I, pp. 271-84, 323.

[9] Kino believed that there had once been a regular trade between the Spanish in New Mexico and the Pimería Alta Indians. He wrote that "we have certain reports that before the revolt of New Mexico the Spaniards of those provinces used to come by way of the Apacheria to these our most remote Pimas Sobaiporis to barter hatchets, cloth, sackcloth, blankets, 'chomitas' [a kind of shirt], knives, etc., for maize." *Ibid.,* II, p. 257.

[10] *Ibid.,* I, p. 358; II, pp. 258-59.

In 1700, Kino began in earnest the search for a California road. During an expedition that year, he reached the Gila, then traveled down that river to its confluence with the Colorado. There the Yumas told him that the head of the gulf lay to the south. This news strengthened his conviction that the gulf did not block the opening of a land route to California. Returning to the same place in 1701, Kino moved down the Colorado until he reached the land of the Quiquimas, about mid-way between the junction of the Gila and Colorado and the mouth of the Colorado. Aided by the friendly Indians, he crossed the Colorado on a raft to the California side. Marching miles westward, the padre received gifts of blue shells which the Indians told him came from a sea that was just eight or ten days' journey west of their villages. They also told him that the Gulf of California was but a day's travel to the south.

Kino was convinced by then that he had found the land passage to California. He was certain that the gulf did not extend as far north as his present position and, according to his reckoning based on the information given him by the Indians, the sea's head ended ten leagues to the south and southwest. In 1702, Kino trekked again from Dolores to the Yuma junction and descended from there to the gulf. From this time forward, he was satisfied that he had not only showed that a land route to California was a possibility, but also had proved that Lower California was a peninsula rather than an island.[11] In all, according to his own count, Kino made fourteen expeditions in order to prove these two claims.[12]

While Kino appeared chiefly motivated by a desire to

[11] *Ibid.,* I, pp. 56, 305-19, 340-44. Kino recorded his arguments for the peninsular theory in a document titled "Cogent Reasons and Clear Arguments which Establish the Certainty of the Land Passage to California." *Ibid.,* I, pp. 351-54.

[12] *Ibid.,* II, pp. 244-45.

extend Christianity and Spanish dominion, he saw additional benefits in his explorations. He felt that his findings would put to rest once and for all time many of the myths associated with North America

> . . . such as a crowned king whom they carried on a golden litter; a lake of quicksilver, and another of gold; a walled city with towers, etc.; the Kingdom of Axa; the pearls, amber, and corals of the Rio del Tizon, the Rio del Coral, and the Rio de Aganguchi, which they represent as emptying into this Sea of California . . . ; likewise the error of the Seven Cities. . .[13]

In spite of this surprisingly enlightened outlook, Kino did not reject everything that he could not prove. For example, he believed without qualification that "Casa Grande . . . [was] . . . a building of the ancients of Montesuma, who set out from these lands when they went to found the City of Mexico."[14]

Throughout almost a quarter century of tramping in the Pimería, Kino usually found the Indians friendly and hospitable. According to his journal, they were always eager to hear him preach and to embrace Christianity. In 1700, for example, during a trip to San Xavier del Bac, Kino was confronted "with so many Indians in this great valley, who were close to three thousand, and also in view of the many prayers of the natives that I should stay with them, I determined not to go further."[15] On all his journeys, Kino was asked by Indians to baptize their children and their sick. Many well adults also sought baptism. The yearning for conversion was not limited to the Pima tribes who were usually considered peaceful and rather receptive to Spanish overtures. On a visit to the Colorado, over 2,000 Yumas, who had been supposed unfriendly, came to talk with and be taught by Kino. Indeed, the padre had decided to visit

[13] *Ibid.*, I, p. 359.   [14] *Ibid.*, II, p. 243.   [15] *Ibid.*, I, p. 234.

MISSION CHURCH OF SAN XAVIER DEL BAC
From *Pacific Railroad Surveys*, Volume II

the Yuma country on that trip only after some Yuma chiefs
had begged him to come see them.

The desire of the Indians for Christianity appears not to
have been a fleeting one. They repeatedly asked for missionaries to come and live permanently with them. In 1701, for
example, Kino visited the Quiquimas who at that time were
considered dangerous. He was accompanied by only one
other Spaniard and some Indian servants. They were received peacefully though Kino's Spanish companion fled in
fright. Before the padre left the Quiquimas, the Indians
were begging him to stay with them. When he finally departed, a body of 500 Indians – Quiquimas, Yumas and
Pimas – followed him.

In 1697, according to Kino, more than twenty chiefs
from the interior came hundreds of miles to mission Dolores
to ask for fathers and baptism for all members of their
"rancherias," or villages. Kino took them to see the "father
visitor" who would be the person to authorize more missionaries to carry out this work. The father visitor assured the
Indians that he would do his best to grant their wishes.
Years later, in 1702, the Quiquimas, Yumas and other distant tribes were still sending appeals to Dolores, requesting
missionaries to come and live among them.[16]

It is interesting, however futile, to speculate on the course
of the history of this region if the Spanish had recognized
the appeals of the Indians as a heaven-sent opportunity and
had granted all their requests. Of what effect a multitude of
gentle padres of Kino's cast could have had on the future of
the Pimería and the rest of Arizona, one can only guess.

Not all of the Indians on New Spain's northern frontier
welcomed the Spanish intruders. The thorn in the side of the
Spanish in Pimería Alta were the Apaches. The term

---

[16] *Ibid.*, I, pp. 312-15, 370-71; II, pp. 246-47.

"Apache" itself is indicative. The Apaches did not call themselves by that name. They referred to themselves as the "N'de" or "Dine" or some variation, meaning simply "the people." Whites called these marauders "Apaches" from the Zuñi word for "enemy." [17] Father Kino was amply aware of the obstacle the Apaches posed to the spiritual and secular conquest. During his stay at Dolores, Apache raiders plunged ever deeper into the lands of the Christian Indians in the Pimería and in Sonora. Urged on by Kino, the Christian Indians, especially the Pimas, fought back and even sent parties on successful punitive raids against Apache camps.

The Apaches were never really put down. Indeed, Kino never penetrated Apacheria. He failed in his desire to connect Pimería Alta with New Mexico because a road would have had to run through Apache lands. Lying between the eastern limit of the Pimería at the San Pedro River and the settlements of New Mexico, Apacheria continued long beyond Kino's day to prevent the union of the two Spanish frontier regions.[18]

Like other frontier missionaries, Kino believed that Indians could not be won to Christ until they were living in towns where they could be ministered to by resident fathers. For that reason, he supported Pima attacks on the Apaches to prevent the Christian Indians from being scattered. For

[17] Dan L. Thrapp, *The Conquest of Apacheria* (Norman, 1967), 237.

[18] For many years following, neither missionaries nor soldiers were able to persuade the Apaches from their way of life. As late as 1870, continuing Apache hostilities led General William Tecumseh Sherman, the United States Army commander, to conclude that the American occupation of the Southwest was neither economical nor wise at that time. "The best advice I can offer," he said, "is to notify the settlers to withdraw and then to withdraw the troops and leave the country to the aboriginal inhabitants." Sherman to W. W. Belknap, Jan. 7, 1870, quoted in Ralph Hedrick Ogle, *Federal Control of the Western Apaches, 1848-1886* (Albuquerque, 1970), 73.

that reason also, he took an active interest in agriculture. During his explorations, he often noted in considerable detail the quality of soils, crops under cultivation, the extent to which irrigation was employed, as well as estimating the agricultural potentialities of various regions. Kino was no mere observer of the processes of agriculture. Under his careful administration, mission Dolores became a model farm, especially in stock-raising. He sent cattle and sheep northward to stock the herds of the missions he had founded, notably Tumacácori and San Xavier del Bac. In the year 1700, for example, Kino sent 700 cattle to San Xavier del Bac to establish the herd for that new mission.[19]

In his writings, Father Kino repeatedly tried to show that the extension of Christianity and Spanish dominion in the Pimería would bring glory and profit to Spain and would not be a drain on the crown's treasury. He balanced the cost of what he doubtless expected to be a peaceful conquest with the advantages of acquiring a prosperous region populated by an industrious people. In 1702, by which time he had traveled throughout the frontier country, Kino wrote:

> There are in this very fertile and rich Pimería . . . many fields of wheat, maize, beans, etc.; and it produces all sorts of vegetables, garden products, and fruit trees, as in Europe. There are already vines for Castilian wine for the missions, a watermill, . . . fields, oxen, lands, level roads, beautiful rivers, abundant pasturage, good timbers for buildings, and mineral lands.[20]

Noting that the crown had allotted 6,000 pesos for support of the five missionary priests in Lower California, Kino explained that such expenditure would not be needed in the Pimería because of its sound economic condition. He asked authorities only that a detail of twenty soldiers be sent from

[19] Kino, *Historical Memoir,* I, pp. 57-58, 241.   [20] *Ibid.,* I, pp. 357-58.

the Sonora garrisons once or twice a year to make the rounds of the missionary establishments. He believed that once these outposts were strong, progress could be made in winning over other tribes, especially singling out the Hopis.

Kino's optimism did not stop there. He pointed out that expansion eventually would take the Spaniards north and west to Cape Mendocino on the California coast and on toward Japan. In the other direction, Spanish dominion would push north and east of New Mexico, eventually resulting in the establishment of direct communications and trade with New France and Europe.[21]

Though not even a small part of Kino's hopes for Pimería Alta were realized, this does not diminish his place in the history of the origins of the southern route. His greatest contributions lay in his discovery that Baja California was a peninsula rather than an island and in showing the feasibility of a land route from the Pimería to California. In his own words: "I discovered the land-passage at 32 degrees of latitude, at the confluence of the Rio Grande de Gila and the abundant waters of the Rio Colorado." As to that land lying west of the Colorado River: "I assign the name of Upper California to the region that extends northward from the 30th degree latitude."[22] Complementing his reputation as an explorer par excellence, Kino is justly famous for his maps of Pimería Alta.[23]

While Kino is best known today for his achievements as an explorer, he undoubtedly considered himself to be, first

[21] Eusebio Francisco Kino, *Kino's Plan for the Development of Pimería Alta, Arizona and Upper California,* trans. and annotated by Ernest J. Burrus (Tucson, 1961), 31-33.

[22] *Ibid.,* 28-29. If Kino's boundary between lower and upper California had been adopted by later authorities, a sizable piece of Baja California today would be a part of California.

[23] For a study of Kino's part in the mapping of this region, *see* Ernest J. Burrus, *Kino and the Cartography of Northwestern New Spain* (Tucson, 1965).

and foremost, God's servant. His spiritual accomplishments were considerable,[24] but the challenge he saw in the Pimería was so great that he could not be satisfied with what he thought meager successes. Aware that his work required official support, Kino never missed an opportunity to remind the viceroy that he received messages almost daily at Dolores from the tribes of Pimería Alta, pleading for him to come baptize them and send them Black Robes to live with them. In a letter to the viceroy, Kino wrote what might have been a fitting epitaph:

> The crosses which the tribes of Upper California and from the areas close to the land passage gave, I am sending . . . to Father Provincial and to your Excellency. Inasmuch as these crosses . . . [are] . . . hallowed by the one on which the Redeemer of the world died for the salvation of all . . . I let them speak and I cease from my poor efforts.[25]

Kino died in 1711 at Magdelena, east of Dolores, and was buried nearby at San Ignacio. He had founded both missions.

For a number of years following Kino's death, Spanish exploration in Pimería Alta came virtually to a standstill. At least, the records for this period give little evidence of any such activity. Fathers Velarde and Agustín de Campos were left almost alone in the Pimería. They continued to receive deputations from distant tribes who asked why the promised Black Robes did not come. Though Campos did journey into the Pimería to visit villages there, his efforts

---

[24] After twenty-three years in the Pimería Alta, Kino wrote that 30,000 Indians had been "reduced to our friendship and to the desire of receiving our holy Catholic faith." He recorded that he had solemnized more than 4,000 baptisms himself and that he could have "baptised ten or twelve thousand Indians more if the lack of father laborers had not rendered it impossible for us to catechise them and instruct them in advance." Kino, *Historical Memoir*, II, p. 252.

[25] Kino, *Plan for Pimería Alta*, 34.

were of little consequence. All Kino's spiritual accomplishments began to fall away. The Indians forgot what they had learned from him and began to drift back to the old ways.

Some few fruitless efforts were made during the next fifty years to revive the spiritual conquest in the frontier regions. For some unexplained reason, the focus moved for a time from the Gila-Colorado area to the distant Hopi country. In 1743, Father Ignatius Keller, then a missionary in Pimería Alta, set out with an escort of soldiers to build a mission among the Hopis. Shortly after crossing the Gila, Apaches attacked the Spaniards and Keller abandoned the enterprise. It was taken up again in 1744 when Father Jacobo Sedelmayr, the resident missionary at Tubutama, set out for the Hopi towns. Crossing the Gila at the Casa Grande, he led his party overland westward to the Colorado, then upstream to the mouth of another river, probably the Bill Williams. Failing to find guides to take them to their destination, Sedelmayr gave up the project and returned to Tubutama.[26] This was the last attempt to take the word of God to the Hopis by way of Pimería Alta. The King of Spain decreed in 1745 that the spiritual responsibility for Hopi souls belonged to the Franciscans of New Mexico, not the Jesuits of Pimería Alta.[27]

Sedelmayr then turned his attention to the Gila and Colorado regions. The records of two expeditions to that country indicate that he was interested more in exploration than conversion. He particularly wanted to reach the mouth of the Colorado River. With a few companions in 1749, Sedelmayr crossed the Gila River and visited the friendly Cocomaricopas on the Colorado north of the mouth of the Gila before

---

[26] Jacobo Sedelmayr, *Jacobo Sedelmayr; Missionary, Frontiersman, Explorer in Arizona and Sonora,* trans. and annotated by Peter Masten Dunne (Tucson, 1955), 5-7, 31-32, 69; Bancroft, *Arizona and New Mexico,* 365-66.

[27] Sedelmayr, *Sedelmayr,* 7.

turning southward. The Spaniards found the Yumas and other Indians below the junction of the two rivers threatening, forcing Sedelmayr to terminate the expedition. Another attempt the following year to reach the Colorado's outlet was no more successful. On this last journey, the Spaniards were forced to fight when hostile Indians, apparently contemptuous of the escort's weapons, harrassed the expedition and finally attacked. Though the Spaniards survived the encounter, killing thirteen Indians and wounding many more, it was enough to convince the padre to turn back to Tubutama.[28]

Sedelmayr's Indian troubles on the Colorado were indicative of what was happening throughout the Pimería Alta. In 1751, there was a full-scale Pima revolt which required many months and much expense to put down. The Apaches also were becoming bolder and raiding ever deeper into Mexico. Missionary work in the Pimería virtually halted as the few remaining fathers struggled to prevent the collapse of the established missions.

Then in 1767, as if to punctuate the declining fortunes of the missionary fathers, came the fatal decree for suppression of the Jesuits.[29] All members of the Society of Jesus in Mexico were taken quickly, secretly in most cases and with-

[28] *Ibid.,* 8, 28, 61-62, 69, 71-72; Bancroft, *Arizona and New Mexico,* 367. It should be noted here parenthetically that Sedelmayr apparently did not know that Kino, his Jesuit predecessor in Pimería Alta, had shown that California was not an island. Calling on one occasion for an extension of Spanish control of the frontier areas, Sedelmayr noted that additional exploration would settle the island – vs. – peninsula controversy. Doubtless, Sedelmayr believed it to be an island since he referred to "explorations in that island" which he understood were to be conducted shortly by California missionaries. Sedelmayr, *Sedelmayr,* 35-36.

[29] The Bourbon King of Spain, Carlos III, had for some time been trying to reform Spanish society toward a secularization of education and culture. The liberal reforms were vigorously opposed by the traditionalist, conservative Society of Jesus. The confrontation that resulted led eventually to the expulsion of the Society from Spain and all its colonies. In banishing the Society, Carlos followed a trend. Portugal and France years before had expelled the Jesuits for the same reasons.

out being told the reason for their removal from their posts, and sent to ports of embarkation. The fathers in Sonora were called to Matape near the Rio Sonora to learn that they were no longer permitted to serve God in Spanish territory. They were then sent to Guaymas to await a ship. They remained there, in disgrace and deprivation, for almost a year before they embarked, eventually to reach Spain and prison in 1769.[30]

The departure of the Jesuits compounded the problems of administering the frontier regions, problems of which civil officials in Mexico and Spain were all too aware. Indian problems in the Pimería were but evidence of a general deterioration of Spanish control in all of its frontier areas in New Spain. Recognizing that something must be done, King Carlos III appointed the Marqués de Rubí to study the problems and recommend solutions. Rubí, a man of influence in political and military circles in Spain, subsequently covered 7,600 miles in touring the frontiers of New Spain in the years 1766-1768.

Accompanying Rubí was Nicolás de Lafora whose duty, it seems, was to study the operation of existing presidios and to suggest to his chief what should be done to improve their effectiveness. Lafora made an exhaustive study and wrote

---

[30] Many of the missionaries were struck with scurvy at Guaymas, and one died. Finally boarding a small ship heading for San Blas, they were blown off course across the gulf to Puerto Escondido, just south of Loreto on the Baja California peninsula. There they fell into the hands of Gaspar de Portola who was good to the former missionaries, though he had been sent to Baja to expel the Jesuits there in favor of the Franciscans.

The Sonoran Jesuits, traveling with others from Sinaloa, finally reached San Blas and crossed Mexico to Vera Cruz. Their numbers were heavily depleted by disease. Arriving in Spain, they were thrown into prison, but eventually were sent to the Papal States to become the Pope's problem. Probably responding to pressure from Spain and France, Pope Clement XIV completed the disgrace of the Jesuits by suppressing the entire Society by decree in 1773. For a more complete account of the expulsion of the order from Mexico, *see* Peter Masten Dunne's "The Expulsion of the Jesuits from New Spain, 1767," *Mid-America,* XIX (Jan. 1937), 3-30, from which the above account is partly drawn.

his report. It painted a dreary picture. In it, he concluded that frontier presidios were ill-equipped and ill-prepared to perform their tasks. He severely criticized the cowardice and ineptitude of the officers and the general lack of training of the men. As solutions, Lafora recommended better equipment and more specialized training for both officers and men, particularly to prepare them for doing battle in their peculiar environment. He strongly emphasized the necessity of effective invasions of the enemy's country rather than waiting for him to enter Spanish territory. Up to this time, Lafora quipped, "When they made large noisy expeditions to the Gila province, they only frightened the game."[31]

Incorporating Lafora's suggestions into his own report, Rubí recommended to the king the establishment of a number of presidios, to be located according to a map drawn by Lafora.[32] The king received Rubí's report favorably and in the Royal Regulations of 1772 directed that it be implemented.

The following year, the task was given to Don Hugo Oconór who subsequently traveled 10,500 miles in the frontier regions, studying the problem. He then settled down to the job of relocating and building presidios and instituting administrative reforms.[33] The line of defense thus

---

31 Nicolás de Lafora, *The Frontiers of New Spain: Nicolás de Lafora's Description 1766-1768,* ed. by Lawrence Kinnaird (Berkeley, 1958), I, 214-17.

32 Lafora's map is reproduced on the inside back cover of Lafora, *Frontiers of New Spain.*

33 The resulting reforms undoubtedly contributed to the decline of the Apache menace in the early 1800s. A sketch map showing the locations of Oconór's presidios appears in Paige W. Christiansen, "The Presidio and the Borderlands: A Case Study," *Jour. of the West,* VIII (Jan. 1969), 31. The study focuses on the second half of the eighteenth century and describes the garrison at Janos as a typical presidio. It is interesting to note that while the operation of Spain's frontier outposts was the responsibility of Hugo Oconór, an Irishman, the commander of the Janos presidio was Captain Juan Bautista Peru, a Frenchman. *Ibid.,* 32. For a more thorough account of Spanish administrative reorganization in the borderlands during this period, *see* Bannon, *Spanish Borderlands Frontier,* chapter 10.

established in effect outlined the northern limits of the vice-royalty of New Spain, though New Mexico lay to the north of the line. With some variations, the line approximated the eventual international boundary between Mexico and the United States. This establishment of a frontier defense line did not mean that Spain gave up its claim to the land that lay north of the line. Spanish activity continued there and in fact increased shortly after the king's declaration which had set the reforms in motion.

Spearheading new explorations in the Pimería Alta were the Franciscans. Following the expulsion of the Jesuits in 1767, the Spanish government appointed royal commissioners to administer the properties vacated by that order. Establishments in southern Sonora were eventually secularized while those in the Pimería were given to the Franciscans of the college of Santa Cruz de Querétaro to administer. Fourteen padres from that college arrived at their new posts in 1768. Among the fourteen was Father Tomás Hermenegildo Garcés who was placed in charge of the mission of San Xavier del Bac, at that time the most northerly Christian settlement on the frontier.[34]

Father Garcés had been cast in Kino's mold. During his short thirteen-year ministry on the frontier, Garcés made five journeys that earned for him a reputation as one of the greatest explorers in the history of the American West. His expeditions took him not only to the Gila and Colorado rivers, but also into distant California and the land of the Hopis.

---

[34] A native of Spain, Garcés entered the College of Santa Cruz at his own request. In 1767, the year of the Jesuit expulsion, he asked for a post in the Sonoran missions, and his request was granted. It required over six months for him and most of his fellow Franciscans to reach their frontier posts. Francisco Tomás Garcés, *On the Trail of a Spanish Pioneer; The Diary and Itinerary of Francisco Gracés,* ed. by Elliott Coues (2 vols.; New York, 1900), I, pp. 2-5, quoting from a eulogy by Fray Juan Domingo Arricivita.

Garcés' first two journeys were brief affairs, the first in 1768 to the Gila where he visited Indians from the region of the Casa Grande to the junction of the Gila and the Colorado, and the second in 1770 to the vicinity of the great bend of the Gila. As in Kino's day, the Indians, especially the Pimas, welcomed his visits and, according to his accounts, followed him in great numbers to hear him preach.

While the first two expeditions were missionary ventures designed to strengthen the influence of the church as far as the Gila, the third was more important as a step toward opening a trail to California. Convinced by the successes of his two earlier journeys that the tribes he had visited were ready for conversion, Garcés set out in 1771 to select the best sites for new missions and to prepare the Indians for the coming of the fathers. With three Indian guides, Garcés marched to the Gila by way of Sonóita, a mission, since deserted, that had been founded by Kino. The road from Sonoíta to the Gila had been pioneered and described by Kino. Striking the Gila, Garcés then headed downstream and passed the confluence with the Colorado without recognizing it as such due to the high waters from recent rains. He eventually reached the mouth of the Colorado, but did not know he had done so, still thinking that he was on the Gila.[35] From this point, we may safely assume that the padre was lost.

Reckoning that he must go westward to reach the Colorado, and hearing from friendly Indians that there were Spaniards who lived seven days' travel in that direction –

---

[35] Herbert Eugene Bolton, "The Early Explorations of Father Garcés on the Pacific Slope," *The Pacific Ocean in History,* ed. by H. Morse Stephens and Herbert Eugene Bolton (N.Y., 1917), 325. Garcés' ignorance of the geography of the Pimería Alta, evidenced by the misconception that he had seen the Gila empty into a great gulf, is illustrative of the failure of Spanish explorers to transmit their findings to posterity.

they probably were speaking of San Diego – Garcés crossed
the river and wandered in the Colorado Desert. Twice he
started from the river with guides. Both times, his guides
deserted him. The farthest point west he reached on the
treks is not known. He did finally come in sight of a range
of mountains and saw two passes through it. But he des-
paired of going further and turned back. Learning that a
war was in progress between Yuma Indians and the Gila
tribes, Garcés decided to return to San Xavier by a more
southerly route. He descended the Colorado River, crossed
it, then trudged through the sand dunes of the Yuma Desert,
a feat that Kino had tried and failed three times.

The significance of Garcés's third expedition is often over-
looked. In the histories, it is customarily given a few lines
along with the first and second trips as background material
for a thorough treatment of the better-known fourth and
fifth journeys. Though he was lost a considerable part of the
time, the ground covered during the trek alone makes the
third expedition impressive. He had traveled approximately
a thousand miles in the course of which he had twice crossed
the Yuma Desert east of the Colorado and had entered the
Colorado Desert west of the river. Though he did not know
it at the time, he pioneered a new trail from the Colorado
toward California. The principal significance of Garcés's
third expedition then was the effect it had on the fruition of
the later Anza expeditions.

The idea for searching out an overland route to California
had been a dream of Captain Juan Bautista de Anza for
many years. Before being killed in a frontier Indian uprising, Anza's father had sought a commission to pioneer a road
to California. The younger Anza apparently inherited his
father's vision.

As early as 1769, Anza offered to lead an expedition for

that purpose. Pima Indians visiting him at the Tubac presidio, of which he was commander, had told him that they had heard that white men had been seen on the California coast. Doubtless, California Indians had seen the Portolá expedition and had told Yumas who relayed the information to the Pimas. Anza reasoned that if news traveled so freely between the California coast and Sonora, then a road could be opened across that same space. He told José de Gálvez, the Visitor, about his theory and at the same time applied for authority to prove it. Gálvez was favorable to the idea, but the viceroy, Marqués de Croix, who would have to give his assent, rejected the plan.[36]

Though disappointed, Anza was not dissuaded. His views were strengthened by Garcés' findings. The friar undoubtedly had told his neighbor – San Xavier was about thirty miles north of Tubac – what he had learned on his journey because he knew Anza was interested.[37] Now that Garcés had seen the California desert, it was no longer an unknown factor. To Anza, who knew arid country from long experience, the mountains that Garcés had seen across the desert meant water. Further, the news that Spaniards lived just

[36] George William Beattie, "Development of Travel Between Southern Arizona and Los Angeles as it Related to the San Bernardino Valley," *Hist. Soc. of Calif. Ann.*, VII (1925), 233; Herbert Eugene Bolton, *Anza's California Expeditions* (5 vols: Berkeley, 1930), I, pp. 44-45. A number of diaries are reproduced in Bolton's volumes. For the sake of clarity, the particular diary from which information is taken in vols. II and III is generally identified in the footnote. For example, a citation from Anza's complete diary, p. 55 of vol. II, would be footnoted thus: "Bolton, *Anza*, II, (Anza), 55." For information on the contents of the five volumes, see the bibliographical entry.

[37] Before Garcés set out on his third expedition, Anza had told the padre about his ambitions. In a letter to his superior, Garcés wrote: "In view of the interest aroused in Mexico over the occupation of Monterrey, and for the service of God and our King, Captain Ansa has told me that he wished to penetrate that region through these parts. And the plan is not repugnant to me, nor does it seem to me very difficult." Garcés to Buena y Alcalde, San Xavier, Feb. 20, 1771, quoted in Bolton, *Anza*, I, p. 46.

a few days' travel from the Colorado River indicated that the desert was not so wide as previously had been thought. All these factors led Anza to conclude that a road connecting Sonora and Monterey was feasible – no one, it seems, denied that the road was desirable – and he reopened his application for a commission.[38]

This time, the request was granted. When the new viceroy, Antonio María Bucareli, received the application, he had asked other knowledgeable people for advice. Two "Californians" who supported the project doubtless influenced Bucareli. Miguel Costansó, an engineer who had been with Portolá in Upper California, told about seeing trade goods there from New Mexico. If Indians could cross the deserts, he said, so could Spaniards. He believed that Anza's land route would permit provisioning the California settlements from Sonora. Junipero Serra also spoke strongly in favor of the plan.[39] Armed with the viceroy's blessing, Anza gathered his force at Tubac, meanwhile communicating with Garcés. At Anza's request, the padre was to accompany the expedition as guide.

The expedition had another guide: Sebastián Tarabal. His arrival in Sonora at this moment was a stroke of luck. Garcés would prove an invaluable guide, but he had not crossed the Colorado Desert. Tarabal had. Originally a "mission Indian" in Lower California, Sebastián was one of a number who were sent with the missionary fathers to Upper California to assist in the conversion process there. He soon tired of the life at San Gabriel mission and ran away, accompanied only by his wife and one relative. The three fled through the San Jacinto Valley, across the mountains, down Coyote Canyon and Borrego Valley and across

---

[38] Anza to Bucareli, Tubac, May 2, 1772, Bolton, *Anza,* v, 3-7; Bolton, "Early Explorations of Father Garcés," 328-29.

[39] Bolton, *Anza,* I, pp. 49-51, 58-60.

the desert toward the Colorado River. Tarabal made it to
the river, but his companions did not. They died from hardship as the little party wandered, lost, in the great sand dunes
of the Colorado Desert.

Following his arrival at the Colorado River Sebastián was
treated kindly by the Yumas. The Yuma chief Olleyquote-
quiebe guided him to the Sonora frontier where Anza found
him. This Yuma chief, the same who would be known to the
Spaniards as Palma, figured often in the fortunes of the
Spanish in Pimería Alta for years to come. Sebastián, or
"El Peregrino" as he became called, referred to Palma as
"Salvador," for the chieftain had indeed saved Sebastián's
life. Tarabal subsequently served as a guide for Anza and
a guide and companion to Garcés.

Anza's expedition was not a large one. In addition to the
commander, Garcés, Sebastián and a soldier named Juan
Bautista Valdés who had been with Portolá in San Diego,[40]
there were: Father Juan Díaz, a missionary at Caborca
mission who had been selected to go along as Garcés' companion, an escort of twenty soldiers, all volunteers from
Anza's presidio at Tubac, a Pima interpreter, a carpenter,
five muleteers and the commander's two personal servants.

Setting out in January 1774, the Spaniards traveled a
well-worn trail toward the Gila via Sonoíta. The route they
followed was frequently used by Papagos and Yumas. Kino
and Garcés had used the road, and more recently, Sebastián
and Palma had come that way. January was a good month
for traveling the arid country, and water was not yet a prob-

---

[40] Valdés had been sent to accompany Anza so that when the expedition reached
the Pacific Ocean, he could lead the way to San Diego without wandering around
trying to decide whether to go north or south. Miguel Costansó to Viceroy Bucareli,
Mexico, Oct. 12, 1772, Bolton, *Anza*, v, 10. In addition to his position as guide,
Valdés also performed invaluable service as courier. Carrying diaries and dispatches
to Mexico, he rode approximately 4,000 miles. *Ibid.*, i, p. viii.

lem, though pasturage in the area was scarce throughout the year.[41]

Shortly before arriving on the Gila, the Spaniards were warned by a passing Papago that a band of Yumas had had a falling out with Palma and planned to attack the expedition. Garcés did not believe the report, but two masses were said nevertheless in anticipation of trouble.[42] The following day, doubtless to the great relief of the company, Garcés was proven right. Throngs of Yumas visited the expedition's camp. According to Anza, the Indians were

> . . . overjoyed at our coming, which they celebrated with cheers and smiles, at the same time throwing up fistfuls of earth into the air and with other demonstrations expressing the greatest guilelessness and friendship.[43]

Hearing that the Spaniards had feared trouble, Palma explained that the malcontents were from other villages and that he had sent them away.

Salvador Palma looms large in the story of the Spanish dream to open a road to California. Principal chief of the Yumas who controlled the gateway to California, he could have prevented, or at least delayed for many years, the realization of the dream. It was indeed fortunate for the Spanish that he chose to favor rather than oppose them. Those Spaniards who left records of their encounters with Palma were impressed with his capabilities and the power he exercised among his people. Even Díaz, who often was less complimentary toward Indians than Garcés, noted that Palma "manifested such capacity and loyalty that he caused us no

---

41 Perhaps the best observer from among those who kept diaries of the first Anza expedition was Father Juan Díaz. Díaz wrote with considerable detail about the route and the countryside. Garcés wrote at length about the Indians, showing both curiosity and insight, but of the country and its flora and fauna, he had little to say.

42 Bolton, *Anza,* II (Díaz), 257-58; II (Garcés), 318.

43 *Ibid.,* II (Anza), 37.

little admiration to see such talent in the midst of such barbarism." [44]

Anza was amply aware of Palma's importance to Spain's fortunes. The expedition's commander decided to confer upon him an honor that would raise his stature as a leader in the eyes of his own people and at the same time woo his loyalty to the Spanish. In a ceremony that apparently was carried out with as much pomp as circumstances permitted, Anza hung around Palma's neck a medal bearing the likeness of King Carlos III and attached by a red ribbon. Anza told the chief that he was confirming him in his office and explained that now he could rule legally and would be recognized in his office by Spaniards. He charged Palma always to wear the medal as a sign of obedience to the Spanish king and his representatives. The chieftain was instructed to respect the missionaries and to maintain friendly relations with the Spanish nation. All these things Palma humbly promised to do. [45]

Father Díaz was impressed by the opportunities he saw among the Indians of the Colorado and the lower Gila. He seconded Garcés' oft-stated opinion that these Indians were good prospects for conversion to the Christian faith. Díaz was pleased to find that they were farmers and not inclined to wander about in the chase. He also found them "very care-free and pleasure-loving, docile and friendly, and they manifest singular affection for our nation." He noted that the Spanish had been successful in bringing peace to the region, which customarily was torn by intertribal war. Yet he was skeptical about the permanency of the peace due to "their barbarity and their lack of laws regulating disruptions." [46]

---

[44] *Ibid.,* II (Díaz), 259.   [45] *Ibid.,* I, pp. 98-99; II (Díaz), 259.

[46] *Ibid.,* II (Díaz), 265-67; II (Garcés), 340.

Satisfied that the Yuma crossing was now secure, Anza decided to move on. The departure of the expedition saddened the Yumas. Palma "rained tears" to see his Spanish friends leaving and, touched by his devotion, many of the Spaniards also wept.[47] The emotion, for the Spaniards at least, dissipated as the solicitous Indians became nuisances. As the column picked its tortuous way through the heavy brush of the river bottom, the Indians

> . . . vied with each other in showing the . . . best trails, clearing them of brush, and competing for the honor of driving the pack mules, horses, and cattle, so that each animal had half a dozen men at his sides or his heels.[48]

Not all of the bottomlands was waste. The commander indeed was quite impressed with the crops grown by the Yumas and the Cajuenches farther south. He noticed that the Indians did not have to irrigate the rich valley soil, relying instead on the annual snow-fed spring flooding which both moistened the earth and fertilized it with a rich silt deposit. As the expedition made its way down the Colorado, Anza saw fields where wheat, maize, beans, calabashes and muskmelons grew in great abundance.[49]

Turning from this oasis, the Spaniards approached the dreaded Colorado Desert. Travelers as late as the nineteenth century would call it the most difficult stretch of an otherwise hard trip. Anza would not have disagreed. Both of his guides, Garcés and Sebastián, had seen the heart of the desert, and Sebastián had crossed it. But both were lost for at least a part of their journeys. Even if Sebastián could have remembered the route he traveled, Anza would not have wished to lead his expedition by way of the Indian's sand-dune route.

---

[47] Ibid., II (Díaz), 270; II (Garcés), 325.

[48] Ibid., I, pp. 102-3, 110-11.   [49] Ibid., I, p. 117.

The expedition's first attempt to cross the desert was abortive. Yuma and Cajuenche guides pointed Anza toward Signal Mountain, a conspicuous peak near present-day Mexicali, but intervening sand dunes prevented his reaching it. Failing to find water – Garcés thought he recognized the vicinity from his previous trek – the expedition was forced to retreat to the Colorado River to recuperate.

As usual, the river Indians welcomed the Spaniards. While the soldiers rested and the stock grazed on the lush grass, the fathers took the opportunity to preach to the Indians. Obviously pleased with the results, Díaz wrote that some of the Indians

> . . . brought the idols which they have and delivered them voluntarily, in order that we might smash them to pieces. Nearly all of them acquired the habit of repeating those sweetest names of Jesus and Mary, and some of them learned how to make the sign of the Cross, although very imperfectly.[50]

Anza found the sojourn less satisfying. He chafed at the delay and finally decided that he would wait no longer. Since the condition of the jaded stock had not improved substantially, the commander entrusted most of the expedition's animals and provisions to Palma's care, planning to recover them on his return journey. The chieftain gladly accepted the trust. The expedition's muleteers and three soldiers also remained to help care for the property. Anza later would have more cause to thank the Indian than the Spanish caretakers.

Mounted on the strongest of the riding animals and carrying only enough provisions to reach the California settlements, the reduced force of twenty-five Spaniards again entered the desert. They were luckier this time. They reached the Cocopah Mountains with no mishap. Passing through

---

[50] *Ibid.*, II (Díaz), 274.

Lower Pass of that range, they camped at the northern end of Laguna Salada. The worst now was passed. This was the first recorded crossing of the Colorado Desert by white men.

As the march continued, Sebastián began to recognize landmarks,[51] and Anza knew that the end of the journey was in sight. Heading almost due north, the expedition passed between the Superstition and Fish Creek Mountains. The Spaniards encountered sand dunes in the passage, but made it through with much difficulty. Water was scarce for a few days, but after passing the dunes, it was found in abundance. In honor of the Indian guide who led them there, the watering place was named San Sebastián.

Sebastián knew the trail from this point forward. Though there was still rough country ahead, Anza's mind doubtless was eased with the knowledge that his guide knew the way and knew where to find water. The weary party marched up Coyote Canyon and finally reached the Royal Pass of San Carlos, as named by Anza, in the San Jacinto Mountains. The desert was behind them, and ahead lay the Cahuilla Valley. From the pass Anza wrote, they saw

. . . beautiful green and flower-strewn prairies, and snow-covered mountains with pines, oaks, and other trees which grow in cold countries. Likewise here the waters divide, some flowing this way toward the Gulf and others toward the Philippine Ocean.[52]

The expedition reached the San Gabriel mission a few days later, on March 22, 1774. Anza had opened the first overland route to California.

---

[51] The area in general also was familiar to Garcés, though his recollections must have been a bit jumbled. On his 1771 journey, he had heard from Indians about Lake Maqueque or Maquata, as Laguna Salada was called, and had actually seen it at the southern end of the Cocopah Range, but he did not reach it. He had named the lake Agua Amarilla or Rio Amarillo, thinking – remember, he was lost at the time – that it might be the Colorado River. Garcés probably had penetrated as far as the area north of Laguna Salada in 1771 before turning back toward the Colorado. *Ibid.,* I, pp. 138-39, 144.   [52] *Ibid.,* II (Anza), 89.

The experiences of the expedition's members in California are only of peripheral interest to our story. The fathers at San Gabriel had expected that Anza's coming meant a relief from their great want, but the members of the expedition themselves were in dire straits.[53] A party was sent to San Diego to try to get supplies for the hard-pressed mission. There a historic meeting took place between Father Garcés and Father Serra. The two padres rode together to San Gabriel whence Serra planned to continue to Monterey. They must have talked about their past accomplishments and their plans for the future. Strangely, the personal records of each of these two pioneers does not mention the meeting.[54]

Arriving back at San Gabriel, Garcés was disappointed to find that Anza had already left for Monterey. The padre had hoped to accompany Anza on the journey and to return to the Colorado by heading east from Monterey. Garcés believed that the San Joaquin River, which he called the San Francisco, was connected with the Colorado just above the Yuma villages, and he had wanted to investigate his theory. Though Anza previously had agreed to the plan, he had changed his mind and left orders for Garcés to lead the expedition's members that remained at San Gabriel back to the Colorado, there to await Anza's return. Undoubtedly disappointed, the padre nevertheless accepted the change in plans, apparently without any hard feelings.

---

[53] The California missions at this time were not the wealthy, extensive establishments that often are shown in the illustrated histories of California. Indeed, for the most part they were in great poverty. Father Fermín Lasuén, one of the ablest padres at San Gabriel, was one of those who felt that the first Anza expedition was to be their salvation. Testifying to the poverty of the mission fathers in 1774, Lasuén explained in a letter that in five years' time, he had not received the value of a single year's salary and had reached the point of destitution. He commented that perhaps that was the reason why the Indians liked him so much: "[W]ith so little clothing I am indeed very similar to them." Lasuén to Pangua, Mission San Gabriel, April 23, 1774. *Ibid.,* V, 142.   [54] *Ibid.,* I, p. 156; II (Garcés), 348.

On April 13, 1774, Garcés set out with his charges for the Colorado. The route he followed was roughly Anza's trail as far as San Sebastián. Instead of heading south from there toward the watering places just north of Laguna Salada, the party marched southeastward directly through the waterless Imperial Valley. Surprisingly, the Spaniards reached the Colorado River in but two days' travel from San Sebastián, cutting off miles from the route followed by Anza on his westward journey. The trip was a credit to Gracés's knowledge of desert travel.

Arriving on the Colorado, the padre and his companions settled down among the hospitable Yumas to wait for Anza. The muleteer and soldiers left by Anza on the outward trip were not there. They had heard a rumor that mountain Cajuenches had killed all members of the expedition, so they had taken most of the animals and provisions and had returned to Sonora. Palma fulfilled his trust by turning over to Garcés all the goods and animals the soldiers had left with him, including some calves that presumably had been born while the cows were his responsibility.

Meanwhile in Monterey, Anza visited Father Francisco Palóu at Mission Carmel. Palóu, who was to become the great historian of early Alta California, was very enthusiastic about the newly-opened road to Sonora. He saw great opportunities in the route and wrote his suggestions to the guardian of the college of San Fernando. In the latter, he proposed that a chain of missions be established along the entire length of the trail from Sonora to San Gabriel. Mail then could be carried every two months over the trail. The California missions thereby would be connected with Mexico in fact. Palóu suggested further that a regular freight service be initiated to succor the missions and settlements in California. Badly-needed settlers, he wrote, inev-

itably would come to California over the trail. The Manila
Galleon would call at Monterey to replenish its supplies and
trade with the Indians. Finally, he concluded, goods from
China could be off-loaded for transshipment to the interior
provinces of New Spain, such as Sonora and New Mexico.[55]

Anza finally completed his business at Monterey and
departed for the return journey to Sonora. He took with
him six soldiers from Monterey who were detailed by their
commander, Pedro Fages, to learn the road as far as the
Colorado River. At San Gabriel, Father Díaz and a few
others who had not left with Garcés, joined Anza. Determined to straighten out his circuitous westward trail, Anza
set out for the Colorado. Crossing the mountains through
the San Carlos Pass, where hostile Indians shot some of
their saddle animals, Anza and his companions arrived at
San Sebastián. There Anza found a note left by Garcés out-
lining the route the padre planned to follow. Anza took this
path for a while, but finding no water, soon left it. Anza's
party finally reached the Colorado in three days' time from
San Sebastián, succeeding somewhat in straightening his
westward route. There the Spaniards were received happily
by the Yumas and were reunited with Garcés.

During the expedition's short stay on the Colorado, an
incident led Díaz to the conviction that the Spanish should
establish a firm control on the Yuma crossing. A rumor
circulated that certain Indians planned to steal some riding
animals and cattle belonging to the expedition, but Palma
and the people of his village prevented it. Díaz commented
on the episode:

> . . . [P]assage through these lands will not be easy unless our
> nation establishes itself at some points on these rivers, for the fickleness

[55] Palou to the guardian of the college of San Fernando, Mission San Carlos,
April 22, 1774. *Ibid.*, v, 135-40.

of the Indians is well known, their inclination to thievery is patent, their consideration is none, and the passage of the river very difficult. And if they should come to be discontented, and disinclined to cooperate in the crossing with their aid, and on the contrary should attempt to impede it, a large force of arms would be necessary to vanquish so numerous although so uncivilized a heathendom.[56]

Though just previously praising Palma and his people for their fidelity in preventing the theft of the expedition's stock, in this discourse Díaz completely overlooks these virtues and characterizes all Colorado Indians as evil. Scores of American travelers in 1849 and the 1850s, however, would agree with Díaz's assessment, likewise the United States government which eventually established the military presence which Díaz was suggesting.

When it was time to leave the Colorado for the return trip to Sonora, Anza again expressed his affection and admiration for Palma and sought to reward him for his services. Leaving with him four cows and some articles of clothing, Anza regretted that he was not able "to reward this heathen barbarian more liberally, for his equal is not to be found among people of his kind."[57] Though condescending, the sentiment cannot be considered other than a great compliment on the part of a proud Spaniard.

Returning to Mexico by way of the Gila River, Anza found a considerable stretch of the river uninhabited due to inter-tribal warfare. When parties of Indians were visited – Cocomaricopas, Opas and Pimas – Anza persuaded most to agree to make peace with their enemies. The Pimas, by this time, were considered subject to Spanish authority, so Anza, acting for the government, filled vacant offices in Pima villages he visited.

Díaz was noticeably impressed with the Gila River In-

---

[56] *Ibid.*, II (Díaz), 298-99.   [57] *Ibid.*, I, p. 182.

dians. He found their means limited, but their production ample. He noted also that there were Christians among them and that

> . . . from what I have observed from communicating with them, all would gladly become Christians, and it would be at the cost of very little labor, if only for this purpose the necessary provisions were made.[58]

Díaz thereby added his plea to the countless other entreaties that had been sent south by missionary fathers in Pimería Alta for almost a hundred years.

At the western end of the great bend of the Gila, Garcés left the expedition. While Anza hastened to return to Tubac, Garcés set out northward to try to communicate with the missionary friars in New Mexico. Realizing that contact by way of Apacheria was out of the question and aware that there was frequent intercourse between the Spanish settlements in New Mexico and the Hopi towns, Garcés planned a journey to Hopi country. From there, he would send a letter to New Mexico. He was forced to turn back short of the mesa country, however, and returned to San Xavier del Bac in early July 1774. Anza had arrived at his home post of Tubac the previous May.

Concluding his diary of the expedition, Garcés attributed its success to the leadership of its commander:

> . . . I think the good conduct which the commander has shown, bearing with the Indians, disciplining the soldiers gently, and respecting and sustaining the fathers, not only with what is necessary, but also with the presents, must have moved the divining mercy to the end that the expedition should be made peacefully, although with impossible equipment, and over bad roads.[59]

Not all of Anza's future companions of the trail would hold the same high opinion of the commander.

---

[58] *Ibid.,* II (Díaz), 305.   [59] *Ibid.,* II (Garcés), 360.

Anza's feat in proving the feasibility of a road to California generated an increased interest in Pimería Alta. There was a call for more missionaries and more missions to convert the Indians and strengthen Spain's hold on that important province. Anza agreed wholeheartedly with these sentiments and suggested that the proposed missions be built on the Colorado rather than the Gila where they would be exposed to Apache attack. He cautioned, moreover, that they should not be built at all unless they could be protected by a strong presidio.

Meanwhile, the decision was made to expand Upper California settlements. Until 1775, both Upper and Lower California had been governed officially from Loreto in Lower California. In that year, a royal decree recognized the growing importance of Alta California and changed the seat of government to Monterey. A lieutenant governor was to be left at Loreto to administer the affairs of Baja California. While the decree was not implemented until 1777, action was taken immediately to increase the Spanish population of Upper California. It was decided that an expedition of soldiers and colonists would be sent to the bay of San Francisco. Anza was selected as the commander. In conjunction with the expedition, explorations were to be conducted in the Colorado River regions, as Anza had suggested.

During preparations for the forthcoming expedition to California, Mexican authorities solicited information concerning travel routes from frontier officials. Governor Crespo of Sonora suggested that Anza leave the Gila before reaching the mouth, then travel directly westward to Jalchedune country north of the Gila's confluence with the Colorado. Crossing the Colorado at that point, said Crespo, Anza would be ideally situated to march straight to Monterey, thus avoiding the Colorado Desert. The Governor further urged that exploration be undertaken, in connection with the expedition, to find the best route to the Hopi towns and New Mexico.[60]

This last was a timely comment, for Mexican authorities were even then questioning officials in New Mexico for their views on the most likely route to the land of the Hopis from the west or southwest. In the early part of 1775, the governor of New Mexico asked Father Silvestre Vélez de Escalante, who was then a missionary at Zuñi, for his views. Escalante, or Vélez as he was known to his contemporaries, was asked to comment on the question of opening communication between New Mexico and Sonora and between New Mexico and the new California capital at Monterey. He was asked also to suggest what policy he thought should be adopted toward the Hopis who long had resisted Spanish overlordship and overtures from the missionaries and who now stood as an obstacle to tying New Mexico with the Pimería and California.[61]

Escalante was very enthusiastic about the project. To gather information for his reply to the governor, he led a small expedition from Zuñi to Oraibe, the principal town of the Hopis. He was quite sure of his purpose. Later the same year, he wrote that he had wanted to investigate prospects of a road to Monterey by way of "the great river of the Cosninas, which I judge to be the Colorado." [62] The Cosninas, whom Escalante would later visit, were ancestors of today's Havasupais.

The padre was not able to reach the Colorado, but he did stay among the Hopis for eight days and formed some definite opinions on the best solution to the "Hopi problem." In the report which he eventually submitted, he strongly urged that the Indians be subdued by force and that a

---

[60] Bancroft, *Arizona and New Mexico*, 391.

[61] Silvestre Vélez de Escalante, *Pageant in the Wilderness*, trans. and annotated by Herbert Eugene Bolton (Salt Lake City, 1960), 1-2. (Citations hereafter are to "Velez.") [62] *Ibid.*, 2.

presidio be built there to prevent and further resistance to Spanish dominion.

Concerning the best route to Hopi lands from the west, Escalante thought a direct trail from the Colorado undesirable. A road from the Gila northward to the Hopi country he thought possible while the best, he considered, would be a trail directly from Monterey to the Hopi towns![63] It should be borne in mind that Escalante's views were based entirely on what Indians told him since he had never been west of Hopi country. He was a man of convictions, however, and eventually took part in an attempt to prove his claim that a northern route to Monterey was the most practical. Escalante was destined to fail in his effort while his fellow Franciscan, Father Garcés, would show that the route which Escalante considered the least likely, directly from the Colorado to the Hopi mesas, was feasible.

In September 1775, Anza set out from Horcasitas, about 200 miles south of Tubac, on his second journey to California. A major expedition, it included 240 persons. Father Pedro Font, who was the father chaplain of the College of the Cross of Querétaro, was selected to accompany Anza all the way to Monterey while Fathers Garcés and Tomás Eixarch were to leave the expedition at the Colorado River. Garcés understood that his instructions were to:

> . . . await their return and in the meantime to look over the country and treat with the near-by Indian nations, determining if they were disposed and ready for religious instruction and for becoming subjects of our Sovereign.[64]

---

[63] Bancroft, *Arizona and New Mexico*, 261, 391-2.

[64] Francisco Tomás Garcés, *A Record of Travels in Arizona and California, 1775-1776*, ed. by John Galvin (San Francisco, 1967), 1. Thus began yet another Spanish expedition to determine whether certain Pimería Alta Indians were ready for Christianity. A Pima or Yuma Indian, in exasperation, might justifiably have said to Garcés during this, his fifth journey from Bac: "Have we not begged you to send us padres to baptize us and live among us? Did our fathers not beg your

The composition of Anza's force emphasizes the uniqueness of the venture. The expedition's members included many families. Some of the soldiers even had their wives and children with them. For this reason, Father Font had little hope that the soldiers could protect the column from Apache attack. The troops were few and green and generally were preoccupied with the needs of their families. Soldiers often were seen carrying two or three children at a time. Font attributed the failure of the Apaches to attack the column not to the presence of the soldiers, but to "our patroness, the Most holy Virgin of Guadalupe."[65] Font might well pray to the Virgin for the expedition traveled on the very edge of Apache country north of San Xavier.

Arriving at the Gila, the expedition was received cordially by the Pimas. Anza had told the Spaniards to expect a friendly reception and had warned them not to molest the Indians or to steal their goods. He had urged them to set a good example and prescribed severe penalties for any who violated his orders. In spite of Anza's favorable picture of the Pimas, the Spaniards were not prepared for the Indians' openness. Doubtless, they had been victims of too many Apache raids to believe that any Indians could be so friendly. Indeed, the colonists had reason to feel a sort of kinship with the Pimas who also often fell victim to the plundering Apaches. As always, the Pimas furnished the travelers all the provisions they needed.[66]

---

fathers to send us missionaries? And did our grandfathers not beg your grandfathers to send us black robes?"

Another useful translation of the same journal is the earlier two-volume work edited by Elliott Coues, *On the Trail of a Spanish Pioneer,* previously cited.

[65] Bolton, *Anza,* IV, 28.

[66] *Ibid.,* III (Anza), 13, 17-18; Garcés, *Record of Travels,* 6. Apparently the Pimas also recognized this kinship-in-adversity with the Spaniards. Some of the Indians told Font that it would be a very good thing for the Spaniards to settle down on the Gila, "for then the soldiers could fight with them against the Apaches." Bolton, *Anza,* IV, 34.

Both Garcés and Font were impressed with the earnest desire of the Indians for conversion. Font found them "gentle and of good heart," noted that they "manifested great pleasure at seeing us in their country" and concluded that they "greatly desire" fathers to live with them and baptize them. Font also acknowledged in his diary that the Indians had asked for fathers several times before.[67] According to Garcés, the Indians "kept asking us repeatedly if we were finally coming to live with them and to baptize them, which seemed to me a sign that these Indians are very well disposed toward Christian teaching."[68] At one village, about 1,000 Pimas gathered before an arbor they had built in anticipation of the Spaniards' coming. In front of the arbor was a cross. When the travelers dismounted, the Indians went to them and kissed their hands, all the while "uttering the name of God, as those other Pimas do who are Christians."[69]

The fathers were moved, but unmoving. Garcés explained his feelings during a visit to one particular village:

> Whenever we have been with these poor heathen they have received me always with the same affection, and I have regretted not being able to fulfill the great desire they show to be Christians; but on this occasion I was the more distressed at seeing so many gathered together who wanted us to stay there to baptize them. . . Yet, even so, the time does not seem to have come for bringing these souls within the fold of the Church. May God so dispose as and when it may please Him most.[70]

Font wrote simply that they could not minister to the Indians or baptize their children because the Spaniards were just "passing through." He added, however, that "we tried to satisfy them by giving them good hopes."[71] The Pimas had been served such poor fare many times before. The tobacco and beads the Indians received proved more valuable than the padre's promises.

[67] Bolton, *Anza*, IV, 43.   [68] Garcés, *Record of Travels*, 6.
[69] *Ibid.*, 7.   [70] *Ibid.*   [71] Bolton, *Anza*, IV, 43.

Moving down the Gila, Anza was happily impressed with the absence of Indian warfare. He attributed the peace to his entreaties during the first expedition. He found Opas and Cocomaricopas living on the open plain, cultivating large fields. Before, he had found them living in secluded hideaways where they could protect themselves from their enemies, the Yumas. The story was the same further downstream. Responding to the repeated thanks tendered him by the Indians for bringing peace to their lands, Anza told them that "they owe this benefit to the king, who is dispatching his soldiers through these parts solely with this purpose, and with greater blessings in view, the spiritual ones, which the reverend fathers will explain to them."[72] This pronouncement must have come as a surprise to the soldiers who, laden with children, understood that the principal reason for the expedition was to plant a colony on the shores of San Francisco bay.

As the expedition visited the villages along the Gila, Anza was pleased to see that the beginnings of a Spanish-styled civil government that he had established the previous year had held firm. During his first expedition, he had "confirmed" Indian leaders in their offices. The chiefs had happily accepted his confirmation as proper, as if it gave them greater authority. Now other Indians approached Anza for appointments or confirmation of positions which they held in their villages. Doubtless with some satisfaction, Anza complied with the requests.[73]

Finally arriving at the Colorado River, the Spaniards received a tumultuous welcome from the Yumas. Captain

---

[72] *Ibid.,* III (Anza), 18, 24.

[73] Anza's charge to the Indian officials apparently was taken seriously by them. On one occasion, as Anza lectured a group of newly-elected officers on their duties, the native governor became overwhelmed with the enormity of his authority and "for more than an hour he did not cease to tremble so hard that he appeared to be shivering from the severest chill." *Ibid.,* III (Anza), 30.

Palma embraced Anza and, it appears, everyone else, men, women and children. We should pause a moment to look more closely at this Yuma chieftain who already had shown his importance in Spain's fortunes.

Salvador Palma is at the same time a powerful, intriguing and pathetic figure. He seems to symbolize the lost opportunity of the Spanish to win the spiritual and temporal allegiance of the Indians and to incorporate them into the life of New Spain. More than that, he symbolizes the failure of the European conquerors of the western hemisphere to carry out promises which, if fulfilled, might have resulted in a happy coexistence of European and native American cultures, or perhaps even a mutually beneficial fusion of those cultures. Either of the alternatives would have been preferable to the results of the policies adopted by most of the conquerors, policies which consciously or unconsciously were designed to destroy Indian cultures, and not infrequently, Indian peoples.

Anza's account of his meeting with Palma on this occasion is particularly revealing:

> This heathen captain had the courtesy to ask me about the health of his Majesty and of his Excellency the Viceroy . . . and that in order to hear them he would gladly take off his ears and put on some Spanish ears so that he might understand what they would say. He begged me to tell him whether the Spaniards and fathers were now coming whom he had requested the governor to send to his country, since for a long time he had desired it, and in order to make himself deserving of it he had strictly fulfilled all the commands which I had given him, and especially that of refraining from war with any tribe. From this he excepted the tribe of the mountain range to the west, because he had heard that these people had gone to our new establishments of Alta California to steal the horses and that they had killed one of our men. [The reference likely is to the murder of Father Jaume at San Diego.] But with the rest he had maintained peace, and now had formed alliances with all, and restrained them from making war with

various other tribes. In this, because of his warlike disposition, he had made no little sacrifice, as a gift to God and the king who had commanded him. And finally, all that he had done and was doing with the tribes, and all that he hoped to do, was in order that all these things might be perpetuated, and that the Spaniards and missionaries might settle here. To this end he offered all his lands in the name of his tribe, since all would be pleased if we should come for these purposes, and especially to Christianize them, for they wished to embrace all the laws of our religion, of which they had some information, and he especially, because he had dealt with our own people in their settlements; . . .

To this I answered that I could not grant what he asked, but I assured him that . . . [his request would be granted] . . . in due time. He accepted my reply. . .

In view of all the foregoing and of my experience with this captain and his tribe since my first visit, I have no doubt that they will embrace our faith and our customs with all complacency. Indeed, I have superabundant evidence that they are attached to both one and the other. One of many proofs is that now when they show us their wives they boast that they have only one. Another is that they still know how to say "Ave Maria," and repeat other words belonging to our prayers, which they ask us to teach them. More than this, we have found them now so well covered for modesty's sake that this has surprised us as much as their nakedness surprised us when they came before us on the first occasion. And finally, we note that they preserve the slight touch of good manners which we instilled in them when we passed, and all, generally speaking, urge us that now we shall remain to reside among them.[74]

Surely no other people in history had ever sought so earnestly and so long to adopt an alien culture.

Font wanted to make sure that the Yumas understood what would be expected of them if missions were established in their lands. He questioned Palma and another Yuma chieftain called "Pablo" by the Spaniards. Pablo, whose villages were more populous than Palma's, was a chief in his own right but appeared to be subordinate to Palma. Font

[74] *Ibid.*, III (Anza), 38-40.

explained that the Yumas would have to learn doctrine and carpentry and would have to cultivate the soil. They would have to end their scattered existence and live in a pueblo where they would build a church and a house for the father. To all this, according to Font, Palma

> . . . replied that they would do these things with great pleasure, although now his head was pretty hard for learning, and that he greatly wished that we would come now and not "soon." . . Then he bade me goodbye with many embraces and demonstrations of pleasure, saying in conclusion that now he was a Spaniard and I a Yuma.

Pablo readily agreed to all that Palma said.[75]

The relationship between Father Font and Anza was not so cordial. Font considered the commander a glory-seeker who slighted the padres at every turn. He complained, for example, that though the viceroy had sent a quadrant for Font's use, Anza unaccountably kept the instrument in his possession except when it was actually needed for an observation. He complained that the commander personally distributed the presents of beads and tobacco, thereby preventing the fathers from winning the affections of the Indians. Anza presented Palma with a suit of clothes in the name of the viceroy in private, wrote Font, because he did not wish to share the glory with anyone. The father disagreed with the commander over the arrangements for the two padres who would remain with the Yumas when the expedition departed for California. Exasperated, Font prayed to God: "A militibus libera nos Domine," meaning, "Lord, deliver us from soldiers." [76]

---

[75] *Ibid.*, IV, 73-74.

[76] *Ibid.*, III (Anza), 47; IV, 23, 80-85. In the prayer, which Font committed to his diary, he was quoting a saying of Fray Antonio Margil de Jesús, a famous Franciscan missionary who had served on the Texas frontier in the seventeenth and eighteenth centuries. If Garcés and Eixarch, the two fathers who were to remain on the Colorado, were not pleased with Anza's arrangements, they did not mention it in their diaries.

The expedition finally got underway for California. Bidding farewell to the Yumas and charging Palma and Pablo to care well for the padres, Anza led the column down the Colorado to the land of the Cojats, a Yuman tribe.[77] From there, the column headed westward to the Laguna de Santa Olaya where a halt was called to rest. The Spaniards must have been surprised to see riding into camp Father Garcés whom they had left at Palma's village but a few days before. The tireless padre was already off on an exploration and had easily overtaken the slow-moving expedition.

Garcés appears to have been much more interested in visiting with the throngs of Indians that hovered about the encampment than with the Spaniards. The father, whom Font considered almost an Indian himself, promptly began preaching to the Indians. He illustrated his words with a canvas, on one side of which he had drawn an image of the Virgin holding the Christ child and on the other, a condemned man burning in hell. According to Font, the Indians were delighted with the one side, saying that they wanted to be Christians so they could be "white and beautiful like the Virgin." When Garcés turned the canvas around, they raised a loud cry and said that they did not like that. In a body, they wished to be baptized, but they were not, wrote Font, because they had not been catechized.[78]

The remainder of the expedition's journey to San Gabriel was made with the usual hardship from exposure and lack

---

[77] Font had an unpleasant encounter here with some curious Cojats who thronged about him. The Indians were "so filthy, because of their vile habits," he wrote, he could not breathe, so he forced them to move away from him. The Indians were offended and became threatening. Withdrawing to his tent, the padre decided that the Cojats were completely depraved. *Ibid.,* IV, 92-93, 110-11. The incident is illustrative of Font's unfitness to minister to "uncivilized" Indians.

Apparently wishing to protect the sensitive reader from the frank language of Father Font, Bolton left untranslated certain passages that deal with the "offensive" habits of the Indians. *See,* for example, *ibid.,* IV, 103-4.   [78] *Ibid.,* IV, 118.

of water. The route across the desert was shorter than that taken on the westward journey by the first expedition. The circuitous southern trail that had taken the first expedition to the northern end of the Laguna Salada was eliminated in favor of a more direct one to the western edge of the desert. Exposure to the cold weather in the closing days of the march seems to have cured the invalids, but it played havoc with the animals, some of which died almost daily. The colonists were distressed at the sub-freezing December weather and apparently were terrified at the sight of snow-covered mountains, something that was unknown to them. Anza calmed their fears by pointing out that when they neared the coast, the weather would moderate. Since many of the colonists were from the warm coasts of Mexico, this explanation appeared to satisfy them. The Spaniards were cheered by the lack of Indian hostility. Indeed, they found the Indians in the desert and foothill regions very timid and among the most destitute they had ever seen.

The expedition reached San Gabriel mission on January 4, 1776. The only death during the entire journey was a woman who had died because of the complications of childbirth. The expedition's numbers indeed had been increased by three babies born during the trip; five women had miscarried. From San Gabriel, the expedition continued the journey to San Francisco bay and the establishment of New Spain's northernmost settlement. Anza's charges were the first party of emigrants to enter California by an overland route.

CHAPTER III

Peak and Decline of the Spanish Northern Frontier

Anza's establishment of an overland route to California in 1774 and his successful march to California with a party of colonists in 1775 would appear to signal a new era for the frontier regions. Indeed, within a few years following Anza's feat, the Spanish population of California increased, the feasibility of a direct route from New Mexico to Monterey was proven, and missions were built on the Colorado River. Even as New Spain's power and interest in its frontier increased, however, the seeds of its decline were taking root, to mature in a rupture that would never heal during Spain's waning sovereignty in Mexico. But that was in the future. In the mid-1770s, Spain's star in the frontier was still rising.

Garcés did not long sit still after Anza set out for San Gabriel in early December 1775. Within days of the expedition's departure from the Colorado River, the padre was off on an exploration southward. He was accompanied by the Indian, Sebastián Tarabal, who had been one of Anza's guides on his first journey to California. It has already been mentioned that Garcés overtook the second expedition at Laguna de Santa Olaya. From there, he continued southward and spent the remainder of the month exploring the lower Colorado. He visited many Indian villages and, according to his account, was welcomed everywhere. Near the mouth of the river, Garcés found Indians who apparently had never seen domesticated animals. They greeted the padre's mules as if they were persons, fed them squash and took one wet, muddy mule to the fire to warm it.

Meanwhile, Eixarch ministered to the Yumas alone. He was well supplied, always having more than he needed, and was constantly attended. Palma, he wrote, "is never absent." [1] With the conviction that the chieftain's attachment to the Spaniards was sincere and deep, the padre told Palma that he should go to Mexico to see the sights and the viceroy who wished very much to see him. Palma replied that he was ready to go with Eixarch immediately and would take his fourteen-year-old son as well! He was disappointed that the padre could not set out at once, but agreed to wait and accompany Anza on his return to Sonora. The ever-optimistic chieftain told Eixarch that on reaching Mexico he would go to the viceroy and ask him to send many fathers to come to his country where they would live with the Indians and would want for nothing.[2]

On Christmas Eve, Eixarch received the disturbing news that there was tribal warfare in the area that Father Garcés had gone to explore and that the padre had been threatened. Though he usually paid little attention to what Indians said, he did not totally disbelieve this news because it was so ominous. He was relieved to learn a few days later that the earlier report had been completely false and that Garcés had been well received and cared for everywhere he went. The wandering padre arrived safe and sound at Palma's

[1] Bolton, *Anza,* III (Eixarch), 314.

[2] *Ibid.,* III (Eixarch), 320. Palma had already visited Spanish settlements in Mexico. In his February 21, 1776, diary entry, Eixarch wrote that the chief was greatly pleased with the Ash Wednesday service and added: "Indeed, in the past year of 1775 he was at Cieneguilla and San Miguel [towns in Sonora], and while there never missed a single Mass or sermon or Rosary, just the same as now. It will be a pity if this Indian is not baptized." *Ibid.,* III (Eixarch), 359-60.

village on January 3, 1776, just one day before the Anza expedition reached San Gabriel.

Eixarch and Garcés taught and preached almost every day. The Indians were exceptionally attentive, and the attendance at the gatherings was always good. Though Eixarch sought with all his heart to minister to his charges, he nevertheless felt personal revulsion at times toward them because of their lack of modesty and good hygiene. Garcés apparently was not bothered. Certainly Eixarch found Indians more compatible than did Father Font, but his tolerance did not approach that of Garcés.

The greatest obstacle encountered by the fathers in carrying out their mission seems to have been a lack of wine. Anza had left some wine for Mass, but it was so foul that it made Eixarch vomit. Eixarch soon suspended the saying of Mass and sent to Caborca for a fresh supply. When weeks passed and the messenger did not appear, Eixarch himself set out for Caborca. He was soon forced to turn back when his guide deserted him. The messenger finally did return from Caborca, much to Eixarch's delight, but brought only a small quantity of the precious fluid. The dejected padre lamented that "unless God should dispose otherwise," he could not stay much longer where he was.[3] Garcés and Eixarch did say a number of Masses thereafter, but soon decided to save their meager supply of wine for feast days.

While the padres were pleased with the spiritual opportunities among the Yumas, they must have been particularly intrigued in early January 1776 when a group of nine Apaches attended Mass. The nine were visiting the Yumas, who were friends of the Apaches. Garcés spoke to the visitors through a Yuma interpreter, asking them how they lived and who their friends were. They replied that they

---

[3] *Ibid.,* III (Eixarch), 334.

were scattered and lived mostly by hunting. They said they supplemented their meat diet by growing a little squash and maize. Their friends were the Yumas and Mojaves; their enemies included the Hopis, Pimas, Cocomaricopas and the Spaniards. The nine added, however, that they had heard that all the Indians were making peace among themselves, and they too wished to make peace. Garcés told the visitors that if the Apaches would gather together in one place and present their children for baptism, he would visit them and help them arrange peace with their enemies. Soon, he added, Spaniards would come to live on the Gila and Colorado and "everything would be all right." The Apaches told the padre that they would relate all they had heard to their people. Garcés ended by pointing out to them that "the Spaniards did no harm to good people and that if the bad stopped being bad there would be no more fighting." [4]

Garcés certainly would have been aware of the possibilities posed by this meeting. If he could bring the Apaches into the circle of peace, the course of the history of New Spain's northern frontier would be drastically altered. But nothing came of it. If Garcés' proposal was in fact transmitted to the assembled Apaches, they apparently thought little of it. At least, the padre left no record of a goodwill visit to Apacheria,[5] and the Apaches continued to resist

---

[4] Garcés, *Record of Travels*, 28-29.

[5] Apaches did, however, continue to visit Palma's village during the padres' residence there. In his diary entry of March 3, 1776, for example, Eixarch wrote: "After dinner the Apaches came and I showed them the vestments for celebrating Mass and likewise the images which I have, and they were much pleased with them." The Apaches were not as intrigued with the Spanish God as the Gila and Colorado River Indians. There is no evidence that the Apaches ever asked the fathers to come to live among them, a request that the Pimería Indians repeatedly made of the Spaniards. Among these latter Indians, indeed, there was even a spirit of competition for the attention of the Spaniards. In May, Eixarch wrote: "The interpreters have told me that the Jalchedunes as well as the Cajuenches and the Jamajabs [Mojaves] are very jealous, saying that the Spaniards love only Palma,

invasion of their lands until near the close of the nineteenth century.

While Eixarch remained on the Colorado preaching to the Yumas and awaiting Anza's return from California, Garcés and Sebastián set out in mid-February on another exploration.[6] From time to time, Eixarch received reports and heard rumors of Garcés' whereabouts. In late April, the Yumas brought the news that he had gone to Monterey.[7] About the same time, a Jalchedun relative of Palma's who lived to the north of the Yumas told Eixarch that Garcés had been in his village. In early May, the two interpreters who had accompanied Garcés on his departure from Palma's village returned. The padre had left them in a Mojave village to care for some animals and goods when he and Sebastián headed westward for Monterey. Receiving no word from the father after the passage of some weeks, they returned to report to Eixarch. Eixarch must have had faith in Garcés' wilderness skills since he did not appear to be particularly disturbed at the news. This was the last word he received about Garcés' movements before the return of Anza and the expedition from California.

Meanwhile, as Father Eixarch labored on the Colorado River, Anza prepared the expedition for the return march from California to Sonora. Reaching the bay of San Francisco in the early part of the year, he had explored in the region before departing. His party reached San Gabriel on the return journey in late April. Anza thought he might find Garcés there. The padre had visited the mission earlier on his outward journey, but he was gone by the time Anza arrived. He left a letter for the commander, telling him that

whom they treat like a king, paying no attention to them. . . . Each and every one of them would like to have a father." Bolton, *Anza*, III (Eixarch), 317.

[6] *See below*, pp. 90-91.

[7] Garcés did enter the California Central Valley, but he did not reach Monterey.

he planned to travel inland to try to find a route directly to New Mexico. Anza sent a messenger to try to find Garcés, but to no avail. Father Font assumed that he had found his road to New Mexico or that he was dead, either from illness or at the hands of Indians.[8]

The expedition tarried only a few days at San Gabriel before departing for the Colorado.[9] The return party, in addition to the commander and Father Font, included ten soldiers, eight muleteers and Anza's personal servants. The eastward journey, though hard, was uneventful except for the fear of Indian hostility in the California passes. The return route was almost identical to that of the first expedition with the exception that the path across the desert was somewhat north of that taken by the first expedition.

Arriving safely in the Yuma villages in early May, the expedition was greeted by Father Eixarch and the Yumas. Eixarch gave the commander a favorable report on his experiences and especially praised Captain Palma for his devotion to the padre's mission and attention to his personal needs. The Indians appeared as happy to see the Spaniards as on the outward journey. Palma soon approached the commander with his request that he be taken to Mexico and presented to the viceroy, as Anza previously had promised. Palma explained that he wished personally to ask the viceroy

　　　. . . that he may be permitted to become a vassal of his Majesty,

---

[8] Bolton, *Anza*, IV, 485.

[9] *Ibid.*, III (Anza), 168. The undercurrent of conflict between Font and Anza had not subsided. When the messenger who Anza sent to search for Garcés returned not with the father but with his animals, Font rebuked him, saying that Garcés might have merely left the animals for a period, planning to return to get them. The messenger replied that he was only following the orders of the commander who had told him that if he failed to find Garcés, but did find his animals, that he should bring them. Font related the incident as typical of "the favors which he [Anza] says he is always showing the fathers." *Ibid.*, I, pp. 485-86.

and that he be granted ministers to instruct his tribe and others, his
allies, in the true faith, to which they are ready to submit themselves.[10]

Satisfying himself that the Yumas wished their chief to
make the journey and that tribal affairs would be carried on
in good order in his absence, Anza consented. He suggested,
much to the delight of the Indians, that three others accompany Captain Palma to serve as witnesses of the good treatment he would receive in Mexico.

Anza had expected to find Garcés at the rendezvous, but
again was disappointed. On hearing that he was in the land
of the Jalchedunes, the commander sent a message to Garcés.
The note told of the expedition's arrival in Palma's village
and informed the elusive padre that if he wished to return
to Sonora with the expedition, he should come promptly.

When the appointed time for Garcés' arrival passed,
Anza decided that the expedition could wait no longer. Four
days were consumed in crossing the swollen Colorado. When
the swift water prevented ferrying the goods by raft, swimmers, mostly women, transported small quantities until all
were across. The Yumas willingly, even eagerly, aided the
transit, leading Anza to reassert the importance of strength-
ening the ties of the river Indians with the Spanish. Without
their help, he concluded, the river could be crossed only
with the greatest difficulty. Faced with their enmity, a crossing would be virtually, if not absolutely, impossible.

Having safely crossed the mighty Colorado, leave was
taken of the hospitable Yumas. Father Eixarch and Palma
joined the expedition for the trek to Mexico. Anza decided
to try to shorten the march as much as possible by leaving
the Gila early and taking a southeasterly direction. He had
heard that there was presently ample water on this route and
figured he could cut sixty leagues off the distance covered

---

[10] *Ibid.,* III (Anza), 177-78.

on the outward journey. The intended trail was not unknown
to Anza. From the Gila to Caborca, the expedition followed
almost exactly the same route taken by the first expedition
on its westward journey. There were only two substantial
variations. The first expedition had traveled west of the Gila
Range, which lies just south of the Gila River, while the
second expedition passed east of those mountains. Another
variation was made just north of the present international
boundary and between the Pinto Range and the Tule Range.
The second expedition passed near the latter mountains
while the first expedition marched closer to the Pinto Range.

This second of Anza's history-making journeys was
brought to a close. Visiting the ruins of Sonóita mission en
route, the remainder of the trip was completed apparently
without incident though an Apache attack was feared near
Horcasitas. From that place, the commander marched to
his presidio at Tubac. Putting his affairs in order there,
Anza continued on to Mexico City where Palma was presented to the viceroy who seems to have been as excited as
the Yuma chieftain about the meeting. During his stay in
the capital, Palma was feted, catechized and baptized in the
cathedral.[11]

The expeditionary force was disbanded without knowing
the fate of Father Garcés. In fact, the padre was alive, well
and as footloose as ever. After he had left Eixarch at the

----

[11] After four months in the capital, Palma and his three Yuma companions returned to their homes on the Colorado River. Anza's service on the frontier of New
Spain was not at an end. He subsequently served as governor of New Mexico where
his greatest accomplishments lay in his handling of Indian affairs. For an interesting
account of Anza's New Mexico experience, see Alfred Barnaby Thomas, ed. and
trans., Forgotten Frontiers: A Study of the Spanish Indian Policy of Don Juan
Bautista de Anza, Governor of New Mexico, 1777-1787 (Norman, 1932).

At the conclusion of the expedition, Father Eixarch returned to his post at
Tumacacori. Soon after, he was appointed missionary at Oquitoa and later served
at the presidial church of El Altar. Bolton, Anza, III (Eixarch), 381, n. 3.

Colorado in mid-February, accompanied only by Sebastián and two Indian interpreters he traveled north to the land of the Mojave Indians, or Jamajabs, as he called them. He was warmly received by these Indians who were to become very attached to the father. The affection was reciprocal.

Garcés still hoped to prove that it was possible to travel directly between Monterey and New Mexico. He learned from his new friends that they sometimes crossed the country west of their villages to reach the Spanish missions on the California coast.[12] The report must have excited his imagination. Perhaps this was the western end of the direct link between California and New Mexico. He determined to investigate the trail and recruited some Mojaves as guides.

Traveling westward from the Mojave villages, approximately at the location of the present town of Needles, the little party made its way over a path apparently known to the guides. It was early March, and finding potable water appears to have been no problem. After a few days on the trail, the travelers met four Mojaves heading eastward. They had come from Santa Clara where they had been trading in shell beads. Garcés was astonished when he saw that they carried no food or weapons for hunting. The Indians explained that they were Jamajabs and could "withstand hunger and thirst for as long as four days." Garcés concluded that they were hardy men indeed. The meeting also could not have failed to influence his speculation that the route he was traveling might prove a favorable alternative to the Anza road. He soon found additional evidence of intercourse between Indians of the interior and the coast. Arriving at the Mojave River, which he named the Arroyo

---

[12] Thereby well within the period of exploration of the West, it would seem that the Mojaves should have earned fame as pioneers. But these Americans, like countless of their contemporaries and ancestors, for lack of a written language are accorded little share in the history of trail-making or being "first to cross . . . ."

de los Martires, Garcés saw some Indians who had baskets similar to those of the Santa Barbara Channel Indians.[13]

Continuing westward along the course of the Mojave River, described by Garcés as a stream-bed with brackish water, the padre and his companions were moving toward the site of today's Barstow.[14] They saw many bands of poor Indians who welcomed them warmly and showed great respect for Garcés. The father's little party suffered much on the trail from cold and rain as well as hunger.

When the course of the river turned to the south just past modern Barstow, Garcés told his guides that he wished to leave the river and head west. He expected thereby to reach the mission of San Luis Obispo which he thought to be at about the same latitude as their present location. The Mojaves refused, telling Garcés that they knew no other route to the coast than the one they were following along the bed of the Mojave River. Reluctantly, the padre abandoned his plan and followed his guides.[15] They continued to march alongside the river to its source, then crossed the San Bernardino Mountains. On March 22, they reached the summit from which Garcés saw the ocean. Two days later, they arrived at San Gabriel mission.

The tireless padre immediately began preparations to continue his journey. He applied to the governor of Upper California, Fernando Xavier de Rivera y Moncada, for assistance in the form of supplies and an escort. He ex-

---

[13] Garcés, *Record of Travels,* 34, 36.

[14] The identifications of present-day place names along Garcés's route in California were taken mostly from Raymund F. Wood, "Francisco Garcés, Explorer of Southern California," *Southern California Quarterly,* LI (Sept. 1969), 185-209.

[15] Garcés, *Record of Travels,* 38. This is one of a number of examples which show that Father Garcés, though justly famous as an explorer, relied heavily on his Indian guides. In this case, while the padre was seeing the trail for the first time, the path was one known to the Mojaves. When his guides refused to help him pioneer a new trail, Garcés decided that he could not or should not go alone.

plained his plans to go to the San Luis Obispo mission, then head eastward to return to the Colorado River in the vicinity of the Mojave villages. To his surprise, Rivera refused any aid, replying variously that such aid was impossible and that he had no authorization from the viceroy to furnish assistance.

Rivera's hostility to Garcés' plans was unmistakable, and the padre soon detected a possible reason. He learned that the governor had recently ordered seized and expelled some Mojaves who were at the mission for trading purposes. The governor admitted that he did not wish to see Indians from the Colorado travel to Monterey over Garcés' proposed trail. The padre was amazed at the governor's attitude. He tried to reason with Rivera, explaining that Spain must have the friendship of all the nations of the Colorado if communications between the Spanish provinces were to pass through their lands.[16] The governor remained unmoved. Finally abandoning any hope of assistance from Rivera, Garcés asked for and received from the San Gabriel mission fathers enough supplies to continue his journey.

In early April 1776, Garcés set out northward, bound for San Luis Obispo. During the remainder of April and part of May, the padre explored in the California Central Valley. Though Sebastián and the Mojaves refused to penetrate deep into the valley, it seems that Garcés was accompanied by a local Indian, perhaps a Yokut,[17] who undoubtedly knew the country and its paths. The padre visited a number of villages and preached to the Indians who welcomed him and tried to persuade him to stay with them. He heard of a great river to the north, probably the San Joaquin, and was told at one point that mission San Luis Obispo was but

---

[16] *Ibid.,* 40.
[17] Wood, "Francisco Garcés, Explorer of Southern California," 195.

four days' travel. But by then his supplies were almost exhausted. He had been in the valley twice as long as he had expected to be, and he knew that Sebastián and the Mojaves would be worried about him.

Indeed they had worried. Though he feared the unknown tribes in the area, the faithful Sebastián had searched for Garcés as far north as the Kern River. In the padre's absence, more Mojaves had arrived from the Colorado, further convincing Garcés that travel from the Mojave country to the coast was rather common.

Leaving the area of Bakersfield, the party did not retrace the outward path. Instead, at Garcés' insistence they marched eastward and southeastward to cross the Tehachapi Mountains. The Mojaves did not know the country, having never come that way. Leaving the mountains, the party passed the site of Barstow and reached the Mojave River. They arrived in the Mojave villages to a tumultuous welcome in late May 1776.

Garcés found letters from Anza and Father Eixarch waiting for him. Anza's message summoned him to return to Palma's village within three days if he wished to return to Sonora with the expedition. Since the letter was written in early May, Garcés assumed correctly that the expedition must have already departed the Colorado. This suited him since he had another journey to undertake before he could consider this exploration completed.

Garcés still wanted to visit the Hopis. His opportunity came when some Hualapai Indians who were visiting the Mojaves said they would guide him to the Hopi towns. Garcés probably was never alone during the ensuing journey, though in spite of Garcés' pleading Sebastián could not be persuaded to accompany him.

The padre's greatest quality illustrated by this exploration was not so much in his pathfinding as his relationships with Indians. Every village through which he passed going to and from Oraibe welcomed him. Because of the warm relations between padre and Indians, he was able to persuade villagers to guide him from town to town. So the wandering friar was in good hands. He literally trod in the footsteps of local inhabitants who knew the country well, perhaps having passed over the trail just days before.

Crossing the Colorado near the site of present-day Needles, Garcés and his Hualapai companions marched northeastward until they reached the land of the Havasupais who were cousins of the Hualapais.[18] Though Garcés was not the first white man to see the Grand Canyon of the Colorado – Cárdenas and his small party had seen it in 1540 – he was the first European to visit the hospitable Havasupais in their village at the bottom of Cataract Canyon. Before leaving the Grand Canyon, Garcés named the magnificent gorge the Puerto de Bucareli in honor of the Viceroy of New Spain, Antonio María de Bucareli y Ursua.

Now guided by some Havasupai Indians, Garcés continued his march toward Oraibe. That long-sought goal was finally seen on July 2. Garcés was chagrined but not surprised to find that he was not welcome in Oraibe. Though contacts between Zuñi and the Hopi towns were not infrequent, the Hopis had no love for Spaniards and had successfully resisted secular or spiritual domination by the Spanish from the first. Father Escalante from Zuñi had visited Oraibe as late as the previous year, but had made no known impression on the Hopis.

---

[18] *Ibid.,* 198. Garcés identified the Havasu Indians as "Yavapais, who differ only in name" from the Hualapais. Garcés, *Record of Travels,* 62-63. Garcés was mistaken, as many other explorers were in their tentative identification of Indian groups. Though the peoples named were of the same linguistic family, they were quite different culturally.

The day after arriving in Oraibe, Garcés' hopes were
raised at a chance meeting with three Indians who had just
come from Zuñi. One of them, a Christian, promptly invited
the padre to return with him to Zuñi. Garcés accepted. By
reaching Zuñi, he would prove that communication between
California and New Mexico was indeed possible. The
padre's enthusiasm was cut short when his Havasupai companions objected strongly to the journey. They would not go
with him to Zuñi, and they could not wait for him among
the hostile Hopis. Without their protection on the return
journey through Hopi lands and without their services as
guides, how would he find his way back to Cataract Canyon?
The father, though courageous and resourceful, decided that
he would not invite martyrdom at this moment and declined
to go to Zuñi.

Garcés might justifiably have rationalized that the trip,
in any case, was not necessary to prove his theory. In California, he had been but a few days' easy march from San
Luis Obispo and Monterey. He had personally traveled
from the California Central Valley all the way to Oraibe.
Escalante had visited Oraibe from Zuñi, and Spanish movement between Zuñi and Santa Fé was commonplace. The
feasibility of a route between Monterey and Santa Fé was
thus proved without the necessity of his actually going to
Zuñi.

Though he was not to go personally to Zuñi, Garcés
wanted to make sure that the authorities in New Mexico
were notified of his having reached Oraibe. Accordingly, he
wrote a letter to "the Father Minister at Zuñi although
I did not know his name."[19] The message detailed not only
his arrival at Oraibe, but also told about the inhospitable
treatment he had suffered. He requested the Zuñi padre to

---

[19] Garcés, *Record of Travels,* 72. The resident padre was still Father Escalante.

forward the letter or a copy to the governor of New Mexico.

After but two days as an unwelcome guest of the Hopis, Garcés set out on the last phase of his last expedition. With his companions, he left Oraibe and once again entered the land of the Havasupai. There the padre rested and feasted on "buffalo and one of the stray cattle." [20] After a few days, Garcés left Cataract Canyon with his Havasupai guides and returned to the Colorado where he was given a rousing greeting by his good friends, the Mojaves. According to Garcés, they embraced him and "knew not how to express their delight." [21] Though he doubtless was tired from the grueling journey from Cataract Canyon, Garcés did not tarry long. He was in a hurry now to return to Yuma. Bidding a sad farewell to the Mojaves who had shown him such kindnesses and who had shared the hardships of the trail with him, the padre took his leave.

Garcés soon brought his journey to a close. He arrived at Yuma in late July. Palma's people were glad to see the padre. They had feared him dead because of his long absence. Garcés shortly left the Yumas to travel eastward along the Gila where he was given a tumultuous welcome by the Pimas. The good padre appreciated the warm reception but was grieved that they celebrated his arrival with an uncharacteristic drunken orgy. Their song, as recorded by Garcés, tells something about the Pimas and their affection for the father: " 'We are good, we are happy, we know God, and we are people who can fight the Apaches. We are glad that the old man'– that is what they call me –'has come back and that the Apaches have not killed him.' " [22] Garcés soon said goodby to the Pimas and ended his long journey with his

---

[20] *Ibid.,* 78. This is an intriguing comment since buffalo did not range into the land of the Havasupai, nor is there evidence that Garcés had ever before seen a buffalo.   [21] *Ibid.,* 81.   [22] *Ibid.,* 87.

arrival on September 17, 1776 at San Xavier del Bac mission.

Before Garcés finished his last major exploration, Father Silvestre Vélez de Escalante of Zuñi was out with a party of nine looking for the same thing Garcés had sought, a northern route connecting Santa Fé and Monterey. Escalante was aware that his Franciscan brother had reached Oraibe. Garcés' messenger, letter in hand, had caught up with Escalante at Santa Fé where the New Mexico expedition gathered. Escalante's determination to find a route to California was unchanged by Garcés' news.

Escalante's part was large in the genesis of the expedition though he was not its head. The official leader of the group was Father Atanasio Domínguez, who was the Superior of the New Mexico Franciscans. Escalante's name nevertheless is today the better known of the two because it was Escalante, not his leader, who wrote the diary that has established the place of the expedition in the annals of western history. Escalante's claim to fame, then, rests as much on his skills as a writer as on those of an explorer, for, wrote a historian of the expedition, "good paper and ink outlast the human body, or the memory of human exploits." [23] Also in the company was Don Bernardo Miera y Pacheco, an engineer from Santa Fé. As custodian of the astrolabe, Miera made astronomical observations which enabled him later to draw a valuable map of the country covered by the expedition. He also wrote an account of the journey which serves as a useful supplement to Escalante's journal.

The objective of the expedition, at least in Escalante's mind, was twofold. The official purpose was to find a direct

---

[23] Vélez, *Pageant in the Wilderness*, 11.

route between Santa Fé and Monterey. Escalante's purpose
went beyond that. He would establish missions along the
route all the way from New Mexico to the California coast.
The father had already determined that the Utes would be
receptive to missionary overtures and hoped that he would
find the Havasupais who Garcés had visited recently, of
a like mind.

The Domínguez-Escalante expedition was not the first
Spanish penetration into the present states of Colorado and
Utah. Traders from New Mexico regularly had journeyed
into Colorado to trade with the Indians for furs. By late
July 1776, when Escalante departed Santa Fé, the area east
of the Colorado River was known fairly well to New Mexicans. Aware that they could not travel due west on a
straight line for Monterey because of Hopi and Apache
hostility, the Escalante party headed north to follow the
traders' trails.

A glance at a map showing the route followed by the
Domínguez-Escalante expedition leads one immediately to
wonder whether the Spaniards had any sort of plan when
they set out. It is almost certain that they did, though the
accounts of the expedition do not reveal it.[24] The party
traveled in a northwesterly direction from Santa Fé to the
southwestern corner of modern Colorado, then generally
northward to the northwestern part of the state, thence westward to Utah Lake in north-central Utah. From Utah
Lake, the expedition took roughly a south-southwesterly
direction.

The course of the expedition ran not much unlike those of
other Spanish explorers. Food was carried on muleback and

---

[24] Bolton speculated on their intended route. *See ibid.,* 14. The trail followed by
the expedition is well-mapped and beautifully illustrated in original landscape
paintings in Walter Briggs, *Without Noise of Arms: The 1776 Domínguez-Escalante
Search for a Route From Santa Fé to Monterey* (Flagstaff, 1976).

on the hoof. The herd of cattle driven along for fresh meat gave the party no end of trouble. Though the diaries of the expedition make little mention of the killing of wild animals for food, it must be assumed that the fare was supplemented by game. Before the Spaniards reached Santa Fé, all their food supplies had been consumed, and they were forced to live off the land.

Father Escalante's experiences with Indians were similar to those of Garcés, his fellow Franciscan. Escalante found most Indians friendly and either willing or eager to hear him preach. Like Garcés and so many other Spanish padres, Escalante planted false hopes that missionaries would be sent to the Indians.

One particular incident, delightful in the re-telling, was not so amusing to Escalante. A group of Sabuaganas in west-central Colorado seemed quite pleased with the padre's preaching, but he soon learned that their pleasure stemmed not from the sentiments which he expressed in the sermon, but those expressed by the interpreter in his translation. Taking great liberties in translating Escalante's explanation of the necessity for baptism, the interpreter stated:

> The Father says that the Apaches, Navajos and Cumanches [sic] who do not become baptized cannot enter Heaven, but go to Hell, where God punishes them, and where they will burn forever like wood in the fire.[25]

The Sabuaganas were overjoyed to learn that their enemies must either be baptized or burn in hell while they themselves were exempted from either. Assuming that the interpreter had altered the text of the sermon in order not to anger the Sabuaganas, Escalante let him off with a reprimand.

---

[25] *Ibid.*, 215-16. We are not told how Escalante was able to render an exact version of the interpreter's translation when the padre did not understand the native language.

Leaving Utah Lake behind them, the expedition took up the trail again, eventually making camp at a place east of the San Francisco Mountains, which lie due south of Sevier Lake in west-central Utah. Here the leaders of the party decided to give up the trek to California. They had failed to find a pass through the rugged San Francisco Mountains, a route which Escalante thought the best to Monterey. At the same time, the weather had turned colder – it was early October – and they already had experienced a heavy snowfall. In every direction, the mountains were covered with snow.

In spite of their leaders' fears, there were others in the party who wished to press on to California. The mapmaker, Miera, appears to have been a leader of the dissenters. Miera, wrote Escalante, "had conceived great hopes of honor and profit by merely reaching Monterey, and had communicated these hopes to these others, building great castles in the air."[26] The dissenters seem to have been strong enough to prevent Domínguez from forcing his will. At this point, the party might yet have earned the distinction of being the first to reach California by a direct route from New Mexico. Or it might have earned the questionable honor of being the first party of white people to die in the snows of the Sierra Nevada. At their camp in western Utah, they were still a long way from the formidable Sierra.

Escalante and Domínguez decided to "inquire anew the will of God" to settle the issue. They would cast lots. Miera and the others agreed to abide by the results. The word "Monterey" was put in one and "Cosnina" in the other. While the former pointed a turn to the west, the latter indicated a southerly direction. Having determined to return to Santa Fé, Escalante hoped to visit the Cosnina Indians,

[26] *Ibid.*, 198.

today's Havasupais, about whom he had inquired at length during his visit to the Hopi towns in 1775. The opposing factions prepared themselves for the toss. The dissenters, noted Escalante, "with fervent devotion . . . said the third part of the Rosary and other petitions, while we said the penitential Psalms, and the litanies and other prayers which followed them." That done, the lots were cast. "Cosnina" came up. "Now, thank God," wrote Escalante, "we all agreeably and gladly accepted this result." [27]

The Spaniards took up the march toward Santa Fé. They continued in a southern direction until they entered the present state of Arizona. Turning eastward, they crossed the Colorado River near the Arizona-Utah boundary at the place that later became known as the "Crossing of the Fathers." En route to Zuñi, they visited the Havasupais. Escalante was impressed with their settlements. While he had found the Indians of present Colorado and Utah principally hunters and gatherers, the Havasupais lived a more settled life. He told of passing good irrigated farms growing maize, beans, calabashes, watermelons, cantaloupes and peaches.

In northeastern Arizona, the expedition visited the Hopi pueblos. They were received with a sort of restrained friendship. Why the Spaniards were not given the same cold reception suffered by Garcés but a few weeks before, we are not told. Perhaps the Hopis had had a change of heart, or they might have remembered Escalante favorably from his previous trip. [28] In any event, the Indians said that they wanted to be friends of the Spaniards, but that they did not

---

[27] *Ibid.*, 199.

[28] Since Garcés had come from the west, perhaps the Hopis did not associate him with the continuing threat of domination from the Spaniards in New Mexico and that, therefore, they need not fear him. Or, possibly Garcés had been too persistent in his attempts to preach to them.

want to be Christians. Though the fathers pled their cause, the Hopis remained firm and declared that they would not abandon the traditions of their ancestors. The Spaniards then departed, following the trail to Zuñi, Acoma and Isleta before turning north to reach Santa Fé and the end of the journey on January 2, 1777.

Members of the Domínguez-Escalante expedition brought back valuable information about the people and the land that they had seen. This fact alone makes the journey historically significant. Whether the expedition should be judged successful beyond that contribution is questionable. They had failed in their principal objective, to find a direct route from Santa Fé to Monterey, but in their failure they at least succeeded in demonstrating that such a route was, for the moment, not feasible. The expedition's members now could be more impressed with Garcés' feat which showed the promise of a central route through the lands of the Mojaves and Hopis.

Father Garcés wasted no time upon his arrival at San Xavier following the conclusion of his 1776 exploration in September of that year. He busied himself in the preparation of his diary for formal submission to the viceroy. He also helped Father Font draw a map which covered the areas of northern Sonora, the western part of New Mexico and most of the territory in present Arizona. The map, which accompanied Garcés' report when it was finally sent to the viceroy, traced Garcés' travels between California and Oraibe and showed the locations of the various tribes in the area.[29]

During this period of post-mortem, it seems that Garcés came upon Coronado's journals for the first time. At least,

---

[29] Garcés, *Record of Travels,* 2, and map following p. 122.

he had never mentioned having seen the journals before. Garcés appeared especially interested in what the accounts had to say about the Colorado River country. He considered the Coronado journals accurate "because I have seen almost everything it speaks of." [30]

Garcés hastened to bring to a successful conclusion what must have been his greatest ambition: the establishment of missions in the farthest reaches of the frontier. The padre had given the Indians hope that fathers eventually would come to live among them, and after generations of promises he meant to fulfill that hope.

Garcés also was motivated by other considerations. He believed that the permanence of the settlements in the Monterey region depended ultimately on Spanish control of the Colorado River. If the Indians of the Colorado were enemies of the Spanish, only at great expense could the Monterey establishments be maintained. Garcés was convinced that the Indians of the Colorado and Gila, far from being enemies, were eager for a lasting relationship with the Spaniards. Therefore, to advance the cause of empire and church, Garcés recommended the establishment of no less than seventeen new missions along the two rivers! [31] Assuming that presidios would be built on the Gila and Colorado to protect the missions, Garcés urged that the soldiers be married men. Undoubtedly, he had in mind one of the main reasons why California Indians hated the Spanish – the soldiers' abuse of young Indian women.

Garcés further suggested means by which the new missions might be supported. A supply route could run from Mexico City to Chihuahua, then to Janos, San Bernardino, Santa Cruz, northward to the Gila, then down the Gila to the Colorado. He dismissed this alternative as too long, too

[30] *Ibid.*, "Reflections," 98.   [31] *Ibid.*, "Reflections," 92-94.

costly, and likely too dangerous, there being so many different tribes located on the route. A second possible supply
route could run by ship up the Gulf of California, thence
up the Colorado River or overland from the head of the
gulf. Still a third alternative could run overland from San
Diego.

In this last case, vessels cruising up the California coast
to provision Monterey would drop supplies off at San Diego
for the inland establishments. This would necessitate the
building of a warehouse at that port. The goods could be
stored there and sent eastward by pack train when conven-
ient. For the sake of efficiency, the detachment at San Diego
would be subordinate to the commander of the Colorado
River district.[32]

Garcés favored this last alternative. In doing so, it appears
that the padre's reasoning was a bit muddled. He had long
argued that Spanish control of the Colorado was essential to
the continued existence of the California settlements. He
was now recommending that the missions and presidios to
be built on the Colorado, which would ensure Spanish control of the region, be supplied from California. One of his
arguments in favor of the San Diego supply point was that
though hostile Indians might cut an overland route from
Mexico, they could not cut an ocean route. While Garcés in
the past had envisioned the Colorado and Gila establishments principally as an essential link in a land route between Mexico and California, it seems that he had come to
think of the establishments as ends in themselves. Perhaps he
now evaluated their worth more in spiritual than secular
terms.

The reports of Garcés, Anza, Font, Eixarch and others

---

[32] *Ibid.,* "Reflections," 99-100.

agreed on the importance of the Colorado River to the fortunes of New Spain. The officialdom of New Spain therefore decided to establish firm control in the Colorado region and strengthen the influence of New Spain in the rest of the upper frontier.

It seems that all interests were to be served by the enterprise. The opening of the missions would at last permit the fathers to live with the Indians and bring them the blessings of life within the true faith. The establishment of presidios would ensure protection of the missions as well as protection for travelers bound for California. Little, if any, resistance was expected from the Indian inhabitants of the regions to be brought under firm Spanish dominion. On the contrary, as already noted, it was understood that the Indians eagerly awaited the coming of the Spaniards.

Though official sanction was given to the project to establish missions, progress was slow. A niggardly attempt in 1779 failed completely. Fathers Garcés and Díaz and a third padre, Juan Antonio Barreneche, all of whom were to serve in the new missions, were allocated inadequate supplies for themselves and no gifts for the Indians. Since the giving of gifts was customary, and the Yumas had been led to believe that a Spanish movement to the Colorado would be accompanied by the distribution of valuable presents, this fact alone doomed the enterprise.

The principal blame for the fumbling progress and ultimate collapse of the Colorado undertaking can be laid at the feet of the commandant-general of the frontier provinces, Teodoro de Croix.[33] To complement the building of missions, Croix ordered in 1780 the formation of small colonies.

---

[33] In 1776-1777, the northern provinces of New Spain were taken out of the hands of the viceroy and organized as the Provincias Internas. As principal administrative official of the Provincias Internas, Croix was independent of the viceroy.

Each tiny pueblo, which would contain about ten soldiers, ten settlers and their families, were to be founded in conjunction with a mission. The padres and others protested against the deletion of presidios from the plan and condemned Croix's small-colony scheme as suicidal. But the commandant-general would not be disuaded. The required number of soldiers and colonists were recruited and sent to the Colorado in 1780 to carve homes from the wilderness. They carried no gifts for the Yumas.[34]

Two mission-pueblos were actually established during the few months following. One, Purísima Concepción, was built on the site of the later Fort Yuma. The location of the other mission, San Pedro y San Pablo de Bicuñer, is in dispute. Older authorities generally locate Bicuñer downstream from Concepción. Later research indicates that it might have been upstream from Concepcion, just below the present site of Laguna Dam.[35] Two padres were assigned to each mission, Father José Matías Moreno having recently arrived on the Colorado to work with the other three fathers. In addition to ministering to the Indians, the original purpose of the missions, the fathers were directed to meet the spiritual needs of the settlers.

Things were not going as Palma and the Yumas had expected. They had not received the promised gifts. They had not reckoned on the attentions of the fathers being divided between themselves and the intruding colonists, nor had they expected the soldiers. No one had told them their long-sought-after padres would come empty-handed, accompanied by unwanted settlers and escorted by guards.

As the disenchantment of the Yumas grew, a new contin-

---

[34] Bancroft, *Arizona and New Mexico*, 396; Wood, "Francisco Garcés, Explorer of Southern California," 202-3.

[35] Wood, "Francisco Garcés, Explorer of Southern California," 203, 209, n. 26. *Also see* below, 189, n. 64.

gent of Spanish settlers under Rivera y Moncada arrived.[36] Though most of the travelers continued their journey to California, Moncada and about a dozen men stayed and set up a camp near a village. Their animals did enough damage to the Indians' crops to bring matters to a head. Yumas previously had been angered when the permanent Spanish settlers on their arrival had taken the best lands along the river and had loosed their cattle to graze in the Indians' corn fields. This last insolence by Moncada and his men was the final insult. The Indians, led by a group of malcontents from Palma's people and other villages, rose in revolt.

In three days, the Spanish presence on the Colorado vanished. Missionaries, settlers and soldiers were killed. Many women and children were carried off to captivity. Palma appealed to his people to end the bloodshed, but he lost control and the slaughter was carried to its conclusion. Father Garcés, who loved the Indians and had been loved by them, was not spared. He died a martyr's death in the service of God and King.

Father Garcés' place in history is well established. With the help of his Indian companions from many tribes, he re-opened trails that originally had been trod by Kino, Keller and Sedelmayr. He pioneered paths across the southern California deserts and showed the feasibility of travel from the California Central Valley to New Mexico. Both contemporaries and later historians have commented on Garcés' stamina and skills on the trail. Yet, the modest padre wrote in his diary that he was "little practiced in matters of out-door life."[37]

Garcés' fame as an explorer does not eclipse his contribution as padre. Though his spiritual ministry to the Indians

---

[36] The same Moncada who in spring 1776 had refused to furnish Garcés with supplies which he needed to continue his journey from San Gabriel Mission.

[37] Bolton, *Anza*, II (Garcés), 326.

was coupled with the secular considerations of empire, his sincere love and concern for the welfare of his Indian friends is undeniable. Perhaps the greatest compliment to Garcés was made unwittingly by Father Pedro Font. Encamped near the Colorado River with the second Anza expedition, Font wrote:

> Father Garcés is so well fitted to get along with the Indians and to go among them that he appears to be but an Indian himself. Like the Indians he is phlegmatic in everything. He sits with them in the circle, or at night around the fire, with his legs crossed, and there he will sit musing two or three hours or more, oblivious to everything else, talking with them with much serenity and deliberation. And although the foods of the Indians are as nasty and dirty as those outlandish people themselves, the father eats them with great gusto and says that they are good for the stomach and very fine. In short God has created him, as I see it, solely for the purpose of seeking out these unhappy, ignorant, and rustic people.[38]

The destruction of the Colorado settlements signalled the beginning of the decline of Spanish fortunes in the north. Within the boundaries of modern Arizona, there were no other significant attempts at settlement or expansion of missionary activities. That part of the upper frontier, though not forgotten, was virtually abandoned.[39]

Though there was no new settlement, there were expeditions into the frontier regions. The initial and understandable Spanish reaction to the "Yuma Massacre," as the destruction of the settlements would be called, was anger. A council, called at Arizpe in September 1781 to discuss the

---

[38] *Ibid*, IV, 121.

[39] Neglect of the upper frontier was made official when the viceroy in 1786 declared that the Yumas were to be left alone until after the Spanish had subdued the Apaches. Bancroft, *Arizona and New Mexico*, 397. The Spanish would not complete this last task, nor would the Mexicans. The Americans would expend many lives and much treasure before finally putting down the proud Apaches 100 years after the viceroy's declaration.

uprising, decided to send a punitive expedition to the Colorado. Command of the force was given to Lieutenant-
Colonel Don Pedro Fages who was "captain of one of the
free companies of volunteers of Catalonia."[40] Don Pedro
Tueros, commandant of the presidio at Altar, was designated
second in command.

The expedition was formed and set out from the Pitic
presidio in September. En route to the Gila River, Fages
enlisted as auxiliaries Papagos and Pimas who appeared
eager to go to war against the Yumas. Striking the Gila, the
expedition turned westward. The Spaniards soon realized
that they were approaching a people who no longer held
them, their king or their God in awe. Reports were received
that the Yumas and their allies were massing to attack the
column, but Fages continued the march.

Arriving at the Colorado, the Spaniards indeed found the
Indians numerous and ready for war, but willing to talk.
Fages already had received from Palma a letter stating that
the Spaniards would be received in peace if they came in
peace. One can only speculate what was in the heart of that
great chieftain. For many years, he had been completely
devoted to the Spanish and had worked hard to cement the
ties between Spaniards and his people. The uprising had
shattered all that. Perhaps, though he had tried to persuade
the warriors to end the bloodshed during the revolt, he had
been carried along with events. Perhaps he was a realist and
had come to recognize that the relationship between Spaniards and Indians could only continue to deteriorate as more
Spanish settlers arrived on the Colorado. Perhaps his love
for the Spanish died with Garcés, whose death surely he
did not wish or condone. That he was still able to write

[40] Pedro Fages, "The Colorado River Campaign, 1781-1782; the Diary of Pedro
Fages," ed. by Herbert Ingram Priestley, *Academy of Pacific Coast Hist.,* III (May
1913), 137.

a letter as the Yuma chieftain testifies to the place he continued to hold among his people. We may not know Palma's
mind, but we do know, from the contents of the letter, that
he wished to avoid further conflict.

Fages' objectives were two: to recover the Spanish prisoners still held by the Yumas and to punish the Indians for
the recent rising. Judging from later incidents, the commander obviously considered the latter of paramount importance. Delivering ransoms of blankets, maize, beads,
cigarettes and other goods, Fages bought the release of
sixty-two captives. Palma promised to send for the remaining prisoners, who were housed in a distant village.

Before the release of these last captives was completed,
Fages was approached and agreed to an alliance with a body
of Jalchedune, Pima and Cocomaricopa warriors who
planned to attack the Yuma villages. The new alliance was
soon tested in battle. About twenty-five Yumas were killed
in the surprise attack, among them a petty chieftain with a
Spanish name, José Antonio. He was Palma's son. Among
the numerous wounded was a brother of Palma and the chief
himself. Amazingly, Fages justified his actions by pointing
to the "lack of good faith and the bad spirit manifested by
Captain Palma." [41] Unfortunately, Palma's thoughts on the
sordid affair were never recorded. Though Fages still had
hopes of recovering the few Spanish prisoners still in Yuma
hands, he and his officers decided by vote that their position
was untenable, the enmity of the Yumas now assured, and
the expedition retreated to Sonóita.

Fages did not disband his force. He was determined not to
do so until his objectives were accomplished. After a month
of resting and reprovisioning, the Spaniards set out again
for the Colorado in November 1781.

[41] *Ibid.,* 153, 155, 157.

Arriving at their destination, the Spaniards found the Yumas uncowed, but still ready to talk. Though Fages was concerned about the fate of the Spanish captives, he was still not above risking their lives to carry out his principal aim. Twice, he laid ambushes in attempts to kill or capture the Indian leaders, including Palma, as they came to discuss the release of the prisoners. Both attempts failed.[42] Though the Indians were not aware of the first attempt – it was called off when things did not go according to plan – there was some ineffectual firing during the second, but not before the last Spanish captive was released to the soldiers. Now there was no necessity for pretense.

A few days later, there was a general engagement when as many as 1,500 Indians attacked the Spaniards. Fifteen or twenty Indians were killed in the battle and many others wounded. The action doubtless was well-planned by the Indians and was bravely executed, but their weapons proved no match for the superior firepower of the Spaniards. All the Yuma chiefs took part in the battle, and some sustained wounds. Palma himself was fired on three times by a soldier, but his pistol misfired every time. The chieftain made his escape on foot, leaving on the field his horse and a gallooned hat that Fages had presented him at their first meeting.

Apparently satisfied that the punitive objective of the expedition had been accomplished, Fages ordered preparations for the march to Sonora. The soldiers gathered the bones and bodies of the Spaniards who had been killed during the uprising the previous year. The remains were burned and the ashes placed in sacks for return to Mexico. The bodies and bones of the four slain padres were not burned,

---

[42] That Fages risked the lives of the Spanish prisoners was confirmed when their release finally was secured, and they were questioned. Did they know what the intentions of the Yumas were toward them? Yes, the Yumas had told them that they would be killed if the Spaniards should initiate battle. *Ibid.*, 171.

but were preserved as they were found. They were taken lovingly to the ruins of the church of San Pedro y San Pablo de Bicuñer.[43] Though the building had been burned, the walls and high altar were still intact. The remains of the fathers were placed on the altar and candles were lighted. The assembled Spaniards then recited the holy rosary with Father Cenizo, the chaplain of the expedition. This sad chore done, the expedition left the Colorado and made its way to Sonora without incident. The remains of the fathers were delivered to the authorities of the presidio at Altar.[44]

Fages arrived at the mission of El Pitic de Caborca on December 30, 1781, there to await the results of his application to lead a party of men to San Gabriel Mission and Monterey in California. He did not confide to his diary why he wished to mount this new expedition. To fill the days while waiting for their next assignment, Fages tells us that the soldiers

> . . . were trained in the duties which become a soldier. They mounted guard in the quarters appropriated to their use, to which they returned at the proper hours. They were instructed in the manual of arms, had the penal laws read to them on the scheduled days, and underwent the inspection of arms and munitions.[45]

Doubtless, the troops were as eager as their commander for the reply to Fages' petition.

The answer finally came, and it was affirmative. Fages was directed to carry messages to the California governor, Don Felipe de Neve. Fages assembled a force of thirty-five soldiers and set out from the mission of Pitic for San Gabriel in California. It was February 27, 1782.

---

[43] Fages noted in his journal that the bodies of Fathers Barreneche and Garcés, the last to be located, were little decayed, especially that of Garcés. The bodies had been buried, he learned, by "an Indian woman who esteemed them highly." *Ibid.,* 183.

[44] Garcés's body eventually was buried at Tubutama.

[45] Fages, "Diary," 195.

The journey to the Colorado was not without some difficulty. In addition to the customary hardships of the trail,
the Spaniards seem to have been poorly mounted at the
start, and the condition of the stock worsened as time passed.
Some worn-out animals were left at one point on the trail,
to be recovered by another expedition led by Don Joseph
Romeu and Don Pedro Tueros which Fages expected would
pass that way shortly en route to the Colorado.[46]

Fages made no attempt to avoid detection as the expedition approached the Colorado River. The soldiers saw
Yuma scouts who rushed away to warn the villagers of the
Spaniards' approach. Fages could not have expected an
open-arms reception. Nor with his small party could he
have hoped to overwhelm the Yumas in case of hostilities.
The commander decided that the best strategy was to march
boldly and directly into the Yuma villages. The tension can
be imagined:

> The band of Indians was watching us . . . but we stopped for
> nothing, taking up our march in column with myself at the head, right
> through the midst of their villages. This apparently was not to the
> taste of the Yumas, who, seeing that we did not halt, came out to meet
> us on the front and rear, as well as on both sides, shouting and raising
> clouds of dust everywhere, so that not even they themselves understood
> each other. But the troop went on in good order, paying no attention to
> all this confusion.[47]

The drilling at Pitic had paid off.

Crossing the Colorado near the ruins of the Bicuñer
mission, the march continued until nightfall. Some of the
Indians who had followed came up and asked where they
were going. Fages replied that "we had come to reestablish

---

[46] *Ibid.*, 197. I have found no record of this latter expedition other than what
Fages says about it. Possibly it was part of a coordinated effort, of which Fages's
expedition also was a unit. In any case, Fages met the Romeu-Tueros expedition at
the Colorado River on April 13.   [47] Fages, "Diary," 201.

ourselves there and make peace." [48] This, of course, was a fabrication. The Indians appeared to take the Spaniard at his word and said that they would return to talk about the matter the next day. The commander had no intention of completing the pretended transaction and continued the march some distance farther before stopping for the night.

The trek across the Colorado Desert brought the usual suffering, relieved only after the expedition reached San Sebastián on March 15. The Spaniards remained at this place a day to rest the animals, then continued on their way. For some unexplained reason, Fages felt the need for haste and decided that he would push on ahead of the main body of the expedition. With eight men, he quickened his pace and arrived at San Gabriel mission on March 26, the balance of the expedition arriving soon after.

In early April, Fages returned to the Colorado River. He had applied for and received a commission from the California governor to deliver messages to the Romeu-Tueros expedition, then encamped on the Colorado. Gathering a group of soldiers, ten Sonorans and ten from Monterey, Fages set out from San Gabriel on the eastward journey. The march, over a trail that was becoming a rather well-known road, was uneventful. Approaching the Colorado, every precaution was taken to avoid being surprised by the Yumas who were by this time assumed to be hostile. None were seen, and a message was sent across the river to the Romeu-Tueros camp.

The Yumas were noticeably absent at the crossing. Some Cajuenches who had taken up residence in the area told Fages that the Yumas had abandoned their villages and lands just after Fages' expedition passed through on its westward journey. Before leaving, the Yumas had burned

[48] *Ibid.*

their towns and whatever belongings they could not take
with them. The Cajuenches could only say further that the
Yumas and the Jalchedunes were at war. Thus assured of
the little likelihood of attack, Fages nevertheless prepared
the camp for that eventuality, then crossed the river to the
other expedition's camp and "passed the remainder of the
day and night in pleasure, without any event whatever."[49]

The next day, his mission accomplished, Fages set out
with his troop once more for San Gabriel. The desert crossing on the whole appeared less severe than usual. Passing
through the sand dunes, some supplies which had been hidden on the eastward journey were recovered. In the cache
was a load of corn which was fed to the animals at intervals
during the remainder of the trek. The only notable incident
in an otherwise routine crossing was the unsuccessful attempt
of some of the soldiers to follow the tracks of some unknown
men and animals that crossed their path.

Resting at San Sebastián, Fages heard that the mountain
Indians near San Diego had turned belligerent. With no
other pressing objective, Fages decided to change his route
of march and headed toward San Diego. He figured that if
he could pass through the lands of the rebellious Indians
with an armed troop, he might be able to learn something of
their plans and also to impress them with Spanish might.

Contrary to expectations, the only crisis encountered during the ensuing march came when Pachula, the chief of the
village at San Sebastián, and thirty armed warriors tried to
attach themselves to the expedition. Fages did not wish to
offend Pachula since his intentions appeared peaceful, but
he did not want to endanger the San Diego mission by leading a band of armed natives to its very gates. Fages diplo-
matically persuaded the chief that the mountain Indians

---

[49] *Ibid.,* 221.

would kill them and that they should not go with the Spaniards. The disappointed Pachula "threw down his cane as if he were offended, saying he no longer wanted to be captain," [50] a title doubtless given him by Spaniards. Nevertheless, he agreed to turn back.

The remainder of the journey passed without incident. The Camillares Indians, supposed to be hostile, were not. They talked amiably with the soldiers, accepted presents of beads and gave the Spaniards fresh milk. The commander found no evidence of an Indian uprising.

After hearing Mass at the mission of San Diego and visiting the presidio and village, Fages continued with his troop northward. En route, the soldiers stayed a night at San Juan Capistrano mission, which Fages found "in a very flourishing condition, both in things spiritual and temporal." [51] On April 25, 1782, the expedition arrived at San Gabriel mission where Fages reported to the governor.

Turning from the troubled Colorado River region eastward to New Mexico, we find Spain's fortunes little brighter. The history of that province during this period is one of almost continuous Indian problems and a procession of governors trying to preserve the integrity of the Spanish settlements. There were a few attempts to extend Spanish domain. In addition to the abortive effort of the Domínguez-Escalante expedition to reach California, other parties from New Mexico explored in Colorado and Kansas and in New Mexico, especially in the southern part.

The New Mexicans continued their attempts to subdue and convert the Hopis. But those stalwart traditionalists continued to resist until they were almost wiped out in the late 1770s by prolonged drouth and disease. Escalante had

---

[50] *Ibid.*, 225.　　　　　　　　[51] *Ibid.*, 231.

counted 7,494 Hopis on his 1775 expedition. That number was reduced by hunger and sickness within a few years to 798. The great Hopi herds almost vanished. Though the Spanish urged the Indians to move elsewhere, many chose to stay where they could die in their own houses and in the old faiths. About thirty families finally were persuaded to leave their parched lands and go with the Spaniards.[52]

Because of the continuing Indian hostility in both New Mexico and the Colorado-Gila region, it was natural that Indian policy should preoccupy Spanish officialdom. A policy dominated, or at least strongly influenced, by the missionary impulse gradually gave way to one which provided for demoralization, deculturation and extermination. As early as 1776, Lieutenant-Colonel Antonio Bonilla of Coahuila advocated in a report an all-out war against the hostile frontier Indians. He considered New Mexico to be important not only for its worth as a Spanish settlement, but also as a buffer and bastion between the savages and the more populous regions to the south. If New Mexico should fall to the hostiles, he warned, the towns of Nueva Vizcaya would feel the loss because the Indians, now adept in the use of firearms and horses, would push their raids deeper into the Mexican interior.[53]

A policy such as that suggested by Bonilla was put into effect by Bernardo de Gálvez after he became viceroy in 1785. A cousin of the visitor-general who was largely responsible for the colonization of California, Gálvez had some knowledge of the northern frontier of New Spain, having served and gathered laurels there as an Indian fighter. In a decree titled *Instructions for Governing the Interior Provinces,* the viceroy ordered the opening of warfare

[52] Bancroft, *Arizona and New Mexico,* 265-66.   [53] *Ibid.,* 263.

against all Indian tribes that were hostile to Spain. As quickly as the Indians were subdued, they were to be re-settled around presidios where they would regularly be given presents. Thereby, Gálvez reasoned, the Indians would soon realize that peace was desirable to war. The presents would include ample supplies of alcoholic beverages and inferior firearms. The weapons would soon become defec-tive, and only the Spaniards would be able to repair them. If the Indians tried to make war against the Spanish, powder and shot would be withheld. Implicit in the plan was the elimination of the Indian way of life. It seems also that the Indian's soul was of less importance to the Spaniards that it had been before.

Another notable feature of Gálvez's plan was a scheme which encouraged Indians to fight among themselves. The various tribes were induced to become friends of Spain, but to remain enemies of each other. The plan, therefore, did not attempt to end warfare on the frontier, but only to extract Spain as a participant. By encouraging inter-tribal hostility, Gálvez hoped that the tribes would not make treaties among themselves and that the resulting warfare would reduce the population of the tribes. The viceroy's plan was implemented and appears to have been somewhat of a success. Peace generally reigned on the frontier, at least as far as Spain was concerned, until 1810 when the Mexican War for Independence began. Thus distracted, the Spanish stopped the distribution of presents and the Indians com-menced raiding Spanish settlements once more.[54]

At the opening of the nineteenth century, Spanish control in the upper frontier was approaching an end. The Colo-rado-Gila region by this time had been abandoned. New

---

[54] *Ibid.*, 267.

Mexico continued to be, but while revolution raged inter-mittently in the south, it existed more as an autonomous region than as a province of New Spain. As the Spanish military presence in the north declined, Indian depredations increased and the towns of New Mexico became islands from which settlers rarely ventured far. For 275 years, Spanish explorers had trekked the upper frontier. By the second decade of the nineteenth century, few of their trails were visible or safe.

CHAPTER IV

Mexico's Frontier Provinces

Following the successful revolution against Spanish rule and the establishment of the Mexican state in 1821, attention was directed once again to the northern frontier regions. The problems there were formidable. Though encouraging signs were appearing, Indian troubles were still unresolved. Russia increasingly appeared to pose a threat in California. Trappers of the English Hudson's Bay Company pushed southward ever deeper into Mexican territory. With the opening of the Santa Fé trade to Americans came an undesirable side-effect: the invasion by American trappers who plied their trade along Mexican streams, legally if possible, but illegally if necessary.

The security of California was seen as the most urgent problem in the north. To investigate the situation there, Emperor Augustín Iturbide of the newly-established Empire of Mexico in 1822 appointed Augustín Fernández de San Vicente, a canon of the Durango cathedral. Paying special attention to the alleged threat posed by foreigners, Fernández made a tour of inspection in California. The report he subsequently submitted confirmed the fears of Mexican officials. Fernández warned that the future of California as a Mexican possession required that Mexico strengthen its position there. This necessitated the immediate opening of an overland route to connect California and Sonora.[1]

---

[1] For accounts of the events leading to the attempts to reestablish the Sonora-California route, *see* George William Beattie, "Reopening the Anza Road," *Pac.*

Fernández believed that a new road would be used immediately. He claimed that the land passage would be preferred by many settlers who might be reluctant to undertake the arduous sea voyage, which in any case had not proved a satisfactory means of populating California.[2] The missionary fathers in California expected to benefit from a new road by establishing a string of missions along it. The padres thereby would be able to reach the then largely inaccessible tribes of the interior. Civil authorities in California agreed that the road would make it easier to initiate contact with the Indians of the interior in order to bring them into the Mexican orbit. The road also would make it easier to put them down should they turn hostile.

The strategic possibilities of such a road had been demonstrated in 1819. Following a devastating raid by Mojaves on the country between the San Gabriel mission and Cajon Pass, Lieutenant Gabriel Moraga led a group of about fifty soldiers on a chase that took them through the pass and into the Mojave Desert beyond. It was the hostility of the environment rather than that of its inhabitants that forced the column to turn back without accomplishing its goals. Though the raiders were not punished, the expedition was not unsuccessful, for the desert was entered and, to the extent posed by necessity, explored.

The first concrete step in re-opening the California-Sonora land route was initiated by Fernández as a result of his inspection tour in California. He suggested to Father Felix Caballero, then assigned to the San Miguel and Santa

---

Hist. Rev., II (March 1933), 52-57, and the introductory comments in Lowell John Bean and William Marvin Mason, eds., *Diaries and Accounts of the Romero Expeditions in Arizona and California, 1823-1826* (Palm Springs, Ca., 1962).

2 Anza's land route had proved a welcome alternative, but in spite of its relative success in moving settlers to California, the Spanish population there in 1822, the last year of Spanish rule, was only around 3,500. Bean, *Romero Expeditions,* 4-5.

Catalina missions in Baja California, that the padre travel direct from his station to Tucson via the region near the mouth of the Colorado. His purpose would be to determine whether the route was practicable as a road to connect the two areas.

Father Caballero took up the task and set out with two Indian companions, one of them a "gentile" or non-Christian Indian named Cota, from the Santa Catalina mission on April 14, 1823. The three travelers drove ahead of them thirty cattle and twelve mares which they intended to present as gifts to the Colorado River Indians. The exact route followed by the trio is not known, but a diary fragment of the journey shows that they were on the Colorado the evening of the next day, April 15. There they were met by the Quamaya or Cocopa Indians. Caballero tried to impress on the Indians that the Mexican Emperor wanted to establish presidios and missions among them.[3] Not only did the Indians welcome this possibility, they even volunteered to escort Caballero to Sonora in order to expedite its fulfillment. Explaining that they would welcome protection from their enemies, the Yumas, the Indians showed the padre a site which they said would be suitable for a mission and presidio.

Leaving the Colorado, the three companions traveled along the Gila River, visiting the friendly Cocomaricopas along the way. The travelers left the Gila somewhere in the vicinity of the Pima villages and headed southward, reaching Arizpe in late May. The account of Caballero's journey eventually was sent to Mexico City by Lieutenant-Colonel Antonio Narbona, the civil governor and military commander of Sonora.

---

[3] Apparently Caballero was unaware that the previous month the Empire of Mexico had been replaced by the Republic of Mexico.

Caballero's feat set in motion a plan that the Sonora governor had been considering for some time. In the previous year, in response to an inquiry from Governor Pablo Vicente Solá of California, Narbona had ordered Captain José Romero, the commandant of the Tucson presidio, to take a force of sixty men and investigate the feasibility of opening a mail route to California by way of the lower Colorado. Delayed for some unknown reason, the expedition had not set out when Caballero appeared in Sonora. Modifying his previous orders, Narbona now instructed Romero to accompany Caballero back to California with ten soldiers, noting sites suitable for presidios and ascertaining whether the Indians along the route would assist in the carrying of mail should that service be opened. The Supreme Government gave its assent to the Romero-Caballero venture and indeed authorized the initiation of mail services over the proposed route.[4]

Romero and his little band set out from Tucson in early June 1823, bound for Baja California. Their route took them to the Gila which they reached in two days. There an age-old ritual was repeated. The Pimas gave the Mexicans a warm welcome and escorted them to the governor's house. Romero thanked the assembled Indians for their kindnesses to Father Caballero on his previous trip through their lands. As for the future, Romero "told them to make arrangements for religious instruction and the arts of civilization. I told them that the new independent government would provide all the means necessary for this purpose." To this good news, the Indians rejoiced, saying "this is good, we have desired this for a long time; so this afternoon you will remain with us."[5] Of course, he did not remain long, for his instructions demanded that he push on to California.

[4] Beattie, "Reopening the Anza Road," 56-57; Bean, *Romero Expeditions*, 13.
[5] Bean, *Romero Expeditions*, 15.

Leaving the Pimas, the Mexicans soon reached the land of the Cocomaricopas farther down the Gila. Romero gave these Indians the same message he had given the Pimas: the Mexican government wished to bring them religion and civilization. Predictably, the Indians were pleased at the news and replied that they had long desired these things. Romero also told them that the government planned to open a mail route to California and asked them if they would be willing to carry dispatches between Mexico and Monterey, via their own country, as they had done in the past. The Cocomaricopas would not so promise because the route lay through the lands of the Yumas and Mojaves, who were their enemies. They had been able to carry mail a few times for the Spaniards only by taking along many warriors. To eliminate that obstacle, Romero urged the Indians to make peace with their enemies. The Cocomaricopas replied that they were willing, but that the Yumas and Mojaves were not.

The issue was unsettled when the expedition departed for the Colorado. Leaving the Gila, the Mexicans marched southward and crossed the Gila Range through the pass at Tinajas Altas, through which Anza had led his first expedition on the westward journey. From there, Romero and his companions crossed the sand dunes to reach the Colorado.[6]

Near the mouth of the river, throngs of Indians, "Cajuines and Quamayas," greeted the Mexicans and brought them food. The Indians were especially eager to see Father Caballero, whom they called their friend. The chief, Captain

---

[6] Though it is not recorded whether Romero had Indian guides in the early stages of the journey, he did have them in this last stretch of country. Romero wrote in his diary that shortly after leaving the Gila, they came across the Yuma road to Caborca, but did not take it "because the gentiles [presumably Cocomaricopas though this is not certain] who guided us were afraid they might meet the Yumas, their enemies, and they did not wish to expose themselves or the padre to danger." *Ibid.,* 20.

Quamaya, led the expedition to various Indian rancherias and pointed out to Romero likely sites for a mission here, a presidio there, and more sites for pasturing animals and growing crops. Romero was pleased with what he saw and noted the locations in his journal.

When it was time for the expedition to cross the river, the Indians rushed to help. They built rafts and assisted in loading them. Certain Indians were detailed to guide the rafts while others drove the horses ahead of them. Romero was so struck with the Indians' friendliness and eagerness to help "that it seemed as though they had been raised among us." [7]

Romero was completely taken in. At mid-stream, the Indians who were driving the horses suddenly turned them back toward the shore they had just left. At the same time, the Indians who were guiding the equipment rafts turned them around, and those who were with the other rafts abandoned them. The hapless Mexicans were left at the mercy of the river which was in flood. They were saved when the Indian, Cota, and two soldiers jumped into the water and pushed the two rafts to the western bank. From there, they helplessly watched the Indians on the other shore dividing the horses and baggage.

The prospects of the Mexicans at this point were not bright. Before boarding their rafts, they had stripped, in case of upset, and piled their clothes on the goods rafts. Now they had lost everything except their weapons which they had kept with them. The desert, the hardest part of the entire journey, lay before them. It was July.

Naked, on foot and without provisions, they gamely set out. In a region where travelers commonly suffered, Romero and his companions suffered uncommonly from hunger, fatigue and exposure. The commander finally split the party,

[7] *Ibid.,* 22.

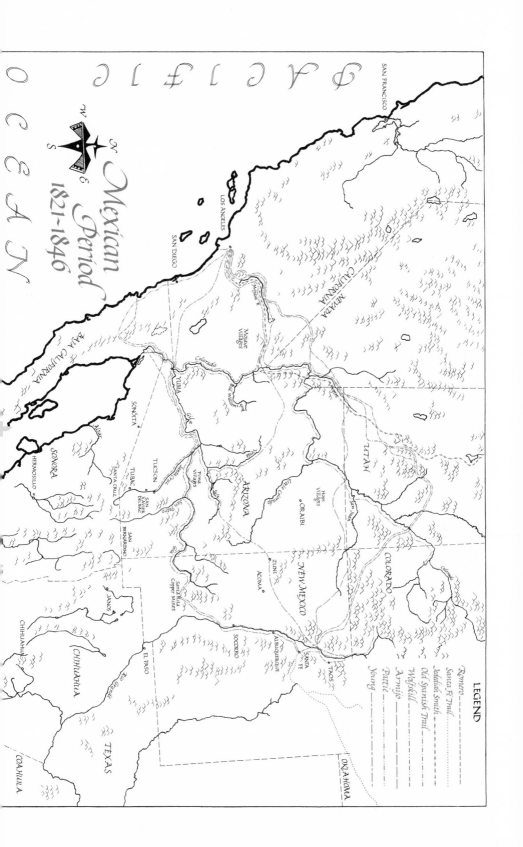

PACIFIC

OCEAN

SAN FRANCISCO

Mexican Period
1821-1846

N
W E
S

LOS ANGELES

SAN DIEGO

BAJA CALIFORNIA

CALIFORNIA

NEVADA

UTAH

Mojave R.

Mojave Villages

Colorado

Gila

Bill Williams Fork

YUMA

SONOITA

SONORA

HERMOSILLO

Altar

SANTA CRUZ

TUBAC
SAN XAVIER
DEL BAC

TUCSON

SAN BERNARDINO

Pima Villages

ARIZONA

Hopi Villages

ORAIBI

Little Colorado

ZUNI

ACOMA

NEW MEXICO

Santa Rita Copper Mines

SOCORRO

ALBUQUERQUE

SANTA FE

TAOS

COLORADO

Colorado

JANOS

CHIHUAHUA

CHIHUAHUA

EL PASO

Rio Grande

TEXAS

COAHUILA

OKLAHOMA

LEGEND

Romero ——
Santa Fé Trail ....
Jedediah Smith —-—-—
Wolfskill —··—··—
Armijo —---—---
Pattie —————
Young ———

sending the strongest ahead to Mission Santa Catalina to secure help for the stragglers. The strategy was successful, and the last of the Mexicans reached the mission safely on July 6, 1823. From there, the expedition marched across the peninsula to Mission San Miguel.

In a letter, Romero reported his arrival to the Governor of California, Luis Antonio Argüello, who had succeeded Solá at Monterey. Romero's evaluation of the trail he had just traveled as a mail route was not favorable:

> The route from Tucson to Santa Catalina is short . . . [and]
> . . . it can be covered in ten or eleven days; but there is the obstacle of the Colorado river, for from the month of May to that of August it remains in flood; and furthermore, the Indian nation that robbed us is there. . . According to my instructions, it only remains for me to see the road by which the Cocomaricopas travel.[8]

With this last statement, it appears that Romero had written off the lower Colorado route in favor of one from the Cocomaricopa country. An investigation of the latter was his next objective.

Romero sent a copy of his diary to Governor Argüello and corresponded with him about his plans to investigate the more northerly San Gorgonio-Cocomaricopa route to determine its potential use as a mail route.[9] Argüello was favorable and ordered the California missions and presi-

---

[8] Quoted in Beattie, "Reopening the Anza Road," 59.

[9] Romero sent another copy of the diary, along with an account of the expedition, to Governor Narbona of Sonora. Narbona in turn sent the documents to Mexico City where they were published, making Romero a famous person. The governor shortly offered to lead a punitive expedition against the lower Colorado Indians to ensure against a recurrence of their treachery. The Supreme Government gave its assent to Narbona's request, but changed the nature of the undertaking. The expedition was not to be punitive. Instead, Narbona was directed to gather scientific data and investigate commercial possibilities of the region, and he was to establish friendly relations with the Indians. The ambitious project never materialized. Narbona lost his position before preparations for the enterprise were completed. Bean, *Romero Expeditions*, 26-28.

dios to furnish animals and provisions for the venture. The governor also arranged for a detachment of thirty soldiers and ten civilians to accompany Romero as far as the Colorado. The commander of the escort, Lieutenant José María Estudillo, then stationed at the San Diego presidio, was directed to bring the troop of forty men back to California after accomplishing his mission.

The expedition left San Gabriel in mid-December 1823, bound for Sonora via San Gorgonio Pass and the Cocomaricopa trail. It was back at the mission at the end of the following month. The desert march had turned into disaster. The Mexicans had endured severe hardships as the trail seemingly was lost and regained, then lost and regained time and again. Eventually the guide admitted that he was lost, and Romero gave the order to turn back, short of the Colorado.

An enlisted man in the expeditionary force, one Rafael Gonzalez, placed the blame squarely on the shoulders of Estudillo who, he said, was a "crazy man," a "drunk" and used his animals "as if it were no concern of his if the horses went to the devil." Gonzalez did not leave Romero blameless, complaining that the commander had carried along a trunk of crockery which had proven a punishing burden for the poor animals. Though neither Romero nor Estudillo seems to have accepted responsibility for the debacle, the latter did confide to his diary that at least seventy-five horses and thirty-five mules had been lost during the six-weeks' journey.[10]

The evaluation of the abortive expedition was mixed. While Father Sanchez of San Gabriel and Governor Argüello regretted the great expense, both Estudillo and Romero could declare the expedition a success in a negative

---

[10] *Ibid.*, 51, 53-55.

sort of way. Romero believed that the usefulness of the Cocomaricopa route at least had been disproven.[11] Estudillo agreed and added that though the route might be used as a foot path for Indians, it was definitely not suitable for cavalry and supply trains.[12]

Back in Sonora, the authorities who originally had dispatched Romero on his expedition had for some time been in the dark as to his whereabouts. They had received no word from him since the report he sent back upon his arrival at the Baja California missions. They therefore sent an inquiry by Indian messengers. The Indians, ten Jalchedun men and nine Jalchedun women, arrived at San Gabriel ten days after Romero's return there from the unsuccessful attempt to reach the Colorado River. To Romero's astonishment, he learned that the Indians had traveled the very route he had failed to find. After hearing about his march, the messengers told Romero that if he had but changed his direction of march from east to south on the very day that he had turned back, he would have reached the river by sunset of the same day.[13]

Buoyed by this news, Romero decided to renew his investigation of the route. He applied to the California governor for permission to leave in early April 1824 and requested that eighty Mazatlán soldiers, then stationed temporarily at Santa Barbara, be detached as an escort to return to Sonora with him.[14] Permission was refused. All available

---

[11] *Ibid.*, 57-58.

[12] Beattie, "Reopening the Anza Road," 62. Bean attributes this reasoning to Romero (*Romero Expeditions*, 58), but Beattie is more convincing, explaining that the information was taken from a transmittal letter by which Estudillo sent his diary to Governor Argüello. The letter reported unfavorably on the San Gorgonio trail to the Colorado.

[13] Bean, *Romero Expeditions*, 60-61.

[14] This troop had been sent from Mazatlan in 1819 to reinforce California garrisons following the Bouchard attacks of the previous year. Hippolyte de Bouchard, a Frenchman, had served in the navy of the "Republic of Buenos Aires" in the

forces were needed to help quiet Indian unrest in southern California.

In mid-April, an Indian named José Cocomaricopa with four companions arrived at San Gabriel. He was carrying letters from Tucson. José volunteered to guide Romero back to Tucson, but urged that they depart as quickly as possible because the approaching rise of the Colorado would present a hazard to crossing later. Romero again sent the governor an urgent request for permission to set out. Again he was refused, and for the same reason.

While Romero chafed at his confinement, he learned that a contingent of twenty-four soldiers, led by Santiago Argüello, a younger brother of the governor, had just returned from the Colorado River. The troop had been in pursuit of an Indian band that had been raiding near San Diego and stealing horses. They did not catch the Indians, in spite of having crossed the entire width of California from San Diego to the Colorado in but three days! The route followed by the soldiers is not definitely known, but it is believed that it corresponded closely to the almost-forgotten Anza road through the desert, crossing the mountains, however, by Warner's Pass rather than Anza's San Carlos Pass.[15] The younger Argüello had unknowingly discovered a new route from the ocean to the Colorado. Romero must have given considerable thought to Argüello's ride. He could not have but measured his own recent failure to reach the Colorado with Argüello's success.

Yet while the crossing from the ocean to the Colorado

revolt against Spain. Finding rebellion profitable, Bouchard gathered an "army" of about 350 men and pillaged throughout the crumbling Spanish empire. In California, his band burned and looted a number of coastal settlements, including Monterey and Mission San Juan Capistrano. Then, Bouchard's two ships sailed away, never to return. By spring of 1824, the Mazatlan soldiers were due to return to their home station.

15 Beattie, "Reopening the Anza Road," 62-63.

River might be easier by a southern route, as Argüello had shown, there remained the obstacle of the hostile Yumas. On this point, it is interesting to note that Don Mariano Urrea, the commandant-general of Sonora, wrote to Governor Argüello, asking him to tell Romero that he was to return to Sonora via Loreto, in Baja California, and Guaymas. Urrea pointedly referred to the risks in returning through the Yuma country. He advised the Loreto route because he had no troops to send to meet Romero at the Colorado, an absolute necessity if Romero were to return that way.

Argüello passed these instructions to Romero in September along with some advice of his own. He informed Romero that he had heard that the American frigate *Mentor* was then at San Diego and probably would be departing soon for Mazatlan. The governor counseled Romero to speak to the captain at once to arrange for transportation for him and his men. In just eight or ten days, he said, they would be home. This course, the governor explained, would save Romero time and the government money.[16]

Romero was not interested. Far from wishing a speedy voyage to Sonora, he still nurtured a hope to investigate the Cocomaricopa route. The break appeared to come in December 1824 when Indian unrest in California had dissipated, and Argüello finally consented to Romero's departure. Controversy continued to swirl concerning Romero's return route, however, and he did not leave. Before the question was settled, there were fresh Indian outbreaks south of San Diego, and the hapless Romero saw his permission to leave revoked as, once again, all available soldiers were to be held in readiness. The months passed.

In August 1825, following considerable correspondence among officials at Monterey, San Diego, San Gabriel and

---

[16] Bean, *Romero Expeditions*, 63-64.

Sonora, Romero received formal orders to prepare for the march to the Colorado. José María de Echeandía who had succeeded Argüello as governor of California, strongly favored the project to open a Sonora-California road via San Gorgonio Pass. The governor's attitude toward the route doubtless was influenced by the fathers at San Gabriel. The padres wanted the road to pass through San Bernardino where they hoped to build a mission. Shortly after taking up his new office, Echeandía ordered that Romero be given every assistance possible. Noting that San Gabriel had borne the expense of lodging Romero's force for a long time, he instructed all missions from San Diego to Purísima to send provisions to San Gabriel to be used on the expedition.

During the summer and autumn of 1825, while Romero had languished at San Gabriel and later as he began preparations for the march to the Colorado, events related to the opening of the road to California were taking place in Sonora. A deputation of twenty-three Gila Pimas appeared at Arizpe, asking for priests to come to their country to establish missions, to catechize them and to teach them in the arts and agriculture. They explained to the authorities there that they had wished this for many years and had been promised priests in 1795 when certain fathers, Bringas and Llorenti, visited them.

The officials weighed the requests in light of the advantages to be gained. They acknowledged that the Pimas were industrious and would benefit from the civilizing influences of a Mexican presence in their country. It was noted that their adherence to Mexico would be of immense value in the project to open communications between Sonora and California, a conclusion reached by Spaniards fifty years before. There remained a substantial obstacle to the completion of that project. Though the Pimas were at peace and allied with the Cocomaricopas, the two nations still considered the Yumas their enemies. It was assumed that the peace would have to be extended to include the Yumas before a route through their lands would be safe. Considerable work had already been done to formalize peace among the three nations, and it appeared that success was near. All that remained was for the chiefs to agree to the terms.

A meeting was scheduled at Arizpe, apparently at the call of General José Figueroa, who had succeeded Narbona as governor of Sonora. It seems that the chiefs had agreed to the arrangements, but they did not appear at the appointed time.[17] The general then decided that he would personally lead an expedition to the Colorado to learn whether the Yumas desired a lasting peace. This was not to be his only reason for going. He would meet Romero at the Colorado and escort him back to Sonora.

Figueroa left Tucson October 26, 1825, with a considerable force of 400 men. The governor purposely included among them men who had experience in dealing with the Indians they would encounter, priests to preach to the Indians and swimmers to test the fords of the rivers. The expedition reached the Gila in two days. After resting a day, they continued their way down the Gila toward the Colorado. A halt was called when they were about twenty-five or thirty leagues from the mouth of the Gila. Figueroa sent two Cocomaricopa women ahead to learn, if they could, how the Yumas would receive the expedition. He apparently was satisfied with their report, for after a delay of three days the march was resumed. The expedition reached the Colorado on November 16 and camped near the ruins of

---

[17] It seems that a meeting was held later in the year, but that the results were inconclusive. *Ibid.*, 74.

a Spanish mission, probably Concepción. Here the Mexicans were confronted from across the river by 4,000 Indians who, wrote Figueroa, were prepared to attack if they were approached.

The governor persuaded the principal chief, identified as Cargo Muchachos, to cross the river to talk. Figueroa assured the chief of his friendly intentions: "I talked peace – about civilization and other objects of interest to him. . . I gave him some gifts. . . I instilled confidence . . . and I demanded proof of his adhesion to us." [18] The proof demanded of Muchachos was that he carry messages to Romero. To this, the chief gladly agreed and added that he would help Romero in his passage through the country of any hostile Indians. For some unexplained reason, Figueroa was not satisfied with this response for he shortly dispatched José Cocomaricopa, who was accompanied by approximately twenty men, to carry messages to Romero and to assist his expedition in crossing the Colorado.

It had been Figueroa's intention to wait on the Colorado for Romero's appearance, but his plans changed. Just three days after arriving there, he received the disturbing news that the Yaqui Indians in Sonora were becoming rebellious. This placed Figueroa in a dilemma. He knew that he must hasten back to Sonora, but he did not wish to desert Romero. Evidently holding little faith in the Yumas' declarations of friendship, he wrote to Governor Echeandía with the request that he send 150 men from California garrisons to the Colorado, presumably to ensure a safe crossing for Romero's expedition. En route to Sonora, Figueroa left a small force of twenty-five men at Agua Caliente with orders to remain there until Romero's arrival. A message was sent to Romero to inform him of the new turn of affairs.

---

[18] *Ibid.*, 79.

Meanwhile at San Gabriel mission, José Cocomaricopa appeared carrying the letter that Figueroa had sent from the Colorado encampment. The message was full of good news: Figueroa was waiting for him at the river – of course, Romero did not learn until later that the general had returned to Sonora; Romero had been promoted to Lieutenant-Colonel in recognition of his services; and Figueroa and his troops had been received well by the Yumas. Assuming at the time that Romero might expect the same reception, Figueroa urged him to reciprocate to the fullest since the Yumas' goodwill was essential to the opening of Mexican travel through their lands. The apparent assurance of Yuma friendship must have reinforced Romero's conviction that a more southerly route was preferable to the Cocomaricopa trail, a conviction that had been growing since the younger Argüello's chase to the Colorado.

Preparations for the departure of the expedition continued. Governor Echeandía assigned a group of laborers to the expedition to work on the roadbed and detached a sub-lieutenant of engineers, Romualdo Pacheco, to erect a fortification at San Gorgonio Pass. Neither Romero nor Pacheco thought much of the idea. They believed that the fortification, meant to protect the California settlements from hostile Indians to the east, was not necessary, now that the Yumas were peaceful. Furthermore, the construction would delay the meeting with Figueroa who had urged haste. Pacheco added the doubtless contrived argument that the winters in the San Gorgonio Pass were so severe that the garrison would be unable to function. Probably, both Romero and Pacheco by that time were convinced that the Cocomaricopa route via San Gorgonio Pass eventually would give way to the Yuma route as the official road, and they did not wish to waste time improving the former.

The expedition finally got underway in late November
1825. Romero could not have been encouraged at the start.
The expedition was not on so grand a scale as all the plans
indicated. Because of insufficient provisions, and those bad,
the force was cut to thirty-four. Riding animals were in
poor condition even before setting out. José Cocomaricopa,
who was to guide the Mexicans to the Colorado, became
impatient with the incessant delays and deserted the train
without a word. The loss did not prove serious. Romero
apparently was assisted by one Julian Valdez who previously
had arrived from the Colorado with José Cocomaricopa.
Figueroa had sent Valdez to guide Romero back to his
Colorado camp.

The march of the expedition seems to have been without
serious incident or undue hardship. Arriving at the Colorado, Romero wrote to Governor Echeandía, notifying him
that Pacheco had assisted in the river crossing and then had
departed with his men for San Diego. Romero's crossing
was made somewhere north of Yuma country, probably
between Arroyo Seco and Blythe.[19] From there, he undoubtedly marched overland to Agua Caliente where Romero's
troops waited. The combined force then made its way to
Sonora.

After seeing Romero safely across the Colorado, Pacheco
led his party to San Diego over the southern or Yuma route.
En route, he wrote Governor Echeandía, expressing his
belief that the southern route was far superior to the
San Bernardino-San Gorgonio-Cocomaricopa trail. He explained that he had not built the planned fortification at
San Gorgonio, but instead had begun the erection of a
building on the southern road at a place called Laguna

19 *Ibid.*, 82; Beattie, "Reopening the Anza Road," 66. Beattie speculates in some
detail on the location of the Cocomaricopa trail and the routes taken by Romero on
his expeditions.

Chapala, presumably for the protection of travelers. Now, he concluded, travel over that trail would be easier.

Echeandía apparently was convinced. Upon Pacheco's arrival on the west coast, the governor reported from his San Diego headquarters to the Minister of War in Mexico that he was testing the route by sending mail to Sonora.[20] Figueroa soon responded to Echeandía, adding his suggestion that the commanders at each end of the road make an effort to open the correspondence.[21]

The San Diego-Yuma route via Warner's Pass eventually was recognized as the official California segment of the California-Sonora road. Crossing California by that path was not easy by any means, nor did the Indians respect this newly-designated highway as Mexican property. Pacheco's outpost at Laguna Chapala indeed was attacked within a matter of weeks after its completion, and Indian troubles flared up frequently thereafter. Nevertheless, the route did in fact become a road of sorts as private persons began to use it for their journeys from Sonora.

As a postal road, the route was not promising. Echeandía had occasion to use the road in early 1826 when he sent a letter to Figueroa, complaining about the refusal of the Spanish padres in California to swear allegiance to the Mexican Republic. The regular dispatch of mail over the route, however, was not common for years thereafter. Even Echeandía's courier, Vincente Gomez, did not complete his journey without a scare from some Yumas.[22] As late as 1829, Echeandía complained that a mail service, which had

---

[20] Bean, *Romero Expeditions,* 83.

[21] Beattie, "Reopening the Anza Road," 67.

[22] Gomez had been a guerrilla leader during the Mexican War for Independence. When he continued to murder and terrorize Spaniards after independence had been won, Mexican authorities exiled him to California. Why Governor Echeandía selected Gomez to act as his courier is not indicated. Bean, *Romero Expeditions,* 86-87.

been agreed upon the previous year, had not been launched.[23]

Undoubtedly, the fathers at San Gabriel were disappointed to learn that the official route to California from Sonora would bypass their mission. They were not cut off, however. According to a study of the route:

> Two roads from San Gabriel connected with the San Diego-Colorado road – one the "Canyon road to the Colorado," running by way of Temescal and Temecula, and entering the San Diego-Colorado road in the San Jose [Warner's] valley; and the other, the road by San Bernardino – later officially designated the San Bernardino-Sonora road – which went to the summit of San Gorgonio Pass, turning south at that point, and leading on through San Jacinto to the vicinity of Aguanga, on the Canyon road.[24]

In any event, it does not appear that Father Sanchez at San Gabriel was too unhappy with the Yuma-San Diego route. Though he had worked long and hard in favor of the San Bernardino-San Gorgonio road, he accepted the official declaration and soon began to argue for the construction of military posts along the southern route to ensure the safety of travelers. There was no doubt in Sanchez's mind that the posts were needed. In a letter to the President of Mexico in 1830, the padre mentioned that four travelers had recently been killed, a tragedy that would reduce traffic until the road was made safe.[25]

That the posts called for by Sanchez and others were not built was indicative of Mexico's problems in the region. Construction of the forts would have required thousands of pesos that the new government just did not have. As Spanish fathers who balked at swearing allegiance to the Republic were deported, frontier missions in some areas declined.

---

[23] *Ibid.*, 87.

[24] Beattie, "Reopening the Anza Road," 68. *Also see* Beattie, "Travel Between Southern Arizona and Los Angeles," 228-30, for a detailed description of the San Bernardino-Sonora road. [25] Beattie, "Reopening the Anza Road," 68.

Loss of the fathers doubtless meant that there would not have been enough padres to staff new missions on the Gila and Colorado Rivers, still being sought by both Indians and Mexicans.

Yet, the trails were used during the late 1820s and 1830s by both emigrants and traders. Traffic was never heavy during these years, though the journey was not a particularly long one, and Indian hostilities seemed to decline. It was not until after the discovery of gold in California in 1848 that the route became crowded with Mexican argonauts.

While the California-Sonora trail was becoming a road, to the north that elusive direct route from New Mexico to California again was being sought. Where Garcés and the Domínguez-Escalante party had pioneered paths, the expeditions of Antonio Armijo[26] in 1829 and William Wolfskill in 1830 from New Mexico to California sparked the development of the route that later became called the Old Spanish Trail. The Old Spanish Trail was more of a "central route" than a southern one,[27] but until the opening of shorter routes from New Mexico to California in the early stages of the war between Mexico and the United States, the Old Spanish Trail was the most heavily traveled trail between the two provinces. Further, it was the first route effectively to tie the two regions together, a goal that had been pursued by Spanish and Mexican officials and explorers for generations.

The trail was not an easy one. The 1,200 mile path has aptly been called "the longest, crookedest, most arduous

[26] Not to be confused with Manuel Armijo who was governor of New Mexico at the time of the American invasion in 1846.

[27] For an example of this view, *see* Harrison Clifford Dale's account of Jedediah Smith's journey over part of the route of the Old Spanish Trail in *The Ashley-Smith Explorations and the Discovery of a Central Route to the Pacific 1822-1829* (Glendale, 1941).

pack mule route in the history of America." [28] Its principal virtue was that it lay north of hostile Indian territory. This was important because the trail was first a commercial route and only secondarily an emigration route. Travel over the trail was slow, and chiefly for this reason it would lose out after 1848 to the more southerly routes as gold-seekers were willing to brave both deserts and hostile Indians to shorten the travel time to California.

The originator of the Old Spanish Trail cannot be pinpointed. Many contributed to its origins. A Spaniard named Juan María de Rivera had a part in opening the country through which the trail later ran. Rivera led at least three expeditions into the region of the San Juan River and Uncompagre Plateau. Fathers Domínguez and Escalante brought back additional knowledge of the country, unknowingly aiding slave traders as well as fur trappers from New Mexico. Armijo's contribution was more in illustrating the economic possibilities of the route than in pathfinding. It was left to the Wolfskill expedition to pioneer the path that largely became the Old Spanish Trail. [29]

Armijo's diary of the journey is agonizingly brief. Some entries note only the name of a geographical feature, a canyon or a spring. Since the party traveled in country that was scarcely or not at all known, the place names mentioned

[28] LeRoy R. Hafen and Ann W. Hafen, *Old Spanish Trail: Santa Fé to Los Angeles* (Glendale, 1954), 19.

[29] A notable member of the Wolfskill party was George C. Yount, who wrote a detailed account of the journey. For more on the Wolfskill expedition, *see below*, p. 183 and Iris Higbie Wilson, *William Wolfskill, 1798-1866* (Glendale, Ca., 1965).

J. J. Warner would have Armijo and Wolfskill share with Ewing Young some of the credit in the opening of trade between New Mexico and California. Warner noted that the members of Young's party, upon returning to New Mexico from California in 1830 "spread among the people of . . . New Mexico . . . a knowledge of California which led to the opening of trade between the two sections. . ." J. J. Warner, "Reminiscences of Early California from 1831 to 1846," *Ann. Pub. of the Hist. Soc. of So. Cal.*, Vol. VII, parts II-III (1907-1908), 189.

probably were those given by the travelers and would have little if any meaning to those who would later read his diary. As a result, Armijo's route cannot be known for certain though it can be traced in a general way.[30]

Leaving Abiquiu, northwest of Santa Fé, on November 7, 1829, the party traveled toward the Four Corners country by way of Cañon Largo and the Mancos River, passing the southern boundary of today's Mesa Verde National Park. From the Four Corners, the trail continued southwestward into northeastern Arizona before turning northeast again to reach the Colorado River near the Utah-Arizona line.

Armijo arrived at the Colorado on December 6 at the Crossing of the Fathers, the same place where the Domínguez-Escalante expedition had crossed the river in 1776. Armijo noted in his diary that members of his party recognized the "ford of the fathers."[31] Whether this meant that they had seen the place before or had merely read or heard about it is not clear.

From the Colorado, Armijo continued westward until he reached the Virgin River. He followed the course of that stream southward as far as its confluence with the Colorado, then headed west again. It required three weeks for the party to reach the Mojave River, a march in arid country that was relieved by too few watering places. Following the

---

[30] *See* Hafen, *Old Spanish Trail,* 371.

[31] Antonio Armijo, "Armijo's New Mexico-California Diary, 1829-1830," in *Southwest on the Turquoise Trail,* ed. by Archer Butler Hulbert (Denver, 1933), 286. The historian, Robert Glass Cleland, during a boat trip on the Colorado in 1946, saw the steps in the sandstone bank that Escalante had cut with his ax. The Armijo party had used the same steps. Cleland was struck with the scene: "As we looked at the ridge and river and walked up and down the roughly fashioned steps, the years fled away, and the past, with its sandaled priests and rugged, unlettered traders, became more real than the troubled world of wars and roaring machines and infinite anxieties that lay beyond the desert's farthest rim." Not far away, the Cleland party found another set of steps of unknown origin hewn from the rock face. Robert Glass Cleland, *This Reckless Breed of Men* (New York, 1950), 267-68.

Mojave toward its source, Armijo's band crossed the mountains, passed San Bernardino and finally reached the mission of San Gabriel on January 31, 1830.

The purpose of Armijo's venture was commercial, to trade New Mexico products for mules. In this, he was successful. Its objective accomplished, the expedition broke up. One group of members started for Santa Fé on February 24, arriving there in just forty days. Another party went south to Sonora. A third group, the remainder of the original force, departed California with Armijo. No one to waste words, Armijo confined his account of the return trip to New Mexico to one paragraph:

> I set out again the first of March on the same route without any adventure other than the loss of worn out horses and mules, until I entered the settlement of the Navajos, among whom I experienced losses of animals which were stolen from me; and I arrived in this province . . . to-day the 25th of April, 1830.[32]

It is certain that Armijo was not a trailblazer for at least part of his journey. It has already been noted that members of the party "recognized" the Crossing of the Fathers, possibly indicating that some had seen the ford before. Further, before leaving the Colorado, one of the group said that he recognized a ford where he had crossed the previous year on a journey to Sonora.[33] Early in the march, Armijo noted in his diary that a Navajo Indian had been hired as a guide, "in order that he might show the way as he knew it."[34] That other Indian guides were similarly employed is evident from a statement made later by José Antonio Chavez, the governor of New Mexico, that Armijo completed the journey with "no other guides than the enterprising natives of this country."[35]

---

[32] Armijo, "Diary," 289.   [33] Ibid., 288.   [34] Ibid., 285.
[35] José Antonio Chavez, Governor of New Mexico, to His Excellency the Minister

Unlike most diarists, Armijo did not dwell on the hardships of the trail, though hardships there were. Having read the journals of more eloquent desert and mountain travelers, one can easily read between the lines of such entries in Armijo's record as "Halting place without water," "We ate a horse," and "We ate a mule belonging to don Miguel Valdes." [36] The Mexicans apparently had no serious trouble with Indians during the journey. They found them generally peaceful and timid.

The governor of New Mexico was pleased with the outcome of the expedition. In a letter to authorities in Mexico City, Governor Chavez declared that the journey had shown that the distance between New Mexico and California was not great, that the route was safe from attack by Indians and that great benefits would accrue to both provinces from an expansion of trade. That said, Chavez urged the Supreme Government "to protect the commerce in that direction." [37] Whatever the governor had in mind, it does not appear that the central government ever involved itself directly in the commerce between New Mexico and California. Trade over the Old Spanish Trail increased nevertheless.

The greatest stimulus to the commerce appears to have been the insatiable American demand for mules. For many years after 1821 when the Santa Fé trade was opened to American merchants, the supply of the hardy animals in

of Interior and Exterior Relations of Mexico, Santa Fé, May 14, 1830, quoted by the editor in Armijo, "Diary," 283-84. The governor's comment doubtless betrays an attitude toward the local inhabitants. Surely no one was better qualified to guide the expedition than the local Indians. Certainly their services were more valuable to Armijo than a map or compass, the lack of which Chavez noted in the same letter.

[36] Armijo, "Diary," 288-89.

[37] Governor Chavez to the Minister of Interior and Exterior Relations, May 14, 1830, previously cited, quoted in Armijo, "Diary," 283-84. Another translation of the letter has Chavez urging the Supreme Government "to promote the commerce of this region." Eleanor Lawrence, "Mexican Trade Between Santa Fé and Los Angeles, 1830-1848," *Cal. Hist. Soc. Qtly.*, x (March 1931), 27.

New Mexico was sufficient to meet the market. But it was soon apparent that local ranchers could not keep up with the demand. New Mexico dealers bought additional stock in Chihuahua and Sonora, but still the demand exceeded the supply. Then the dealers learned about the great horse and mule herds in California which, by 1830, were so great that the animals were regarded as pests.

The opening of the Old Spanish Trail made it possible for New Mexico mule dealers to tap this new source. Caravans from New Mexico bound for California carried mostly woolen goods, blankets and silver. They returned with horses and mules to feed the American market. Profits were enormous. Quite a number of New Mexico traders were loath to spend even the small purchase price and began stealing rather than buying stock in California.[38] A few American mountain men participated in this illicit trade toward the end of the fur trapping era.[39]

Trade over the Old Spanish Trail flourished during the 1830s and early 1840s. Though some American fur trappers took part in the traffic, legitimate and otherwise, for the most part it was a Mexican commerce from beginning to end. The trail was the safest route between New Mexico and California. Traders often were accompanied by their families, and after 1841 the trail also was used by emigrants.

[38] The practice apparently was widespread. The California legislative body passed a law which prohibited New Mexicans from visiting ranches without the permission of the Alcalde and specified that the traders pay prices for stock set by Justices of the Peace. Officials in Los Angeles required the traders to submit their herds for inspection before departing California. If stolen animals were found in the herds, they were recovered and the thieves apprehended. Lawrence, "Mexican Trade," 29.

[39] The mountain-man-as-horse-thief theme is treated in Cleland, *Reckless Breed of Men,* 270-75; Virgil L. Mitchell, "California and the Transformation of the Mountain Men," *Journal of the West,* IX (July 1970), 413-26; Francis J. Johnston, "San Gorgonio Pass: Forgotten Route of the Californios?", *Journal of the West,* VIII (Jan. 1969), 132.

As the population increased in California following the gold discovery, the whole nature of commerce and travel between New Mexico and California changed. The trade in woolens and mules virtually ended. After 1848, there was no longer an excess of riding animals in California. The new arrivals bought mounts as well as gold pans. Gold became the principal export. New Mexico traders were quite willing to accept California's gold in exchange for New Mexico's sheep and cattle to feed California's exploding population.[40] Like the argonauts who favored the faster trails south of the Gila, impatient traders soon abandoned the Old Spanish Trail and plied the southern route instead.

The Old Spanish Trail was not the first direct route from New Mexico to California, nor were Armijo and his companions the first white persons known to have reached California directly from New Mexico. Doubtless, there were a number of crossings made before Armijo's 1829 journey which have gone unheralded for want of first-hand chroniclers. Sufficient personal records have survived, however, to prove beyond question that the southern trails extending from New Mexico to California were familiar to a certain group of men by the mid-1820s. These were the American trappers who had been attracted to the rivers of northern Mexico, reputed to be teeming with beaver.

Even before American backwoodsmen recognized the economic potential of Mexican streams, merchants in the United States had sought to trade with Santa Fé. Until 1821, Spain's mercantilistic policies prevented the trade. In that year, the protectionist wall came down. The new Mexican state welcomed trade with the United States.

---

[40] An interesting account of the trade over the Old Spanish Trail during the years 1830-1848 can be found in Lawrence, "Mexican Trade," from which much of this material has been extracted.

American merchants were quick to oblige. Hugh Glenn and Jacob Fowler took a small caravan to Santa Fé in late 1821. Glenn and three others anticipated an era when they secured a trapping license and returned to the southern part of the present state of Colorado to work the sources of the Rio Grande. Captain William Becknell, a veteran of the War of 1812, and four companions were in Santa Fé the same fall. These traders sold their small store of merchandise for a tidy profit and returned to Missouri to tell all that the door to Santa Fé was wide open. With William Wolfskill, a Missouri frontiersman, Becknell in 1822 led the first party to drive wagons over the Santa Fé Trail. Trade over the trail was brisk and profitable from that moment until the mid-1840s when the tensions that would erupt into war closed it. Some Americans, businessmen mostly, came to live in New Mexico, a few to become Mexican citizens, others to live there as aliens, almost all to remain Americans at heart.

Within the first waves of the invasion came the fur trappers. A cursory reading of the personal accounts left by the mountain men often leaves one with the impression that each diarist was the leader of his own expedition and that his companions were largely nameless and shadowy figures. A closer reading of the journals and also the secondary literature of later years leads one, on the other hand, to the conclusion that fur trapping in the New Mexico-Arizona region at this time was carried on by one big, loose-knit fraternity of men who for the most part knew, or knew about, each other. In more than one case, two or more individual narratives, which at one time were thought to describe different journeys, have been found on close inspection to describe the same expedition. It is not unlikely that most trappers knew what parties were out at any one moment and where in general they were bound.

At first, Mexicans welcomed American trappers along with the merchants. Glenn's party apparently encountered no difficulty in obtaining permission from the governor to trap Mexican streams. Ewing Young, a Tennessean who came to Santa Fé with the Becknell-Wolfskill wagon train, joined with Wolfskill in forming a small party to trap along the Pecos River in the fall of 1822.[41] The following January, Wolfskill with a single companion, probably not Young, trapped down the Rio Grande. This appears to have been the general pattern of American trapping during the first two years: small expeditions, working local streams, and carrying licenses from the governor which granted permission to trap in Mexican territory.

In 1824, the official attitude toward American trappers changed. The central government in Mexico City notified the governor of New Mexico that in the future he must not permit foreigners to trap in his territory. The genesis of this order is not known, but it is obvious that the officials decided that it was not in the best interests of the new republic that aliens exploit its resources, a conclusion that developing nations in the twentieth century would reach even more quickly.

The order was not immediately obeyed by the New Mexico governor.[42] Indeed, Governor Bartolomé Vaca in 1824

---

[41] This probably was Young's second trip to New Mexico. It seems that he came to New Mexico in 1821 with Becknell and a man named Ferrel who had some sort of contract to supply the Mexican government with powder. If this is true, Young returned to Missouri, then rode back to New Mexico the following summer with Becknell's train. Failing to find a handy source of nitre, an essential ingredient in powder-making, the venture fell to pieces. It was then that Young and Wolfskill turned to fur trapping. Joseph J. Hill, "Ewing Young in the Fur Trade of the Far Southwest, 1822-1834," *Ore. Hist. Soc. Qtly.,* XXIV (March 1923), 6-7.

[42] In fact, it was physically lost at an early date. The year following the date of issuance, a copy of the order could not be produced by the governor of New Mexico. Though Armijo, when he became governor in 1827, claimed to have found a copy, it too was soon lost. In 1828, when the Mexican government protested to Joel Poinsett, the American minister to Mexico, that American trappers were holding a rendezvous

and his successor, Antonio Narbona,[43] continued to issue licenses to American trappers. A new condition was added, however, that they employ a certain number of Mexicans who would go along on the expeditions to learn the trapping trade,[44] a technique adopted by new nations of the following century during the transitional period from dependency toward a measure of self-sufficiency. Government officials in New Mexico undoubtedly knew, furthermore, that they could not police a total exclusion of American trappers.

There were at least two important trapping expeditions in 1824. Young, Wolfskill and a third partner, Isaac Slover, led a party out of Taos in February of that year bound for the San Juan River to the northwest. The trappers found an abundance of beaver and stayed out until June, eventually selling their furs for about $10,000.00. Encouraged by this success, another party, or parties, totaling about eighty men returned to the same region during the fall of the year.[45]

During the closing months of 1825, more Americans entered New Mexico. One particularly large trading party of 116 men led by Sylvestre Pratte departed Council Bluffs in late July. Two notable members of the expedition were

---

in northern Utah, then claimed by Mexico, Poinsett asked to see a copy of the law which prevented foreigners from taking game in Mexican territory. The Mexican Secretary of Relations seems not to have had a copy himself and, though the national archives were scoured, no copy could be found. The archivist, apparently exhausted, expressed his opinion that no such law existed. David J. Weber, "Mexico and the Mountain Men, 1821-1828," *Jour. of the West,* VIII (July 1969), 371, 375.

[43] The same Narbona who was governor of Sonora during the years of the Romero expeditions.

[44] Josiah Gregg, perhaps the greatest authority on the Santa Fé trade, and himself a Santa Fé trader, wrote that "as there were no native trappers in New Mexico, Gov. Baca [Vaca] and his successor (Narbona) thought it expedient to extend licenses to foreigners, in the name of citizens, upon condition of their taking a certain proportion of Mexicans to learn the art of trapping." *Commerce of the Prairies,* ed. by Max L. Moorhead (Norman, 1954), 160.

[45] It seems that Young was not on this trip. He returned to Missouri in 1825, but reappeared the following year in New Mexico at the head of another expedition. *See below,* p. 160.

Sylvester Pattie and his son, James Ohio. The latter's record of his adventures in northern Mexico, though not entirely reliable, still makes interesting reading.[46] The two Patties had left their Missouri frontier home, planning to engage in the Indian trade on the upper Missouri River. Failing in this – they neglected to procure the necessary license – they threw in their lot with Pratte.

The caravan's progress toward New Mexico was marked by adventure, according to the romantic, younger Pattie.[47] There were peaceful encounters with Indians, when the Americans ransomed a captive Indian child and later returned him to a grateful father. Other confrontations ended in violence. Members of the expedition attacked a party of Crows whom they suspected of having killed some unidentified whites. Later, a large body of Comanches fell upon the caravan, only to be driven off by a rival Comanche force

---

[46] The edition used here is James Ohio Pattie, *Pattie's Personal Narrative of a Voyage to the Pacific and in Mexico; June 20, 1824-August 30, 1830,* ed. by Reuben Gold Thwaites (Cleveland, 1905).

Pattie recorded his adventures after the fact, from memory. It has been suggested that he made brief entries in some sort of record during his travels and referred to this document later, especially for place names and dates, when he sat down to write his narrative. *See* Clifton B. Kroeber, ed., "The Route of James O. Pattie on the Colorado in 1826: A Reappraisal by A. L. Kroeber," *Arizona and the West,* VI (Summer 1964), 123. If there was such a document, it has not survived. Certainly, Pattie would have placed a high sentimental value on the record, and it seems unlikely that he would have neglected to mention it, had it existed, somewhere in his published journal. I tend to believe that no such record was kept during his travels and that the close attention to detail in the published narrative points neither to a phenomenal memory nor to a contemporary record, but instead to a skilled and pragmatic editor. In any event, Pattie's facts are sometimes exaggerated, in some passages suspect, and occasionally unreliable. His dates are confusing and, in a number of cases, have been proven wrong.

[47] Pattie's account of the journey from Council Bluffs to Taos reads like a western dime novel of later years. And well it might, for it is almost certain that either he or Timothy Flint, his editor, or both, embellished the facts to add to their readability and, undoubtedly, saleability. It is also quite possible that Flint, a Congregationalist minister and missionary, invented or enlarged Pattie's anti-Catholic bias that is repeatedly expressed in the mountain man's journal.

that was bent on settling an old score. The traders rewarded the leader of the victorious band with their thanks and goods valued at $100.00.[48]

The animal life on the trail to New Mexico apparently proved as dangerous to life and limb as hostile Indians. Pattie told of seeing great packs of wolves, 1,000 in a single pack. Grizzly bears were numerous – Pattie says that he saw 220 of the "white bears" in one day – and attacked the camp almost nightly. Less dangerous, but thoroughly humiliating, was Pattie's attempt to capture alive the calf of a buffalo cow which had been killed for meat. The little beast charged Pattie, flattened him, then bowled him over each time he tried to get up.[49]

The caravan arrived in New Mexico in late October 1825. At Taos, Pratte paid the duties on the goods they were carrying, then led the party to their destination in Santa Fé. There, as the caravan broke up, some of the traders asked the governor for permission to trap the Gila River. What followed is a bit unclear. It is possible that a license was granted to Pratte under the arrangement which required the American licensee to take a certain number of Mexicans on the expedition so they could learn the trade.[50]

Pattie tells a different story – a delightful, and perhaps fanciful narrative. According to Pattie, the governor at first refused to issue a trapping license. While he was considering a bribe of five per cent of the catch, news arrived that Comanches had attacked some settlements nearby, probably near the Pecos River. Some whites were killed, and five women were carried away. To gain the favor of the governor and the Mexican people, the Americans joined the force

[48] Pattie, *Personal Narrative,* 67-69.   [49] *Ibid.,* 56, 63-64.

[50] Weber, "Mexico and the Mountain Men," 371; David J. Weber, *The Taos Trappers: The Fur Trade in the Far Southwest, 1540-1846* (Norman, 1971), 95.

gathered to pursue the Indians. The raiders, driving before them a large herd of stolen sheep and horses, were soon over-taken and attacked. The Indians killed three of the captive women at once, but two were rescued. One of those saved was the beautiful Jacova, daughter of the former governor who had been removed following the Mexican revolution because he was a European. Pattie's contempt for Mexicans, Mexican men at least, is evident in his telling of the incident, as he repeatedly charges them with cowardice in the affair. When the Americans returned to Santa Fé, according to Pattie, they received the thanks from the citizens, including the ex-governor, and their reward: permission to trap the Gila.[51]

Armed either with a license of their own or with permission to trap under Pratte's license, the Patties with five companions set out down the Rio Grande in late November, bound for the "Helay, a river never before explored by white people."[52] Pattie's ignorance of the history of the country was typical of travelers at least into the 1850s.

The beginning of the expedition was pleasant enough. En route to their home, Jacova and her father overtook the mountain men on the trail from Santa Fé and persuaded the Americans to visit them. Resuming their journey after three days, the trappers joined company with seven hunters, all agreeing that the combined strength of the two parties would discourage Indian attack.

Leaving the Rio Grande, the mountain men passed the Santa Rita copper mines, located east of present-day Silver City in southwestern New Mexico, and reached the Gila. Though thirty beaver were taken the first day, hard times

---

[51] Pattie, *Personal Narrative*, 78-81. Whether Pattie here relates a true account of an actual incident or merely a fantasy created by the imaginative mind of a young egotist, we can never know. The whole affair has been discounted as the most questionable of a number of exaggerations in Pattie's journal.   [52] *Ibid.*, 85.

followed. The hunters deserted Pattie's group and worked ahead of them, thereby trapping, killing or scaring all animals from the country. The trappers were somewhat successful on the untrapped San Francisco River, as the Verde was then called, and cached over 250 skins on their return to the Gila.

The trappers began to move down the Gila again, but found it still worked out by the party ahead of them. Cursing the hunters, Pattie's group continued their search for untrapped streams. Instead, they found the hunters, battered and wounded from an Indian attack. The trappers gave the hunters some horses and provisions and saw them depart for Santa Fé. The hunters were sure they would never see the trappers again.

Though their competition was gone, the mountain men found little beaver or game, and their condition worsened. During the ensuing weeks, according to Pattie's account, the trappers were threatened and attacked by Indians and forced by hunger to kill their animals for food. A single raven fed all of the men on one occasion, a buzzard on another. More than once, they were saved by robbing poor Indians of their meager provisions. "Hunger knows no laws," wrote Pattie.[53]

On a particularly rough stretch of the Gila, the men left the river and wandered in broken country for nearly two weeks in bitterly cold weather. They almost starved before they regained the Gila. On another part of the river, Pattie saw quantities of broken pottery and traces of ditches and stone walls, leading him to conclude that the country had been settled in the distant past. Doubtless, these were the same remains that would be seen and described by members of the United States Army en route to California in 1846-1847.

---

[53] *Ibid.*, 107.

Apparently despairing of any change of their fortunes, the mountain men set out finally for Santa Fé. They checked their caches – they had buried more than 450 skins in two locations and ten gallons of oil extracted from the carcass of a bear – found them unmolested, and left them for recovery later. The trappers reached the copper mines in New Mexico in late April 1826.

Leaving his father at the mines to recuperate, Pattie set out for Santa Fé to pick up some goods they had left with a merchant and to get some horses which they would need to collect their cached furs. Though he does not say so in his diary, Pattie presumably also needed to report the results of the expedition to Pratte. En route to the capital, Pattie and his four companions stopped at the home of Jacova and her father. After resting there a few days, they continued on their way, each riding a good horse given them by the ex-governor. On their arrival in Santa Fé, they were happy to find their former trading companions, but saddened to see Pratte ill in bed.

Pattie took some of his goods and set out for the mines. His four companions refused to return with him because of danger from Apaches, so Pattie hired a man to accompany him. Stopping again at Jacova's home, Pattie received from her father a gold chain as a remembrance of his daughter. For her part, Jacova said that she would always mention Pattie and his father in her prayers. The remainder of the journey was uneventful, and the two travelers arrived safely at the mines.

Receiving provisions from the sympathetic mine superintendent, the Patties set out to recover their furs. They were accompanied by ten laborers which the superintendent assigned to go with them. Marching directly to the largest of their caches, they were disappointed to find the furs gone.

They did succeed in recovering the small cache at the San Francisco River, little compensation for a year's labors. They returned to the mines, undoubtedly with long faces.

Abandoning trapping for the moment, the Patties agreed to the superintendent's request that they stay to guard the mines from Apaches. They refused the proffered wages because the superintendent had been so generous to them. There was little trouble in the months that followed because, according to Pattie, the Indians believed that the mines were owned at least partly by the Americans, who the Indians respected while they mistrusted and hated the Mexicans, with whom they had vowed never to make peace.[54]

Early in 1826, as the Patties settled into the comparatively quiet life at the mines, the attitude of New Mexicans toward American mountain men hardened. It will be remembered that though the order from Mexico City in 1824 had flatly excluded all foreigners from trapping in Mexican territory, officials in New Mexico had continued to issue licenses with the "apprenticeship" condition. This scheme, however, was a deviation from the intent of the central government's order and was struck down in the spring of 1826.

The Mexican Secretary of Relations, who sent the directive to Governor Narbona to halt all foreign trapping, was doubtless influenced by a report he had received from Pablo Obregón, the Mexican minister in Washington. Obregón had written to the Secretary, telling him that he had learned that Americans were then trapping rather widely in New Mexico. The latest caravan bound for Santa Fé, he reported, included 300 men who planned to trap the Gila River. He urged the Secretary to take action to prevent this illegal activity as contrary to Mexico's best interests. The Secretary enclosed a copy of Obregón's letter in his order to Narbona.

---

[54] *Ibid.*, 114-15.

The expedition to which Obregón referred might have been the original Pratte group which left Council Bluffs in July 1825 or that led by the four Robidoux brothers which left the Bluffs in September of the same year,[55] or both. Or perhaps the minister had heard of another large party that was gathering in anticipation of trapping in Mexico, a venture that was open and publicized. The *Missouri Intelligencer* for April 14, 1826, stated:

> A company of nearly one hundred persons . . . will start from this place [Franklin, Missouri] and vicinity in a few weeks for New Mexico. It is the intention of some of this party to penetrate to some of the more remote provinces, and to be absent several years.[56]

The new official policy altered the legality of American trapping, but only slightly limited the actual freedom of movement of American mountain men. In May of 1826, the trapping licenses which had been granted to Pratte, and more recently to the Robidoux brothers, were cancelled, and an order was issued for the confiscation of their furs. It was then that many American trappers adopted the ruse of posing as merchants, with the appearance of participating in the quite legal trade between Mexico and the United States. Other Americans disdained even this facade of legitimacy. They just avoided the officials and headed straight for the beaver streams upon entering New Mexico.

There is little evidence to indicate that the new hard-line policy had the desired effect of eliminating foreign trapping in Mexican territory, an activity which was considered by Mexican officialdom an insult to the nation and a threat to its commercial interests. On the contrary, the policy must have made less an impression on American backwoodsmen

---

55 Weber, "Mexico and the Mountain Men," 372; Weber, *Taos Trappers,* 91-93.
56 Quoted in Joseph J. Hill, *The History of Warner's Ranch and Its Environs* (Los Angeles, 1927), 71.

than the tales being brought back to the States of Mexican streams rich with beaver. The very year the total prohibition order was issued saw a great increase, rather than a decline, in American trapping in New Mexico. Even as the order was being publicized in that province, expeditions were forming up in Missouri, composed of men who were bound to mine the furry gold of New Mexico's streams in disregard of the reception they might receive there.

In that same year of 1826, there was an event on the western edge of present-day Arizona that would have a far-reaching effect on Mexico's northern possessions. Jedediah Strong Smith led an expedition out of northern Utah and into southern California, thus becoming the first white American known to have completed an overland journey from the United States to California.

Smith, a partner with William L. Sublette and David E. Jackson in the Rocky Mountain Fur Company, set out from northern Utah's Bear River Valley in August 1826, to investigate trapping prospects in the Southwest. The party of fifteen or twenty men traveled along the Sevier River and eventually down the Virgin to its confluence with the Colorado. Continuing down the Colorado to the Mojave villages in the vicinity of modern Needles, the mountain men turned westward toward the Mojave River. Their route must have been close to that followed by Father Garcés westward in 1775 and eastward in 1776.[57] Like Garcés, Smith employed Indian guides, two runaways from the mission San Gabriel. Though they understandably did not return all the way to the Mexican settlements, the Indians assisted the trappers across the desert.

---

[57] *See above*, pp. 91-92, 94. *Also see* George R. Brooks (ed.), *The Southwest Expedition of Jedediah S. Smith: his personal account of the journey to California, 1826-27.* (Glendale, Ca., 1977.)

Striking the Mojave River, Smith and his men followed it toward its source, then crossed the mountains and arrived at Mission San Gabriel in late November 1826. The Americans were not welcome in California. Governor Echeandía denied them permission to trap and told them to get out of the province. Leaving most of his men at a camp in California's Central Valley, Smith crossed the Sierra Nevada, the first white man known to have done so, and arrived at Bear Lake in July 1827.

Smith traveled the Mojave route once more that same year when he returned to California, in violation of his promise to the governor never to return. Smith was determined to rendezvous with the men he had left there. The trail followed by the party of nineteen was roughly that of the previous year, but the trappers' luck had run out. Mojave Indians attacked the party and killed ten men. Smith brought the survivors into San Gabriel where they were received hospitably. Mexican authorities were not so generous and once again told the Americans to leave the province. The trappers complied and, late in the year, left California for Oregon.[58]

As the year 1826 drew to a close, the drama in the Southwest was beginning to unfold. The new Mexican state had recognized the threat both to its integrity and economy posed by the rough American mountain men. Accordingly, an attempt had been made to discourage their coming and action taken to penalize those who came nevertheless and broke the law. Yet, they continued to come, and in ever-increasing numbers. At the same time, a trail from the Great

---

[58] Smith survived an Indian attack in Oregon the summer after leaving California that wiped out his entire party with the exception of himself and two others. He plied his trade for two more years before going to Missouri with Jackson and Sublette to take up the life of a Santa Fé trader. Smith then returned to the Southwest, but only to die. See below, p. 185.

Basin to southern California was opened, and Americans were seen in the interior of California as well as in the ports. The American presence in the northern provinces of Mexico was growing at an alarming pace.

WILLIAM WOLFSKILL
The only known picture of Wolfskill, taken in 1866 by Henry Panelon
in Los Angeles six days before Wolfskill's death on October 3rd.
Courtesy John C. Wolfskill

CHAPTER V

The First American Invasion

The peak of American trapping in what are now the states of New Mexico and Arizona came in the year 1826. We cannot know for sure the composition and routes taken by the various parties that year. The records left are scant, and these are often vague and contradictory. But we can piece together the essential facts and support them with cautious assumptions to get a picture, from the contemporary American point of view, of a banner year in the fur trade of the Southwest, and, from the contemporary Mexican view, of a glimpse of the subtle onslaught of a foreign invasion which Mexican officialdom recognized, abhorred, but could not prevent.

An unknown number of American trappers arrived in Mexico during the summer and fall of 1826, swelling the numbers of those plying their trade there already. The most visible newcomers were those posing as merchants. In August, Governor Narbona issued passports to at least four groups of Americans who claimed to be traders bound for Sonora. Why the governor issued the passports is not known for certain. Perhaps he believed their story at first. Or perhaps he feared to do otherwise in the presence of so many determined men who must have been armed. A less likely explanation is that he believed the report given him by one of the applicants that they were going to Sonora to get a trapping license.[1]

Whatever his reason for granting the passports, Narbona's

---

[1] *See* Weber, "Mexico and the Mountain Men," 373.

suspicions of their true intent – they had no trading goods with them, and their conversation indicated more interest in beaver pelts than cotton goods – led him to warn the governor of Sonora two days later. In a letter, Narbona told the governor about the passports he had issued, described the make-up of the four parties and stated his opinion that their real purpose was to trap the Gila, Colorado and San Francisco (Verde) rivers.

Narbona's description of the parties is indicative of both the size and the leaders of some of the expeditions of 1826. Seran Sombrano (Ceran St. Vrain) and J. William (identified by Narbona elsewhere as "S. W. Williams," perhaps refers to Isaac Williams [2] or, more likely, William Sherly – "Old Bill" – Williams [3]) were said to be leading a party of more than twenty men. Miguel Rubidu (Michel Robidoux, the youngest of the Robidoux brothers) and Pratte (Sylvestre Pratte [4]) had about thirty men. A third party of eighteen was under the leadership of Juan Roles (probably John Rowland) and a fourth, also eighteen, under Joaquin Joven (Ewing Young).[5] It has been suggested that these four parties originally came from Missouri in a single body under the leadership of Ceran St. Vrain,[6] but this interpretation is either disputed or ignored by most writers.[7]

---

[2] Hill, "Ewing Young," 8.

[3] Hiram Martin Chittenden, *The American Fur Trade of the Far West* (2 vols.; New York, 1935), II, pp. 974-75. Cleland agrees that Old Bill "accompanied St. Vrain on the expedition down the Gila in 1826." *Reckless Breed of Men*, 254. Also *see* Weber, *Taos Trappers*, 120.   [4] Weber, *Taos Trappers*, 123.

[5] *Ibid.*, 119-20; Joseph J. Hill, "New Light on Pattie and the Southwestern Fur Trade," *The S.W. Hist. Qtly.*, XXVI (April 1923), 244. Gregg suggests that Governor Narbona issued Young a trapping license with the "apprenticeship" condition that he employ Mexicans to learn the trade. *Commerce of the Prairies*, 160. This is unlikely since the practice had been forbidden by the central government early in 1826.

[6] Thomas M. Marshall, "St. Vrain's Expedition to the Gila in 1826," *The Pacific Ocean in History*, ed. by H. Morse Stephens and Herbert E. Bolton (New York, 1917), 430-33.

Though concern about the intruders mounted, Governor Narbona felt that his hands were tied. In correspondence with the Minister of Foreign Relations in Mexico City and with the governor of Chihuahua, he complained that he was so short of troops, riding animals and equipment that he could neither patrol the border effectively nor search out the offenders. Indeed, he wrote, only "with certain miseries and sacrifices I have been able to maintain a small detachment of ten men on the frontier of Taos."[8] The few remaining soldiers available to him, he said, had to be stationed in the villages to quell the disturbances caused there by Americans. Unless something was done immediately to halt the illegal trapping, he wrote, there was danger that the beaver would shortly be extinct in parts of northern Mexico.[9] No help, it appears, came to Narbona or to Manuel Armijo, his successor.

It is difficult to judge whether Mexicans in general and New Mexicans in particular were aware or concerned about the American trappers. Certainly there were some complaints. One James Baird, a Mexican citizen, lodged a strong protest from El Paso in late October 1826. Baird complained in great detail that the haughty Americans deprived Mexico of wealth and Mexicans of occupation. He called on all Mexican citizens who were proud of their nation to let the government know what they thought about these transgressors. He appealed to the authorities to force the foreigners to respect the laws of Mexico to the end "that we Mexicans may peacefully profit by the goods with which the merciful God had been pleased to enrich our soil."[10]

[7] For example, *see* Hill, *Warner's Ranch*, 73, and Weber, *Taos Trappers*, 119-20.

[8] Narbona to the Minister of Foreign Relations, Santa Fé, Sept. 30, 1826, quoted in Weber, "Mexico and the Mountain Men," 373.

[9] Marshall, "St. Vrain's Expedition," 436; Weber, "Mexico and the Mountain Men," 373.

The full impact – and humor – of Baird's complaint cannot be appreciated without some knowledge of his background. Baird first came to New Mexico in 1812 with a
trading party of Americans, hoping that the Hidalgo uprising in 1810 had opened Mexican trade to Americans. It had
not, for the Hidalgo revolt had failed, and the Spaniards
jailed the Americans as suspected spies. Released in 1821,
Baird returned to the United States, but soon made his way
back to New Mexico where he became a citizen and eventually took up trapping.[11]

Baird's complaint prompted a lively correspondence between Mexico City and officials in Chihuahua and Sonora
in an attempt to get more information on the composition
and movements of various groups of Americans. The Secretary of Relations was particularly concerned about the
multitude of Americans who were said to have descended on
the Gila country in the fall of 1826. Joel Poinsett, the
American minister in Mexico, tendered the official regrets
of the United States government and promised to investigate.[12] There is nothing in the record to indicate that the
United States government subsequently did anything to halt
the illegal activity.

It has been suggested that hordes of American mountain

[10] Archivo de Gobernación (Mexico) Comercio, Expediente 44, quoted in Marshall, "St. Vrain's Expedition," 435.

[11] Baird was only one among many whose occupations became legitimate when
they changed their citizenship. Among the better-known trappers who became Mexican citizens were Antoine Robidoux, Richard Campbell, David Waldo, William
Wolfskill, Antoine Leroux and Ceran St. Vrain. Weber, *Taos Trappers,* 183-85.
Others, not wishing to go that far, adopted the subterfuge of paying Mexican citizens to get trapping licenses for them. Marshall, "St. Vrain's Expedition," 437.
Indeed, there is some evidence that the practice of issuing licenses to Americans in
the name of Mexican citizens was utilized by Governors Vaca and Narbona as a
means of evading the government prohibition on foreign trappers. *See above,* p.
148, n. 44.

[12] Weber, "Mexico and the Mountain Men," 374.

men converged that fall of 1826 in the Gila-Colorado country. Doubtless, a number of these illegal transients made
their way there clandestinely, plied their trade illegally and
left Mexico secretly, either having quietly disposed of their
pelts in New Mexico or carrying the bundles of skins to
sell in the United States. Of their identities and activities,
nothing is known, and they likely will forever remain phantoms. Whether their numbers were great or small is not
known.

The only parties known to have trapped the Gila country
during the 1826-1827 season were the four identified by
Narbona, totaling less than a hundred men. Of the party
under Juan Roles, or John Rowland, nothing is known.[13]
The second group, led by Williams and Ceran St. Vrain,
was on the Gila in October. Visiting a Maricopa village,
the outnumbered Americans submitted to being robbed and
withdrew toward Apacheria when they learned that the
Indians had sent a messenger to Tucson to tell the Mexicans
about the intruders. Soldiers from Tucson searched for the
trappers, but failed to find them.[14] The Williams-St. Vrain
party then vanishes from the record.

Of the remaining two parties identified by Narbona, one
led by Ewing Young and the other by Michel Robidoux and
Sylvestre Pratte, more is known for they had their diarists.
In spite of the agonizing contradictions and omissions in
the journals left by these backwoodsmen, the progress of
these last two expeditions can be pieced together, though not

13 A shadowy figure in southwestern history, Rowland remained in New Mexico
until 1841 when he was a co-leader in an expedition of Americans to California.
See below, p. 197.

14 Weber, *Taos Trappers,* 120. The soldiers then went to the Maricopa village
where they were given documents the Indians had taken from the Americans. Included were passports issued by Governor Narbona to Seran Sambrano and S. W.
Williams. *Ibid.*

in a continuous thread and not without some liberal assumptions.

The party, whose leaders were identified by Narbona as Robidoux and Pratte, arrived at the Santa Rita copper mines in early fall, probably September, bound for the Gila. Sylvestre Pratte had stayed behind at Santa Fé, leaving Michel Robidoux as the sole leader of the expedition.[15] The Patties, who had been guarding the mines since the completion of their last expedition, decided to join Robidoux.[16] Fearing for the security of the mines if he should lose his guards, the superintendent tried to persuade them to stay by offering to lease the mines to them. The elder Pattie accepted the generous offer, but James declined, telling his father that he wanted to return to trapping and "to see more of this strange and new country."[17]

Soon after departing the mines, the expedition, composed of Frenchmen according to Pattie, became more preoccupied with Indians than beaver. The first encounter was settled peacefully enough. Working down the Gila, the trappers came upon a second band of Indians who the year before had attacked Pattie's party and subsequently taken their cached furs. In the showdown that followed, the Indians, being a small party, agreed to return Pattie's goods. Pattie accepted the Indians' explanation that they had used some of the furs and had been forced to eat some of the horses. This done, the pipe was passed around, and all smoked as friends.

It was not long before another confrontation proved fatal for most of Pattie's companions. Passing through the villages

[15] *Ibid.,* 123.

[16] Pattie's dates are disregarded here. Joseph J. Hill has shown convincingly that Pattie was off as much as nine months in his dating. "New Light on Pattie," 251-54. *See also* Weber, *Taos Trappers,* for corrections of Pattie's dates.

[17] Pattie, *Personal Narrative,* 119.

of the friendly Pimas, the trappers arrived at a "Papawar" village. The identity of this tribe is disputed, but they probably were Maricopas.[18] Pattie was suspicious of the friendly reception and warned his comrades to remain alert. They ignored him and thus were not prepared for the attack that came that night as they slept within the Indian camp. Only three of the mountain men survived the slaughter. Pattie had persuaded one man whom he had known in Missouri to sleep outside the camp with him. The next morning, they found Robidoux who had been wounded, and the three escaped.[19] At dusk, the trio stumbled purely by chance upon the camp of the Ewing Young expedition.

Before continuing with the adventures of the combined party, we should go back to trace the journey of Young's

---

[18] Young identified the Indians who later attacked the Robidoux party as Pimas and Maricopas, implying that the present village was the latter. Charles L. Camp, "The Chronicles of George C. Yount," *Calif. Hist. Soc. Qtly.*, II (April 1923), 8. Other writers have claimed that the Indians were either Apaches or Yavapais. *See* Kroeber, "Pattie on the Colorado in 1826," 124, and appended comments by Albert B. Schroeder, 135. For additional evidence supporting the Apache-Yavapai view, *see below*, pp. 167-68, n. 24 and n. 25. More substantial evidence appears to verify the Pima-Maricopa claim. *See below*, n. 19, and p. 173, n. 37.

[19] Why the Indians attacked the trappers remains a mystery. Pimas and Maricopas had a reputation for befriending travelers. Forbes speculated that perhaps the Mexican commander of the Tucson garrison incited the Indians to attack the Americans. Forbes, "Yuma Route," 110. This is a reasonable assumption. It has already been noted that the Maricopas robbed another party of Americans under Williams and St. Vrain and promptly notified the Mexican garrison at Tucson. *See above*, p. 163.

Stephen C. Foster makes an interesting comment that may relate to the attack on the Robidoux expedition. He noted that a party of French trappers on the Gila in 1826 were attacked at Gila Bend by Maricopas. The trappers, he said, then made their way to Tucson. Stephen C. Foster, "A Sketch of Some of the Earliest Kentucky Pioneers of Los Angeles," *Hist. Soc. of So. Cal. Ann.* (1887), 30. He appears to be describing the Robidoux party. But Pattie said that only he, Robidoux and one other survived the slaughter and eventually joined Young. If Foster's recollection is correct, either he is speaking of a different party of Frenchmen, or some of Robidoux's men escaped during the attack, unknown to Pattie, and fled southward to Tucson.

party from New Mexico to this point. The origins of the expedition which Pattie and Robidoux joined on the Gila are confusing. But it seems safe to say that members of the party included George C. Yount, the expedition's chronicler, who probably arrived in New Mexico in late 1825 and who is today equally famed as a fur trapper and California pioneer, Milton Sublette, brother of William Sublette, and Thomas "Peg-leg" Smith. While Wolfskill was associated with Young in a number of trapping ventures, it is doubtful that he was a member of this expedition.[20]

The Young party followed somewhat the same route as that of Robidoux, but some days later. They stopped in the vicinity of the copper mines for about three weeks. If the trappers visited the mines, surely Sylvester Pattie talked with Young about Robidoux's party and told him that his son had joined it, but there is no record of such a meeting. Leaving the mines, Young struck the Gila and shortly blundered into the middle of a war between Apaches and their enemies, the Pimas and Maricopas.[21] The trappers took hostage seven Apaches who entered their camp, probably as decoys or spies, then waited as the army of "more than One Thousand" hostile Apaches

> . . . kept at a respectful distance evidently waiting the concerted signal – The seven dare not give it, well knowing that it must secure to them speedy death – It was a long day – very hot, no water for themselves or their animals – Every rifle cocked & every pistol with loosened holsters.[22]

---

[20] Hill, "Ewing Young," 9; Weber, *Taos Trappers*, 125.

[21] It is not clear from Yount's account whether the incident that follows involved just a small trapping party that had gone off to work a tributary stream of the Gila or the main body of the expedition after the return of the small party. Nor is it clear whether the encounter took place on the Gila or the tributary, the San Francisco River in western New Mexico. *See* Camp, "George C. Yount," 7.

[22] *Ibid.*, 8.

The tension mounted as the day wore on. Only the Indians' respect for the white man's rifle prevented the annihiliation of the trappers, according to Yount. At nightfall, the seven hostages were permitted to escape, and the confrontation ended.

Near the confluence of the Salt and the Gila, the three survivors from the Robidoux party joined the expedition. Young's force, now numbering thirty-two, subsequently attacked the offending Indians so successfully that all of the trappers' stolen goods and horses were recovered. One hundred ten Indians were killed, and the rest fled. Their revenge now complete, the mountain men resumed trapping, working the Salt and the Verde to their sources before returning to the Gila.

Moving down the Gila, the trappers reached the junction with the Colorado, the first Americans to do so. Here they traded with the Yumas, ribbons for beans. Yount commented in his narrative that the Yumas were "generous & humane & might easily be civilized."[23] The ghosts of Kino and Garcés – and Palma – must have nodded sadly at Yount's discovery.

Turning up the Colorado, the trappers entered the land of the Cocomaricopa.[24] The Indians at first fled at their approach, but were coaxed into the expedition's camp with gifts of coals and skinned beavers. Lounging about the camp later, the Indians noticed some scalps that had been taken by the trappers following the punitive attack on the Indians who had destroyed Robidoux's party. The Cocomaricopas

[23] *Ibid.,* 11.

[24] Pattie called them "Cocomarecoppers." According to Kroeber, they were the Jalcheduns of Father Garcés, later called Halchadhoms, who farmed on the Colorado between the Yumas and Mojaves until about 1828 when they fled from Mojave incursions to settle in Sonora. Eventually they returned to the Gila to live and merge with the Maricopas. Kroeber, "Pattie on the Colorado in 1826," 125.

said that they were at war with that tribe and asked for some of the scalps to dance around.[25] The trappers complied, and the Indians did their "horrid anticks"[26] around them.

Working up the Colorado, the trappers found the Indians less hospitable. When they refused a Mojave chief's demand for a horse in payment for beaver taken locally, the Americans had to fight a number of skirmishes before working clear of the Mojaves' country.[27] On another occasion, probably in the vicinity of today's Boulder Dam, there was a hostile encounter with a group of "Shuenas," variously identified as Havasupais[28] and southern Paiutes.[29] A few days later, three trappers were killed by Indians while scouting for beaver sign. A search party routed the offending Indians as they roasted pieces of the trappers' bodies before a fire. When the other members of the expedition heard all this, they were saddened. Pattie's comments on the occasion dispel the notion that the rough backwoodsmen were indifferent to death and immune to grief at the loss of companions.

[25] Kroeber cites this incident as further evidence that the Indians who attacked the French party were Apaches or Yavapais rather than Pimas and Maricopas. The Apaches and Yavapais were aligned with the Yumas and Mojaves, who were the enemies of the "Cocomarecopper"/Halchadhoms, while the latter were friendly with the Pimas and Maricopas, with whom they later merged. Therefore, the "Cocomarecopper"/Halchadhoms would have wished to dance around the scalps of Apaches or Yavapais, their enemies, but not around those of Pimas and Maricopas, their friends. *See* Kroeber, "Pattie on the Colorado in 1826," 125.

[26] Pattie, *Personal Narrative,* 133.

[27] Jedediah Smith had preceded the Young expedition to the Mojave villages on his 1826 trip to California. When he passed the villages again in 1827, once more en route to California, the Indians told him about the American trappers. Dale L. Morgan, *Jedediah Smith and the Opening of the West* (Lincoln, 1964), 238.

[28] According to Reuben Gold Thwaites, the editor of Pattie, *Personal Narrative,* 136.

[29] Kroeber believed that the Shuenas were the Southern Paiutes, the same tribe that the Mojaves knew as "Shivintas." Kroeber, "Pattie on the Colorado in 1826," 129. In appended comments to Kroeber's article, both Albert H. Schroeder (136) and Robert C. Euler (134) agree that they probably were Paiutes, though Euler thought they could have been Walapais.

As the trappers moved up the Colorado, the country became rougher. According to Pattie's own account:

> . . . [W]e reached a point of the river where the mountains shut in so close upon its shores, that we were compelled to climb a mountain, and travel along the acclivity, the river still in sight, and at an immense depth beneath us. . . It is perhaps, this very long and formidable range of mountains, which has caused, that this country of Red [Colorado] river, has not been more explored, at least by the American people. A march more gloomy and heart-wearing, to people hungry, poorly clad, and mourning the loss of their companions, cannot be imagined. . . Our provisions were running low, and we expected every hour to see our horses entirely give out. . . [W]e arrived where the river emerges from these horrid mountains, which so cage it up, as to deprive all human beings of the ability to descend to its banks, and make use of its waters.[30]

The members of the Young expedition were the first white Americans to travel the entire length of the Grand Canyon. Pattie was not impressed with the beauty and majesty of the sight. The awesome gorge was to him just another obstacle. Unfortunately, none of his companions kept diaries on this part of the expedition's journey – at least, none are known today except Pattie's – so we cannot know what they thought of the spectacle. Many mountain men, especially when they were not in great want, were not blind to the attractions of their wilderness existence.

There is considerable controversy concerning the route followed by the expedition from this point back to Santa Fé. Neither the route nor the controversy will concern us, for here the expedition left the Arizona-New Mexico area.[31]

---

[30] Pattie, *Personal Narrative*, 137-38.

[31] In addition to Pattie's incoherent account of this leg of the trip, *see* Hill, "Ewing Young," 17-18; Cleland, *Reckless Breed of Men*, 186; Camp, "George C. Yount," 12-13. William H. Goetzmann believes that Pattie's description of the route may be more reliable than heretofore believed. *See* Goetzmann's *Exploration and*

The trappers certainly worked northward until they crossed
the Rocky Mountains and entered the Great Plains, thence
to return via a circuitous route to Santa Fé, arriving there
probably in early May 1827.[32]

Why Young brought the expedition to Santa Fé with
a load of furs is not explained. Governor Narbona had
granted him a passport to trade in Sonora, not to trap
Mexican streams. Perhaps Young meant to convince the
authorities in New Mexico that the expedition had acquired
the furs by trading in Sonora. Other trappers used this ruse
with success. If Young's actions are inexplicable, the governor's should have been predictable. Manuel Armijo, who
had succeeded Narbona, promptly confiscated the hard-won
pelts, explaining that the Americans had trapped without
a license from him. Pattie apparently replied that he did
have a license, but was told by the governor that the license
previously granted him was not valid for the current expedition. Pattie confided to his diary that if he had not been
restrained out of a sense of duty to his own country, he
would have taken the furs back by force of arms.[33]

There is persuasive evidence, though incomplete and
contradictory, of another party of trappers in the field in
1827. It seems that Richard Campbell, a resident of Santa
Fé, led an expedition with pack animals from New Orleans

Empire: The Explorer and the Scientist in the Winning of the American West (New
York, 1966), 73-74, n. 1.

The expedition's route in northern Arizona is no less confusing. For debate on that
stretch of the journey, _see_ Kroeber, "Pattie on the Colorado in 1826," 129-30, a map
between pages 122 and 123, and objections to Kroeber's interpretation in comments
by Euler and Schroeder, appended to Kroeber's article, 133-36. There is strong
evidence, indeed, that Young's party divided – perhaps "splintered" is the more
accurate term – at some point after passing the Mojave villages. _See_ Weber, _Taos
Trappers,_ 126-27.

[32] If the party split near the Mojave villages (_see_ previous footnote), this group
was just a part of the original expedition.

[33] Pattie, _Personal Narrative,_ 144; Camp, "George C. Yount," 13; Hill, "Ewing
Young," 19-20.

via Zuñi to San Diego that year. The size of the party has been numbered at seventeen, thirty, thirty-five and sixty. One report has Campbell selling 500 skins to a Russian vessel in San Francisco in October. While in Monterey, Jedediah Smith heard about a party of Americans in southern California. Though Smith discounted the report, Governor Echeandía appeared to give it some credence. Remaining in California until some time after January 1828, the shadowy Campbell party eventually bought horses, presumably with the proceeds of the sale of the skins, and departed California by the same route over which they had entered. Then, for want of a chronicler, the expedition seemingly vanished.[34] If the story is true, Campbell and his companions were the first Americans known to have traveled directly to California from New Mexico.

Since leaving the Young expedition at Santa Fé in May 1827, Pattie had been traveling, hunting and trapping, alone or with a few companions. He eventually returned to the

[34] Alice B. Maloney, "The Richard Campbell Party of 1827," *Cal. Hist. Soc. Qtly.,* XVIII (Dec. 1939), 347-49. Campbell reappears in the records in 1833 witnessing, as a godparent, the baptism of a baby, said to be the child of his friend, Ewing Young. (*See below,* p. 191, n. 68.) He is seen again in 1849, probably at Santa Fé, being interviewed by Lieutenant James H. Simpson who was investigating likely wagon routes from Santa Fé to California. In his official report of the conversation, Simpson wrote that Campbell recounted his 1827 trek to California via Zuñi and the Rio de Zuñi, a tributary of the Little Colorado River. Campbell said that he had had no trouble during the entire trip and, wrote Simpson, assured the Lieutenant that ". . . there is no question that a good wagon route, furnishing the proper quantum of wood, water, and grass, can be found in this direction, both to San Diego and the Pueblo de los Angeles. He informs me, however, that in order to reach the Rio Colorado, the Rio de Zuñi [actually, the Little Colorado] would have to be diverged from at the falls, within a few miles of its confluence with the Colorado and a valley running southwardly followed down to its junction with the valley of that river." James H. Simpson, *Navaho Expedition: Journal of a Military Reconnaissance from Santa Fé, New Mexico, to the Navaho Country . . . in 1849,* ed. by Frank McNitt (Norman, 1964), 160-61. It appears that Campbell had followed the Zuñi River to its confluence with the Little Colorado, thence downstream to the Great Falls south of the present Wupatki National Monument, then westward to cross the Colorado, perhaps in the Needles area.

copper mines, determined to end his wandering and settle down. But such was not his fate. Sylvester Pattie, who had prospered in his son's absence, lost his lease on the mines when his trusted superintendent absconded with his capital. The elder Pattie, though severely disappointed at the turn of events, declared that he would put all unhappiness from his mind and return to trapping as quickly as possible. James agreed to accompany his father, and the two men started for Santa Fé in mid-summer.

At Santa Fé, the Patties joined a party that was preparing to set out for the Colorado region. Though accounts differ, it is virtually certain that this was the Yount expedition of 1827-1828. Strangely, as in the case of the expedition of Ewing Young in 1826-1827, neither of the diarists, Pattie or Yount, mentions the name of the other. In his reminiscences, Yount places himself at the head of the expedition of twenty-four men.[35] Yount's claim to the leadership is supported by evidence that he had obtained a license from New Mexico authorities to trap on the Gila.[36] Pattie says only that he and his father joined a party of thirty men and that his father was chosen commander of the expedition. Since both Pattie and Yount recorded their experiences long after the events transpired, and in view of the conflict that developed between the two men during the journey, differences in their accounts are understandable. In any case, the expedition left Santa Fé, probably in the fall, marched down the Rio Grande, passed the copper mines and reached the Gila without incident. They trapped the Gila with little success until they reached the Pima and Maricopa villages.

---

[35] Camp, "George C. Yount," 17.

[36] Stephen C. Foster stated in his recollections that Pattie, following the split later on the Gila with Yount, arrived in California with a copy of the trapping permit which Yount had obtained from the authorities in New Mexico. Foster, "Kentucky Pioneers in Los Angeles," 32.

Yount was amazed that these Indians harbored no resentment at the trappers for the defeat they had suffered at the hands of the Young expedition. He noted that the Indians recognized them as their former enemies, but showed them respect and offered the peace pipe. They gave the members of the expedition their permission to trap their streams at will and vowed that never again would they molest their "pale brothers."[37] It seems that they had once again become the gentle folk known by so many travelers through their lands.

As their luck at trapping began to improve, Sylvester Pattie thought it best to draw up an "articles of agreement" to protect the interests of all members of the party. The agreement stated that all in the company were in partnership and that any who should try to separate from the group should be shot dead because he would be weakening the ability of the company to resist Indian attack. Furthermore, the deserter might wish to trap ahead of the company, thus ruining the trapping for the followers.[38] The articles, even if they were accepted by all, proved to be a weak binding cement.

The good luck did not last. Beaver became scarce, their provisions began to run out, and the party soon was in great need. Still working down the Gila, they began to argue over what route to take. Probably at some point between Gila Bend and the mouth of the Gila, the Patties proposed that they continue downstream to the confluence with the Colorado. They were opposed by a majority of the party who

[37] Camp, "George C. Yount," 17. Yount's comments here appear to support the identification of the attackers of the Robidoux party as Pimas and Maricopas.

[38] Pattie, *Personal Narrative*, 182. Yount does not mention the agreement. It seems altogether logical that the Patties would favor some such arrangement. Sylvester undoubtedly was remembering the unpleasant experience with the breakaway hunters on their expedition in 1825-1826.

wanted to cut across country directly for the Colorado. The elder Pattie reminded the company of the articles, but they, being the majority, replied that they were not bound by it.

Finally agreeing to part in friendship, the expedition split into two groups. The Patties and six others, two of whom were Sylvester's hired men, remained to trap the Gila to its mouth while the other larger party, probably under Yount, left the river and set out overland for the Colorado.[39] Yount's group worked its way back to New Mexico, and Yount is next seen accompanying Wolfskill on a journey to California in 1830.

The fortunes of the Patties from this point declined. Arriving at the mouth of the Gila, the trappers were welcomed by the Yumas, but soon lost their horses to raiders from the same tribe. Failing to recover the animals, the mountain men built dugout canoes and set out down the Colorado to try to find settlements the Yumas had mentioned. The Americans assumed they would find Mexican villages where they could buy horses and provisions. They reached a point near the head of the gulf before they gave up the search. They learned about tides the hard way as their riverside camp was flooded one night by the incoming tide, and their boats were almost swamped by the rush of the tide on another day.

Some encounters with Indians during the floating trip

---

[39] This is Pattie's account of the split. *Personal Narrative,* 187. Yount says only that eight members of his party "became insubordinate & parted from the main body." Camp, "George C. Yount," 17-18. There is little doubt, however, that the Pattie and Yount journals refer to the same expedition. Attesting this fact are the comments made by Foster in his recollections:

"Capt. Yountz's party were very successful, and on the Gila, the two Patys, [N]athaniel M. Pryor, Richard Laughlin and Jesse Ferguson concluded to leave Yountz, who returned to Santa Fé, and came to California with their beaver. . .

". . . Capt. Paty had a copy of Capt. Yountz's permit from the New Mexican Authorities to trap on the Gila River." Foster, "Kentucky Pioneers in Los Angeles," 30-32.

down the Colorado had been hostile; others had been friendly. One group, probably Cocopas who, according to Pattie, were "frightened to insanity" [40] at their meeting, told the trappers that there were settlements of white people to the westward. Though they could not learn how far away the settlements were, they decided that their only salvation lay in reaching them. [41]

It is unlikely that anyone in the party had the faintest notion of the country which they then entered. It is almost certain that they would have perished without the assistance of local Indians. Shortly after leaving the river, already in desperate circumstances, they chanced upon some Indians who, once their fears were quieted, agreed to guide the trappers to the Mexican settlements to the west.

The desert proved a greater obstacle than they had expected. The Indians, who spoke no Spanish, had not been able to tell them the extent of the desert or that it was waterless. The sand, wrote Pattie, was "almost hot enough to roast eggs in." [42] Resorting in their extremity to drinking their own urine, they only aggravated their thirst. The trappers feared that the Indians would desert them, for their guides, long accustomed to desert travel, quickly outdistanced them, but they remained faithful to their promise. They finally reached the mountains where they found a spring. In early

[40] Pattie wrote that the Indians appeared not to have seen white men before. *Personal Narrative*, 197. Perhaps he was wrong. These might have been the same Indians visited by Father Caballero on his journey from Baja California to Tucson in April 1823. *See above,* p. 123.

[41] Foster suggests that Pattie's trip to California was not an accident, but was planned. Foster explains the reason for the break with Yount: "[The Patties] had heard that there were American vessels trading on the coast, and they reasoned that if their beaver could bear a land carriage to the Atlantic coast for a market, they could realize more by selling to American traders in California than they could by selling in Santa Fé." Foster, "Kentucky Pioneers in Los Angeles," 31. For additional evidence on this point, *see* Weber, *Taos Trappers,* 138.

[42] Pattie, *Personal Narrative,* 211.

March 1828, the Patties and their comrades met some Christian Indians from the Dominican mission of Santa Catalina in Baja California. Discharging their guides with a blanket each for their labors, the mountain men followed the Christian Indians to the mission.

Pattie's run of bad luck did not change upon reaching San Diego. There, the Americans were imprisoned for lack of passports. Sylvester Pattie died during the confinement. An embittered James finally gained his freedom as recognition for his services as an interpreter and his assistance in vaccinating mission Indians during a smallpox epidemic. Later in 1829, he helped put down the rebels in the Solis revolt. For this service, he was offered Mexican citizenship. He declined and instead showered on the governor a recitation of the wrongs he had suffered since arriving in California. In May 1830, Pattie took his complaints to Mexico City where, according to his account, he saw the president and the American minister. Obtaining no satisfaction, he left the capital for Vera Cruz, en route suffering the then common inconvenience of being robbed on the road.

Arriving in New Orleans from Vera Cruz, Pattie, now penniless, borrowed enough money for steamboat passage to Cincinnati, whence he returned finally to his native Kentucky. What happened to him in later years is not known, for here his diary ends. It is hard to imagine this wanderer, yet a young man, settling down to a sedentary existence on a small Kentucky farm.[43]

Meanwhile in New Mexico, a new attempt was launched to prevent any further American trapping on Mexican streams. In spring 1828, shortly after the Patties were im-

---

[43] Bancroft suggests that he turned up in San Diego following the American acquisition of California. *History of California,* III, p. 171, n. 44.

prisoned in California, Mexico City granted two petitioners, Julian Wilson, a United States-born Mexican citizen, and an English merchant named Richard Exter, an exclusive monopoly in the taking of sea otter, beaver, bear and other animals throughout New Mexico and Alta California.[44] For their part, Wilson and Exter were obligated to keep foreign hunters and trappers out of Mexican territory and to pay a tax on all furs taken.

When news of the concession reached California and New Mexico, the governors and the public alike reacted unfavorably. The chief argument seems to have been that the granting of a monopoly deprived the citizens of the northern provinces of a potential livelihood. They, the local residents, not Americans or concessionaires, should have the right to harvest the furs. Mexico City replied to the governors, assuring them that the concession was not meant to be exclusive and would not be prejudicial to the best interests of local citizens. The apparent contradictions in the terms of the permit and the assurances were not explained by the authorities.

The scheme came to nothing. The partners made but a feeble effort to exploit their monopoly. They placed an advertisement in a Missouri newspaper in the fall of 1828 which announced their exclusive rights and warned that "any person who shall infringe this privilege, by hunting on these lands without authority from the grantees, shall be treated accordingly."[45] American trappers along New Mexico and Arizona streams, if they ever heard about the monopoly, might have looked in vain for Wilson or Exter or their agents. There seems to be no evidence to indicate

---

[44] This account of the Wilson-Exter scheme, above and below, is taken largely from Weber, "Mexico and the Mountain Men," 375-76.

[45] St. Louis *Missouri Republican,* Nov. 4, 1828, quoted in Weber, "Mexico and the Mountain Men," 376.

that they ever entered the field. That such a grandiose scheme should have been swallowed by the Mexican authorities was an admission that government action was powerless to halt the illegal trapping.

Certainly Ewing Young paid no attention to the paper monopoly, if indeed he was aware of it. Young's whereabouts for the year following his return to Santa Fé and the confiscation of his furs by Governor Armijo in the summer of 1827 are vague. But he reappeared in New Mexico during the summer of 1828 when he seems to have been associated in a trading enterprise with William Wolfskill at Taos. He had not given up trapping by any means. That same summer, he sent a party out to trap the Colorado. It was not a successful hunt. Hostile Indians forced an abandonment of the venture. The following year, another expedition was formed. This one Young led. The party of about forty men set out from Taos, bound for the Colorado, in August 1829.

This was to be Ewing Young's first journey to California. As usual, we know little about the members of the expedition. Besides Americans, we are told that there were Canadians and Frenchmen, probably French-Canadians. Accounts of particular incidents in the course of the expedition tell us a few names. James Higgins, a member of the party, shot James Lawrence, another member. In California, three deserters appeared before Mexican authorities to request passports to New Mexico. They were Francois Turcote, Jean Vaillant and Anastase Carier.[46] Also in the party was the young Kit Carson who kept the only known record of the journey.

Carson was no stranger to New Mexico and the life of the frontiersman. Apprenticed to learn the saddler's trade in

---

[46] Hill, "Ewing Young," 23.

Missouri, the sixteen-year-old Carson had run away and arrived in New Mexico in 1826.[47] There he worked first as a teamster, then as a cook for Ewing Young, as an interpreter for Colonel Trammell, a merchant, later as a teamster for Robert McKnight at the New Mexico copper mines.[48] Carson went to Taos in late summer 1828 where he heard about the failure of Young's expedition to the Colorado that summer. It was here that Carson joined Young's California expedition of 1829.

Since the Mexican government still was not issuing licenses to Americans, Young led his expedition northward from Taos to make it appear that they were bound for the United States. After about fifty miles of trekking through the San Luis Valley, now safely out of view of Mexican authorities, they turned to the west, then southwestward to pass through the Navajo country to Zuñi. From there, the expedition marched to the headwaters of the Salt River where they were confronted by the same band of Indians that had routed Young's expedition of the previous year. A well-laid ambush scattered the Indians.

The Salt was worked to its confluence with the Verde, which Carson called the San Francisco, then up that river to its head. At this point, Young divided his force. Part was sent to Taos to purchase traps to replace those that had been stolen by Indians and to dispose of skins they had taken thus far. The other group would go west to the central valley in

---

[47] Christopher Carson, *Kit Carson's Own Story of His Life,* ed. by Blanche C. Grant (Taos, 1926), 9-10. Grant's publication is reputed to be the material exactly as it was recorded from Carson's dictation. For a discussion of Carson's six journeys to California, *see also* Charles L. Camp, "Kit Carson in California," *Cal. Hist. Soc. Qtly.,* I (Oct. 1922), 111-51.

[48] This is the same McKnight who led a trading expedition from Missouri to New Mexico in 1812, hoping that the Hidalgo revolution had resulted in an easing of Spanish trade restrictions. James Baird was a member of McKnight's party. *See above,* p. 162.

California which, Indians told them, was teeming with beaver. Of the party that returned to Taos, nothing for sure is known since the expedition's only diarist, Carson, was included in the California group.

Young decided to cut directly across country to get to the Colorado. Learning from local Indians that the area they had to cross was rough and arid, Young had three bears killed and their skins fashioned as water bags. The trappers set out and found shortly that the Indians had told the truth. Water was so scarce that they had to post a guard over the water bags to prevent any man from taking more than his share. They passed south of the Grand Canyon, completing their journey in two forced marches of four days each.[49] By the time they reached the Colorado, they were suffering greatly from hunger. They bought a mare in foal from a band of Mojave Indians and feasted. They found the Indians friendly and traded with them for beans and corn.

After resting for three days on the banks of the Colorado, the party marched westward for three days until they reached a dry river bed, probably the Mojave. They followed the bed for two days before finding water. Continuing up the Mojave, the mountain men likely passed through Cajon Pass and finally arrived at San Gabriel mission. The date of their arrival is not known, but it probably was early in the year 1830.

Turning north, Young took his trappers into the California Central Valley. They found few beavers, doubtless due to the presence of a Hudson's Bay Company party under Peter Skene Ogden. They nevertheless had skins to dispose of and, gaining the favor of Mexican authorities by recov-

---

[49] About fifteen miles northwest of Truxton is a watering place identified on early Arizona maps as "Young Spring." This might have been the oasis where the party refreshed themselves at the end of the first of the four-day marches. Hill, "Ewing Young," 23.

ering some runaway Christian Indians, subsequently sold the pelts to the captain of a trading ship.

With the proceeds, Young bought horses and mules. It seems that he had decided to get into the business of selling horses and mules in Mexico and perhaps even in the United States. Though he lost some stock to Indians and almost lost control of his men in a drunken brawl in Los Angeles, he held his party together and returned to the Colorado River.[50]

There they set about their business. They trapped down the river to tidewater, then back upstream to the mouth of the Gila and up that stream. Near the confluence with the San Pedro, the mountain men stole well over 200 horses from two different bands of Indians. According to Carson, the Indians had taken the animals in raids on Mexicans in Sonora.[51] Now owning more horses than they needed or could care for, the trappers picked the best animals from the herd for riding and packing, then killed ten horses and dried the meat. The remainder, they set loose.

The expedition ended peacefully and profitably. The trappers continued to work up the Gila until they left it to march to the copper mines, then in the hands of Robert McKnight. With McKnight's permission, the expedition's beaver skins were concealed in one of the deep holes of the mine. Young knew that he could not take the furs to the settlements since he had no trapping license.

If he could not trap, then he would trade. Young sent the majority of his party to Taos and took Carson with him to Santa Fé where he obtained a license to trade with the Indians on the Gila. He then sent some of his men to the mines to fetch the cached skins. Returning to Santa Fé, they disposed of 2,000 pounds of skins "to advantage," Carson

[50] Carson, *Own Story*, 13-15; Hill, "Ewing Young," 24.
[51] Carson, *Own Story*, 19.

noted, while "[e]veryone considered we had made a fine trade in so short a period." After receiving their wages, Carson and the others

. . . passed the time gloriously, spending our money freely never thinking that our lives were risked in gaining it. Our only idea was to get rid of the dross as soon as possible but at the same time, have as much pleasure and enjoyment as the country could afford.[52]

It was probably April 1831, though Carson erroneously recorded the year as 1830.

Other expeditions were in the field during Young's journey of twenty months. Though sources are scant, it seems that a party from the Great Basin in 1829 trapped the Virgin and other rivers in the vicinity. The trappers were fortunate to find virtually unworked streams and within a few weeks had taken all the skins they could manage. Since the season had many weeks yet to run, it was decided that two members of the party should take the skins to Los Angeles to dispose of them while the remaining trappers stayed on the streams. Peg-leg Smith, the only identified member of the party, was one of those selected to make the hazardous journey to Los Angeles, probably arriving there in early 1830.[53] Little else of this expedition is known.

There were also two California-bound expeditions about this time that originated in New Mexico. One was the Armijo party, previously discussed,[54] that left Abiquiu in November 1829 on a mule-buying venture. Traveling a northerly route, part of which was incorporated later into the Old Spanish Trail, Armijo returned to New Mexico in April 1830. The other expedition from New Mexico, which figures even more prominently in the origins of the Old

52 *Ibid.,* 20.
53 Weber, *Taos Trappers,* 141; Hill, *Warner's Ranch,* 86-87.
54 *See above,* pp. 140-41.

Spanish Trail, was led by William Wolfskill. There were about twenty men in the trapping party, George C. Yount among them.[55] It seems that Wolfskill had plans to join Ewing Young, then in California, trap the San Joaquin valley and return to New Mexico via the Great Salt Lake.

Departing in late September 1830, Wolfskill followed a route from Abiquiu northwestward into the Great Basin. The expedition crossed the Grand River just below the mouth of the Dolores, then turned westward, crossing the Green and finally striking the Sevier River. The trappers worked southward along that stream and wandered by mistake into the plateau of the southern Wasatch Range. Traveling in fall and winter, the mountain men suffered great hardships from hunger and the bitterly cold weather. There in the high country, the worst snowstorm they had ever experienced struck them. They huddled with their animals for warmth under a hastily-constructed brush hovel with a blazing fire in the center. For days the storm raged, and the snow deepened. No one ventured from the camp. Some of the animals froze to death. The snow finally gave way to rain which was followed by a hard freeze.

While the accumulating snow had threatened to snuff out their lives, the chance turn in the weather saved the mountain men. The deep snow, which would have been almost impossible to negotiate, was now covered with a thick layer of ice which supported their heaviest animals. They could travel now, but they were lost. According to Yount, whose diary is the only record of the expedition, he and Wolfskill

> . . . ascended a lofty peak of the mountains for observation – In the whole range of human view, in every direction, nothing could be discerned, in the least degree encouraging, but only mountains, piled on mountains, all capped with cheerless snow, in long and continuous

[55] For a list of the members, *see* Weber, *Taos Trappers,* 144.

succession, till they seemed to mingle with the blue vault of heaven and fade away in the distance – It was a cheerless prospect, and calculated to cause emotions by no means agreeable in the stoutest heart.

But they did find their way down from the plateau and into the valley of the Virgin River, a "perfect Elysium" where "calm zephyrs played around them" and game was plentiful. After their narrow escape, they were reluctant to leave this Eden, but the lure of California had them in its grip [56]– argonauts and emigrants for generations after would understand – and they took up the trail again.

The mountain men worked southward along the Virgin to its confluence with the Colorado, thence down that river to Mojave country. There they were threatened by hostile Mojaves who were frightened off by a small brass cannon mounted on a mule's pack-saddle.[57] Leaving the Colorado, Wolfskill led his party westward toward the Mojave River. They followed along the course of the Mojave, crossed the mountains at Cajon Pass to reach San Bernardino and finally Los Angeles in February 1831. The trappers had just completed a journey over a route that would largely become the Old Spanish Trail, the first regularly-traveled route between New Mexico and California.

The expedition's members were destitute. The planned rendezvous with Ewing Young did not materialize. Young already had left California for the return to New Mexico. If indeed he had agreed to meet Wolfskill, he had conveniently forgotten about it. In any event, Wolfskill and his companions were without means to return to New Mexico and engaged themselves in whatever activities they could find. Wolfskill and some of the others worked for a time at otter hunting on the California coast. Wolfskill eventually

[56] Camp, "George C. Yount," 40-41.
[57] General Kearny reportedly used the same cannon. *Ibid.,* 41.

left the business of fur hunting altogether and turned to vineyard and fruit farming. Yount also remained to settle and give his name to the northern California village of Yountville.

Ewing Young did not remain idle for long after his return to New Mexico from California that spring of 1831. Young always seemed a businessman of sorts, and the arrival of a certain trading caravan from Missouri the following summer offered him an opportunity. The train had left Independence under the leadership of the former partners, Jedediah S. Smith, David E. Jackson and William Sublette, the same trio that had bought Ashley's fur interests in 1826 shortly before Smith's first journey to California. Smith was killed by Indians en route to New Mexico, and Sublette shortly set out to return to Missouri, but Jackson remained to enter into an association with David Waldo and Ewing Young. The partnership entered the fur business under the name of Jackson, Waldo and Company.

The new company sent two expeditions to California in the fall of 1831. The first, under Jackson, was to purchase mules for eventual sale in the United States, and the second was directed to trap the waters of the San Joaquin and Sacramento valleys. Jackson's party of eleven men left Santa Fé in September 1831. Jonathan Trumbull Warner, who had been a clerk in the trading expedition of Smith, Jackson and Sublette, was among the eleven and left a record of the journey. Only two other members are known: Peter Smith, a younger brother of Jedediah, and Jim, Jackson's black slave.[58] The company carried no trade goods. Instead, five of their seven pack mules were loaded with Mexican silver coins. Jackson took the by now well-traveled trail along the

58 Hill, *Warner's Ranch*, 94-95.

Rio Grande south from Santa Fé, then west to the copper mines.

The route followed from that point took the traders to the abandoned San Xavier del Bac mission and the presidio of Tucson before striking the Gila River at the Pima villages. They marched alongside the Gila and crossed the Colorado a few miles below the junction of the two rivers. Apparently negotiating the desert with no undue difficulty, the party passed Temécula and the San Luis Rey mission on the road to San Diego. This would seem to indicate that they had passed through the San José Valley. If so, Warner got his first glimpse of the valley where he would later build his ranch, destined to be a mountain oasis on the trail between the Colorado and the ocean.

Jackson and his companions probably had an easier time of it than they had expected. They had been depressed by the absence of identifiable trails and their inability to find guides. Warner later wrote that

> . . . there could not be found in either Tucson or Altar – although they were both military posts and towns of considerable population – a man who had ever been over the route from those towns to California by the way of the Colorado River, or even to that river, to serve as a guide, or from whom any information concerning the route could be obtained, and the trail from Tucson to the Gila River at the Pima villages was too little used and obscure to be easily followed, and from those villages down the Gila River to the Colorado River and from thence to within less than a hundred miles of San Diego there was no trail, not even an Indian path.[59]

With neither trail nor guide to show the way, the traders had expected the worst. But their hardships seem not to have been severe. From San Diego, the party followed the coast to Los Angeles, arriving there in early December 1831. Jackson and his men then busied themselves purchasing

---

[59] Warner, "Reminiscences," 188-89.

horses and mules, in the process traveling as far north as the missions on the southern shore of San Francisco Bay.

Meanwhile, Jackson, Waldo and Company's second expedition got underway for California. Reflecting its purpose, the size of this trapping party was larger than the mule-buying venture. Under the command of Ewing Young, the group consisted of thirty-six men, twenty-nine of whom have been identified. The only known journal kept by a member of the party was written by Job F. Dye.[60]

Young's party left Taos in October 1831. Passing through Zuñi, where provisions were purchased, the trappers crossed the mountains to the headwaters of the Black River, thence down that stream to its junction with the Salt. Taking little beaver or game thus far, the men were elated to find both plentiful here. They feasted on a fat bear which Dye killed. Bear meat was highly prized by mountain men who found beaver flesh poor fare. Dye and Young had begun hunting together, but Dye separated from Young, "Capt. Young not being a very good hunter and yet over-anxious to kill game." [61]

---

[60] Job Francis Dye, *Recollections of a Pioneer, 1830-1852: Rocky Mountains, New Mexico, California* (Los Angeles, 1951). Dye and some others, probably all novices, had tried their hand at trapping in 1830 on the Arkansas and Platte Rivers, but soon gave up and headed for Taos. There, the governor ordered them to leave, but the citizens permitted them to stay. After a period of illness, Dye determined to go to California at the first opportunity.

For a list of the members of the Young expedition, *see* Dye, *Recollections*, 18, and Weber, *Taos Trappers*, 148. A notable member of the party was Isaac "Don Julian" Williams of Rancho del Chino fame. Located near the present town of Chino, Rancho del Chino originally was a San Gabriel mission ranch. It lay at the end of the southwestern trail and was visited by countless immigrants. The record book kept by Williams shows signatures and comments of many of the travelers who stopped there. Benjamin David Wilson, "Benjamin David Wilson's Observations on Early Days in California and New Mexico," Foreword by Arthur Woodward, *Hist. Soc. of So. Calif. Ann.*, XVI (1934), 136-37, n. 3. *Also see* Isaac Williams, "The Record Book of the Rancho Santa Ana del Chino," ed. by Lyndley Bynum, *Hist. Soc. of So. Calif. Ann.*, XVI (1934), 1-55.

[61] Dye, *Recollections*, 20.

The balance of the journey to the Pima villages was tumultuous. Cambridge Green shot James Anderson as Anderson stood peacefully by the campfire, smoking his pipe. There had been an argument over the setting of traps, each claiming that the other had encroached on "pre-empted ground." [62] Later, when Indians were harrassing the trappers day and night, an edgy night guard, James Green, by mistake shot and killed a Mexican from Taos, Santiago Cardero, who appears to have been just passing by. Green cried bitterly when he learned what he had done. Troubles with the Indians finally culminated in a battle with 100 Apaches. Doubtless, the trappers were relieved to reach the Pima villages at last, where they were welcomed and entertained.

The visit was but a respite. Taking on provisions – pinole, pemmican and frijoles – the expedition set out once more, and hard times returned. Meat supplies ran out, and beaver became scarce. Passing the junction with the Colorado, the mountain men worked down that river. At tidewater, they discovered the ruins of an old mission and pitched their camp there. It was around New Year's Day, 1832. For some reason, they remained in this camp a considerable time. It could not have been a bountiful harvest of beaver that kept them there, for they were forced to kill and eat twenty-three of their horses while in the camp. And although a mountain man might get awfully tired of a diet of roast beaver, he would never kill a precious horse as long as he had any other source of sustenance.

Perhaps it was fatigue that prompted the trappers to remain encamped on the Colorado so long, for Dye wrote

---

[62] *Ibid.,* 23-24. The trappers' sense of justice apparently was outraged at Green's cold-blooded act. When the expedition arrived in Los Angeles months later, Green was turned over to Mexican authorities. He was confined in prison for a year before escaping and, according to rumor, joining the Apaches. *Ibid.,* 27.

that "[a]fter being thoroughly rested,"[63] they crossed the river to continue their journey.[64] On the California side of the Colorado, thirteen members of the party, including Young, decided to strike out across the desert for the coastal settlements. Why the larger group declined to accompany them is speculative. Perhaps the hardships were too much for them. It seems they returned to New Mexico, trapping on the way.

A three-day trek of hunger, thirst and thorns brought Young and his companions to a watering place. They slaughtered a horse for meat, and all were happy. Two days more carried them finally to "California, where we found large herds of cattle. To our eyes this was a glorious feast,

---

[63] *Ibid.,* 26.

[64] The implication is that they crossed at or near the site of their encampment, which was at an undetermined distance downstream from the mouth of the Gila. Joseph J. Hill has questioned this conclusion. He notes that the expedition encamped around Jan. 1, 1832 and arrived in Los Angeles in mid-March 1832. What happened to the intervening two-and-a-half months? Dye does not account for them. Hill suggests a possible explanation: "In 1849, he [Dye] crossed from Sonora to California by what, he said, was the same route that he followed in 1832. But in the 1849 expedition he states that he crossed above the mouth of the Gila. On the later expedition he claims to have discovered New River, which he says did not exist in 1832. This might lead one to conclude that, although they reached tidewater on the 1832 trip, they returned up the river to the mouth of the Gila, where they crossed as in the later journey and then proceeded across the desert to Los Angeles, where they arrived March 14, 1832." Hill, *Warner's Ranch,* 97. I have suggested an alternative explanation that would indicate that they were indeed camped on the Colorado for quite some time. Admittedly, there were thirty-six hungry men to feed, but twenty-three horses killed for food "while in this camp" (Dye, *Recollections,* 26) would have gone a long way, considering the aversion of mountain men for traveling on foot. Dye himself wrote that they remained in this camp "for several days." *Ibid.*

The question of the expedition's campsite and itinerary also may have implications for the dispute over the site of Bicuñer mission. *See above,* p. 107. Dye did not, and probably could not, tell which mission they discovered. It would seem proper to place the mission downstream from Yuma since Dye saw the ruins of the mission at tidewater. On the other hand, if Hill is correct, that the expedition after reaching tidewater traveled back upstream to a point north of the mouth of the Gila before crossing the Colorado to the California side, then Dye still could have seen the ruins of the mission at the point of the crossing.

but not so much as it was to our appetites." Dye's concluding comments in his journal could well serve as a paean and a lament for all those thousands who would follow him to California over southwestern trails:

> We . . . [have] . . . just crossed the continent, suffering worse than torture, from savages, hunger and thirst, heat and cold, want of rest and clothing, amidst mountains and deserts, traveling without a road or any friendly device or trail to direct our way, and worn out with care and ceaseless vigilance in . . . avoiding savage tribes of Indians. You may well believe we were grateful for our deliverance, and felt glad to once more meet with even the semblance of civilization.[65]

The trappers reached Los Angeles in mid-March 1832.

In early April, Jackson returned to southern California from his horse and mule buying trip in the north. The Americans were driving about 600 mules and 100 horses. The herd did not number as many as Jackson and Young had hoped to find, and this changed their plans. They previously had agreed to merge their parties to drive the animals all the way to Louisiana. The smaller herd would not require all hands, so it was decided that Young and his men would accompany Jackson only as far as the Colorado.

The company broke camp on the Santa Ana River at the site of modern Corona and set out for the Colorado in May 1832. The route taken to the Colorado is not known, only that they arrived there in June and found the river very high. The crossing was made with some difficulty and not without the loss of a few animals. According to the revised plan, Jackson and his men continued the trek with the herd, arriving in New Mexico probably in July 1832.[66]

---

[65] Dye, *Recollections,* 27.

[66] Weber, *Taos Trappers,* 149. There is a later statement attributed to Young that Jackson absconded with property that belonged to the Jackson, Waldo and Company partnership. Hill, *Warner's Ranch,* 100.

Young, meanwhile, with about five men, one of whom was Warner,[67] probably returned to Los Angeles.[68] Young subsequently led an otter-hunting expedition up and down the California coast, then journeyed inland to the central valley for beaver trapping. The expedition eventually moved north until reaching Oregon, then turned southward,

---

[67] Warner later settled in California and, around 1838, changed his name from Jonathan Trumbull Warner to Juan Jose Warner. The name, "Trumbull," was hard for Mexicans to pronounce, and there was no equivalent for it in Spanish. The land in the San José Valley where he built his famous ranch was granted to him in 1844. This oasis in the mountains, about mid-way between the Colorado and the California coast, is justly acclaimed in the history of southwestern trails. Anza's route passed just to the east of the ranch. The road from California to Sonora ran through the San José Valley. The Army of the West and the Mormon Battalion passed through Warner's, and countless desert-crazed argonauts stopped there. Until the coming of the railroad, overland stages and freight wagons were regular visitors. To all, Warner's Ranch was a half-way station for refreshment and replenishment. Hill, *Warner's Ranch*, ix, 101, 110, 113.

[68] It is generally believed that Young never returned to New Mexico, but there is contrary evidence. The story is told that a baby boy was born on April 8, 1833, to one "Maria Josefa Tafoya, a single lady inhabitant of the place of our Lady Guadalupe" and christened Joaquin Joon four days later in a parish church in Taos. Witnessing the christening as a godfather was Richard Campbell, a friend of Young's. The presiding priest was Father Martinez, probably the same who had baptized Ewing Young on May 11, 1831, at which time Young was living with Senorita Tafoya.

If the boy was Young's son, that would place Ewing in the vicinity of Taos and Maria Tafoya sometime around July 1832, the same month the Jackson party probably arrived back in New Mexico. It is unlikely that Warner errs in his recollections that he accompanied Young back to Los Angeles from the Colorado after helping the Jackson expedition across the river. Though Warner details Young's activities in California in late June and early July, he does not account for Young's whereabouts for most of July, or August or September. If Young went in early July to New Mexico instead of Monterey, as Warner states, he could still have returned to California by October when, says Warner, Young began a series of hunts that lasted for two years.

Whether the child was Young's is debatable. Warner recalled that Young died with "no lawful heirs, either in Oregon or New Mexico." The Oregon legislature was convinced to the contrary when the young man turned up in Oregon a few years following Young's death to claim his inheritance. Kit Carson was among a number of men who signed sworn statements verifying the claimant's identity. Maloney, "Richard Campbell's Party," 349-50; Warner, "Reminiscences," 179-80, 187-88; Harvey L. Carter, "Ewing Young," in LeRoy R. Hafen, ed., *The Mountain Men and the Fur Trade of the Far West* (10 vols: Glendale, 1965-1972), II, pp. 388-90.

trapping all the way. Spring of 1834 found Young with a few men trapping on the Colorado and the lower reaches of the Gila. Moderately successful there, he returned finally to Los Angeles in the early summer of 1834. Soon after, Young met Hall J. Kelley who persuaded him to go to Oregon where he settled down and became a respected and influential member of the community. He never returned to the Southwest.

A number of southern California pioneers who crossed the southwestern trails have already been introduced in this narrative. In the fall of 1833, another, Benjamin David Wilson, who was destined to be the first American mayor of Los Angeles, arrived in Santa Fé. For a time, he trapped the Gila with James Kirker.[69] In his recollections recorded years later, Wilson has little to say about his experiences with Kirker except that they "were quite successful" and that they "explored the Gila River."[70] Later Wilson returned to the Gila at the head of his own party of six. During this expedition, he became entwined in the events surrounding the murder of Juan José Compá.[71]

Juan José, a chief of the Mimbres Apaches, had been educated in Chihuahuan Catholic schools for the priesthood. It seems that he was a model student until his father

---

[69] Wilson was new to trapping, having gone west on the advice of physicians, but Kirker was an old hand. Kirker had been employed by the Rocky Mountain Fur Company and later trapped in New Mexico, sharing the distinction with others of having his furs confiscated by Governor Narbona. While working for Robert McKnight at the Santa Rita copper mines, he trapped each winter on the Gila. It was one of these annual expeditions that Wilson joined. Wilson, "Observations," 77, 128-29, n. 4. Kirker often combined trapping with an illicit trade in arms and powder with the Apaches. *See* Weber, *Taos Trappers,* 221-23.

[70] Wilson, "Observations," 77.

[71] The following account of Juan José's death, including events leading to and following the incident, is taken largely from Wilson, "Observations," 77-84. *Also see* Gregg's account, *Commerce of the Prairies,* 205-6.

was killed by Mexicans, a tragedy that completely trans-
formed him. He became a renegade, a leader of his people
in a bitter war against the Mexicans. The evolution of Juan
José seems to typify the trend in Mexican-Indian relations
at this time.

Juan José's relationships with Americans were of the
most cordial nature. Here too, the chieftain's attitudes
appear to have been typical of Apaches in general: enmity
for Mexicans and friendliness for Americans. During the
years Wilson trapped in Gila country, he became personally
acquainted with Juan José. The chief's visits to the trappers'
camps were more than social. He regularly intercepted dispatches from Mexican officials, who were desperately trying
to destroy him, and passed the information on to the Americans who had equal reason for avoiding detection. They had
no Mexican trapping license.

The governor of Sonora decided that what could not be
accomplished by military action might be done by assassi-
nation. His willing instrument was an American named
James Johnson, a merchant and part-time scalp-hunter liv-
ing in Oposura, the present-day Moctezuma in northern
Sonora.[72] It had not escaped the governor's notice that Juan
José often visited Johnson's caravans between Oposura and
New Mexico.

Johnson's opportunity came with the arrival in Oposura
of a mule-buying expedition of ten or eleven Missourians
under a Mr. Eames. The only other person identified was
William Knight, the same man who later gave his name to
"Knight's Ferry" on the Stanislaus River and "Knight's
Landing" on the Sacramento River, both in California.

[72] It has been suggested that Johnson was an Englishman, but Wilson, who was
closer to the facts of the tale, says without qualification that he was an American.
Wilson, "Observations," 78; Thrapp, *Conquest of Apacheria*, 10.

Finding no mules to buy, the Americans were on their way back to New Mexico when Johnson offered to guide them. He assured them that though the trail he selected lay through Apache country, there was not the slightest danger. He said nothing to the Missourians about his plans.[73]

Adding to the entourage an accomplice named Gleason, or Glisson, also a resident of Oposura, Johnson set out with the Missourians. A few days' travel brought the party to the Gila River where Juan José found them.[74] By means of an intercepted message, the chieftain had learned of their coming and the details of the arrangement between Johnson and the Sonora governor. Being a forthright man and placing great faith in those he judged his friends, Juan José confronted Johnson with the report and asked him whether it was true. When Johnson assured him that it was completely without foundation, nothing more was said of it, and Juan José invited the Americans into his camp.

There the tragedy was played to its conclusion. Johnson gave a sack of pinole to the Indians, and they crowded around it, men, women and children. Into this crowd Johnson fired a "blunderbuss," or small cannon, that he had secreted into the camp. A score were killed. Gleason, who had called Juan José aside to make sure of him, shot the chief but did not kill him. As the two grappled, the Apache, with knife drawn, was soon on top of Gleason. Trusting to

---

[73] On the question of motivation, Gregg suggests that Johnson and his party, composed mostly of foreigners, were inspired by a Sonoran government proclamation which declared that any "booty" taken from Indians was the legal property of those who captured it. *Commerce of the Prairies,* 205. This overlooks Wilson's statement that members of the Eames party, with whom Johnson was traveling when he killed Juan José, were unaware of Johnson's scheme. Wilson's version is the more convincing.

[74] Juan José was based somewhere near the Santa Rita copper mines in southwestern New Mexico, but his raiders ranged far from there. Thrapp, *Conquest of Apacheria,* 10.

the end, the chieftain called to Johnson: "For God's sake save my life, I could kill your friend, but I don't want to do it." Johnson replied with a shot, and Juan José fell dead on Gleason. "Thus perished that fine specimen of a man," Wilson later wrote, "I knew the man well, and could vouch for the fact that he was a perfect gentleman, as well as a kind hearted one." [75] Johnson's shot did more than kill an important Apache leader. It also irreparably damaged the fragile friendship that had, until that moment, largely characterized relations between Apaches and Americans.

The response of the Apaches to the treachery was immediate and then sustained in a wave of vengeance. The Indians quickly gathered a large war party and fought the Americans all the way back to Oposura, killing some of the innocent Missourians, though Johnson and Gleason escaped.

Meanwhile, the Wilson party, unaware of the whole affair, was camped on the Gila about thirty miles from Juan José's camp. Some forty miles downstream from Wilson's camp was a group of twenty-two trappers under the leadership of Charles Kemp. Leaving the battered remnants of the Johnson-Eames party in Oposura, the Apaches descended on the Kemp encampment and killed them all. Other companies in the field suffered a like fate. Wilson and two companions named (Lucien?) Maxwell and Tucker, who by this time were on the return trail towards the New Mexico settlements, were lucky to be merely taken prisoner. The other members of Wilson's party managed to avoid detection and eventually reached New Mexico.

Happily for the captives, the chief of their captors was Mangas Coloradas who did not wish their death. Mangas, one of the most outstanding Apache chieftains of the nineteenth century, still felt that it was in his people's best

---

75 Wilson, "Observations," 80-81.

interest to remain friends of the Americans. When he could not persuade his young warriors, who were intent on the death of the three, that they should be spared, Mangas helped them escape. In the confusion, Wilson was separated from his two companions and walked alone over 100 miles to Santa Fé. Wilson learned later that Mangas had a "row" with his angry people – probably they learned about his part in the escape – and that they broke his arm.[76]

When the Missourians who had survived the Apaches' vengeance returned to Santa Fé, Eames stayed with Wilson. Eames told Wilson the whole story of Juan José's death. Wilson finally knew the reason for his capture and the destruction of the Kemp party. Until that moment, he had not been sure of the cause.[77]

By the fall of 1841, Wilson and a number of other Americans decided that it was no longer safe for them to remain in New Mexico. Governor Armijo, who had no affection for Americans, apparently was trying to implicate certain Americans with the Texan Santa Fé Expedition of summer 1841. The hapless Texans had hoped to establish the authority of Texas in New Mexico, at least as far as the Rio Grande, by military action. They failed and were imprisoned in Mexico.[78]

---

[76] Wilson did not forget what Mangas did for him. He wrote that Mangas "frequently visited me in Santa Fé afterwards, and in consideration of his services to me and my companions, was a pensioner of mine." Wilson, "Observations," 84.

[77] Wilson, "Observations," 84. There are a number of accounts of the Juan José murder, but Wilson's is likely to be the most accurate since he got the details from an eyewitness. Wilson noted with some satisfaction that Johnson was never paid by the Mexican government for his deed. Because of Apache hostility, he was forced to leave Oposura and his family and go to California where he lived and died in poverty. *Ibid.*

[78] The expedition of from 300 to 400 men set out from Austin and crossed the barren Llano Estacado or Staked Plains of northwestern Texas in a westward direction for the first time by whites. (Coronado's expedition had crossed the high plain from New Mexico to Texas in 1541.) The so-called Santa Fé Pioneers never reached

Wilson had not been involved in the affair, but he rightly judged that the political climate in New Mexico was not favorable to argument against the government. Determined to leave New Mexico for good, Wilson joined with other Americans similarly threatened to form a party of about twenty to travel to California. A few members of the group are known. The leaders were John Rowland and William Workman, long-time residents of New Mexico, then living at Taos. Others were William Gordon, David W. Alexander, William Knight [79] and a creole gambler from St. Louis named Tiboux. The Americans were soon joined by a number of New Mexicans.

The expedition – by now it must have been quite a respectable number – set out from Abiquiu in September 1841. Of the journey, Wilson wrote only that they had no accidents, drove sheep for food and arrived in Los Angeles in November. According to Alexander, their route lay through the Wasatch Mountains and Little Salt Lake over the "Old Mexican Trail," undoubtedly the Old Spanish Trail.[80]

Wilson and his companions narrowly missed the distinction of being the first party of American emigrants to enter California by an overland route. Just days before, in October, the Bartleson-Bidwell party had arrived over the more northerly California Trail.

Most of the members of Wilson's expedition, it seems,

Santa Fé. They suffered severely on their thousand-mile journey through arid west Texas and fell easy prey to the Mexican militia. The Pioneers gave up without firing a shot and were marched 2,000 miles to ridicule and imprisonment at Mexico City. Though the author goes a bit far in suggesting that the unsuccessful expedition of the Texans brought on the Mexican War, an interesting account is Noel M. Loomis, *The Texan-Santa Fé Pioneers* (Norman, 1958).

[79] Knight, as noted above, was with Eames and his Missourians, and it must be assumed that Wilson questioned him about the Juan José killing. In California, Knight was involved in the Bear Flag Revolt and, like most other Californians, was swept up in the gold rush.   [80] Wilson, "Observations," 86, 136, n. 11.

arrived in California determined to make their homes there. Wilson had no such intention. He was merely on a circuitous route that would eventually take him home. His plans were to return to his home by sea – via China. Three unsuccessful trips to the port of San Francisco discouraged him from this plan, and he decided to stay in California, for a time at least. Though some of his comrades from New Mexico, notably Rowland and Workman, received grants of land from the government, Wilson did not because he would not apply for Mexican citizenship. In 1843, he purchased the Jurupa Ranch in present-day Riverside County and settled down to a rancher's life. He soon not only became reconciled to his new home, he

> . . . arrived at the conclusion that there was no place in the world where I could enjoy more true happiness and true friendship than among . . . [the native Californians] . . . There were no courts, no juries, no lawyers, nor any need for them.[81]

The name of Kit Carson reappears often in the annals of New Mexico during the years leading to the Mexican War. After 1831, when he returned to Santa Fé with the Ewing Young expedition,[82] Carson trapped the northern plains, hunted for the traders at Bent's Fort and guided and hunted for Colonel Charles Fremont. Always he returned to Taos where he made his home and, in 1843, was married. He continued his wandering, however, and it was with Fremont's 1845 expedition to California that he got involved in the Mexican War.

By the early 1840s, trapping in New Mexico and Arizona was on the decline.[83] The trend was general throughout the

---

[81] *Ibid.*, 87.   [82] *See above*, pp. 181-82.

[83] But not at an end. As late as 1844, a large party of forty-eight men was trapping on the Rio Verde. They were nightly fired on by Apaches who wished to steal

West. Beaver everywhere had been overtrapped, to the point of virtual extinction in some areas. Contributing to the ultimate collapse of the fur business was a change in London styles. Fashionable Englishmen decided that they preferred the new silk hats to those made from beaver skins.

The contributions of mountain men in the development of southwestern trails were considerable. During the twenty-five years or so they trapped the streams of New Mexico and Arizona, they became familiar with every water course of any size and the Indian trails that criss-crossed the country. Almost always traveling without Indian guides, they trekked between New Mexico and California at will, though not without hardship. Some of the mountain men eventually settled down in California. Others returned to the United States. Some remained in the Southwest where officers of the invading American Army of the West would seek their services as guides and interpreters in the country they had come to know so well. Perhaps the mountain men also contributed to the conquest in a more subtle way. Perhaps New Mexicans, before 1846, had come to accept Americans as sometimes disagreeable, but usually compatible, compatriots.

---

their mules. The party lost a number of traps to the Indians, and at least one man, an oldster who had been in the mountains for forty-five years, was killed in a raid. One LeVonoceur, who had been a member of that trapping expedition, returned to the vicinity in 1846 as a member of William H. Emory's party in the Army of the West. William H. Emory, *Notes of a Military Reconnoissance from Fort Leavenworth . . . to San Diego,* H.R. Doc. No. 41, 30th Cong., 1st Sess. (1848), 86. Even later, in the fall of 1846, Philip St. George Cooke and the Mormon Battalion met a party of trappers on the Rio Grande, near the present town of Rincon, New Mexico. *See below,* pp. 254-55.

CHAPTER VI

Conquistadors from the North

As the waning fur trade in Mexico's northern provinces foretold a declining American presence there, the war between Mexico and the United States erupted, thereby ensuring a permanent American presence. While Mexico had been unable to prevent the illegal activities of a few score American trappers in its territory, it was even less able to repel the invasion by the Army of the West in the opening stages of the war.

The United States went to war with Mexico in 1846 for a number of complex reasons, not the least of which was a widely-held desire to acquire California. The American interest in this Mexican province was not new. President James K. Polk was only the last of a number of American presidents who coveted California. When the United States Army, bound for Mexico and California, invaded New Mexico, that province was tied to the United States for all time. Pushing the conquest westward, two military expeditions marched through the Southwest, deepening the trails, opening a wagon road between New Mexico and California and influencing the later selection of a railroad route to the Pacific coast.

As American power in California began to show itself in the Bear Flag Revolt in June 1846 and the seizure of Monterey in July by Commodore John Drake Sloat, an army was organized at Fort Leavenworth, Missouri, for dispatch to New Mexico. Under the overall command of Colonel Stephen Watts Kearny, the Army of the West consisted of a number of units, among them two companies totaling 300 regulars of the first United States dragoons under Major Edwin V. Sumner, a regiment of mounted Missouri volunteers under Colonel Alexander W. Doniphan, a small group of topographical engineers under Lieutenant William H. Emory, an infantry regiment of volunteers from Missouri led by Colonel Sterling Price and the Mormon Battalion. In all, the army numbered 1,700 men, mostly volunteers with no military experience.[1] Captain Abraham Robinson Johnston, Kearny's regimental adjutant, was all too aware of the task of making soldiers of this great body of recruits:

> To fit regular troops for so long a march is a great undertaking, but to equip and put in fighting order fifteen hundred volunteers, all of whom (even the officers) being ignorant of their duties, is a task requiring a large stock of patience.[2]

The advance units of the army, which included Kearny and his staff, moved out of Fort Leavenworth in late June 1846 and the first part of July. Other units were to follow later. The march was hot and tedious, with but infrequent diversions. The troopers did not neglect to celebrate Independence Day properly. Marcellus Ball Edwards, a Missouri volunteer, reported that "our captain procured a keg of whiskey . . . and . . . in commemoration of the glorious '76, each man drank his fill and in good *spirits* proceeded on [his] way rejoicing through the hottest day that ever shone."[3]

Buffalo herds along the way provided sport and comedy. The same frenzy that seized most western travelers at the

---

[1] For a detailed listing of the units, numbers and officers of the Army of the West, *see* Bancroft, *Arizona and New Mexico,* 410.

[2] Abraham Robinson Johnston, "Journal of Abraham Robinson Johnston, 1846," in *Marching with the Army of the West,* ed. by Ralph P. Bieber (Glendale, 1936), 73.

[3] Marcellus Ball Edwards, "Journal of Marcellus Ball Edwards, 1846-1847," in *Marching with the Army of the West,* ed. by Bieber, 125.

first sight of buffalo worked on the soldiers. They broke ranks and fired wildly at the beasts, endangering their fellows as much as the buffalo. Typically, most of the soldiers thought nothing of leaving most of the carcasses to rot, though some commented on the tragic waste.[4] It seems that the soldiers had as much use for buffalo chips as buffalo meat. The chip fires provided heat for cooking and smoke to ward off the gnats and mosquitoes which were fierce during the early part of the journey.

Some of the soldiers, many of whom lived on or near the frontier, showed a surprising open-mindedness in comparing white and Indian cultures, especially in attitudes toward the dead. Passing the unmolested prairie grave of a white man who had been killed by Indians, Lt. J. W. Abert, one of Emory's topographical engineers, noted how often urban cemetaries were leveled to make room for new buildings. "Who now shall we call the rude man? the wild man?" he mused.[5] On another occasion, when some soldiers desecrated an Indian burial place, Edwards condemned the action, saying:

> Let some Indians be passing through our country and go to our place of interment and break them open, we would at once say they were the worst of savages and not one whit above the brute creation, and be for murdering them at once. This says at once that civilized men is [sic] not entirely perfect. . .[6]

By late July, the Army of the West was encamped at Bent's Fort. While the troops relaxed after an uneventful but fatiguing march of 650 miles across the prairie, Colonel

---

[4] *Ibid.*, 129-30; James W. Abert, *Western America in 1846-1847,* ed. by John Galvin (San Francisco, 1966), 9. One of Emory's topographical engineers, Abert was an exceptionally good observer. He noted not only the details and trials of the march, but also the flora and fauna. He appeared especially interested in plants and birds.

[5] Abert, *Travel Diary,* 10.   [6] Edwards, "Journal," 142-43.

Kearny was busy. He persuaded William Bent and six of his men to accompany the army as guides. They joined the mountain men, Thomas "Broken Hand" Fitzpatrick, already serving as guide, and Antoine Robidoux who was the interpreter. While at the fort, one of the information-gathering parties that Kearny had sent ahead to New Mexico arrived with the word that the New Mexicans would fight.[7] The Colonel then ordered Captain Philip St. George Cooke to go ahead with a party of twelve men under a flag of truce to try to convince Governor Armijo that resistance was futile.

Cooke was not happy with the assignment. Indeed, he was not pleased with his attachment to the Army of the West at all. He would much rather have been assigned to a unit destined for the battlefields in Mexico.[8] Apparently conscious of Cooke's disappointment at the lack of prospect for glory, and the resulting promotions, Kearny tried to convince him of the importance of their mission. Failing in that, the Colonel disclosed his instructions for the conquest of California. Until that moment, Cooke had not been aware of these secret orders. The army had been told only that New Mexico was their objective. Cooke was delighted. He wrote later of his reaction to the news: "New deserts to conquer! That was giving to our monotonous toils a grandeur of scale that tinctured them with adventure and excitement."[9]

---

[7] Bancroft, *Arizona and New Mexico*, 410-11.

[8] When orders to report to the Army of the West caught up with him, Cooke was en route to San Antonio, a journey which likely would have led to an assignment with Zachary Taylor and the conquest of Mexico. Kearny's desire to have Cooke attached to his command – Kearny had requested that Cooke be assigned to the Army of the West – doubtless was influenced by his knowledge that the captain was familiar with at least a part of the Santa Fé Trail. In 1843, Cooke twice commanded a large escort force for caravans as far as the Arkansas River. *See* Gregg, *Commerce of the Prairies*, 21.

[9] Philip St. George Cooke, *The Conquest of New Mexico and California* (Oakland, 1952), 4.

Included in Cooke's advance party was James Magoffin who planned to confer personally with Governor Armijo. Magoffin was a long-time Santa Fé trader who spoke Spanish and knew many influential men in New Mexico. Armijo, in fact, was his cousin by marriage. Magoffin had served his country before, in 1828 as United States consul at Saltillo, and as Commercial Agent at various times between 1830 and 1846 at Chihuahua and Durango. When Senator Thomas Hart Benton heard that President Polk was looking for someone, known and respected by the Mexicans, to precede the United States army as a peace commissioner, he suggested Magoffin. Polk interviewed Magoffin, agreed with Benton and sent the new commissioner to catch up with Kearny at Bent's Fort.[10] Shortly after arriving, he set out with Cooke for Santa Fé.

The army left Bent's Fort for New Mexico in early August. It was a hard march, and water and grass were scarce because of drought. The soldiers were hungry most of the distance due to supply problems. As the column neared Las Vegas, Mexican farmers offered a variety of wares for sale: milk, bread, mutton, cream, cheese, eggs, fruit, pepper, chickens and vegetables. Kearny already had warned the soldiers that he meant to cultivate the goodwill of the Mexican people and that there would be no confiscations of property, no looting, no pilfering. The hungry soldiers, who had been on half-rations for some time, bought the goods at inflated prices out of their own pockets until

---

[10] Thomas Hart Benton, *Thirty Years' View* (2 vols.; New York, 1856), II, p. 683; Susan Shelby Magoffin, *Down the Santa Fé Trail and Into Mexico: The Diary of Susan Shelby Magoffin, 1846-1847*, ed. by Stella M. Drumm (New Haven, 1962), x, xx, xxiv-xxv. At Bent's Fort, Magoffin also found his brother and sister-in-law, Samuel and Susan Magoffin. Samuel Magoffin, a veteran of the Santa Fé trade, was on his latest trek to the New Mexico capital. His caravan was following in the tracks of the Army of the West. Susan, his eighteen-year-old wife, wrote a delightful account of her experiences on the trail and in New Mexico.

their money was all but gone.[11] The troops must have thought this a strange war indeed.

Intelligence reports and rumors gave conflicting predictions of what lay ahead, but it appeared that there would be a fight. According to the report of one Mr. Towley, or (Charles?) Town, Armijo had placed the entire country under martial law and had called all citizens to arms. The Pueblo Indians, largely indifferent to the crisis, would be made to fight. A force of 300 Mexican dragoons had just arrived in Santa Fé, and 1,200 others were expected momentarily. Governor Armijo, said Town, did not really want to resist, and had so expressed himself at a council of the leading men of the country held in Santa Fé, but he was overruled. Another report indicated that Taos was prepared to halt the army's advance. Still another disclosed that 600 men were ready to battle the invaders near Las Vegas. An American who had just escaped from Santa Fé warned that the governor was preparing his defense with 12,000 troops about fifteen miles from Santa Fé. Armijo himself sent a message to Kearny indicating that he would lead his people in a defense of their land.[12] Such was the blend of facts, half-truths and fiction that reached the advancing column.

At Las Vegas, which the army entered peacefully, Kearny had the town officials and citizens assembled and delivered a speech. He presented the Americans as deliverers rather than conquerors. The townspeople, who henceforth should consider themselves Americans, were absolved from allegiance to Armijo. They were free to continue practicing their Catholic religion and would retain their government

11 John T. Hughes, *Doniphan's Expedition,* S. Doc. No. 608, 63d Cong., 2d Sess. (1914), 32.

12 Emory, *Notes,* 22-26; Henry Smith Turner, *The Original Journals of Henry Smith Turner,* ed. by Dwight L. Clarke (Norman, 1966), 70-71; Bancroft, *Arizona and New Mexico,* 145.

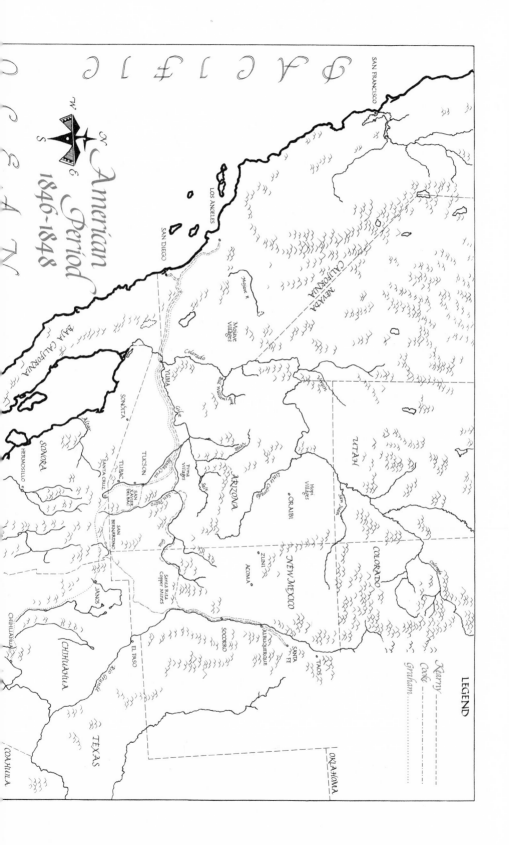

PACIFIC OCEAN

SAN FRANCISCO

LOS ANGELES

SAN DIEGO

N
W   E
S

American Period
1846-1848

BAJA CALIFORNIA

SONORA

HERMOSILLO

ALTAR

SONOITA

SONORA

Mojave R.

Mojave
Villages

Colorado

YUMA

Gila

Bill Williams R.

Virgin R.

ALTA CALIFORNIA

UTAH

COLORADO

Santa Cruz

TUCSON
TUBAC
SANTA CRUZ
SAN XAVIER
DEL BAC
SAN
BERNARDINO

Pima
Villages

San Pedro

Salt

Gila

Little Colorado R.

San Juan R.

ARIZONA

Hopi
Villages
ORAIBI

ZUNI
ACOMA

NEW MEXICO

Colorado

JANOS

Santa Rita
Copper Mines

SOCORRO
ALBUQUERQUE
SANTA FE
TAOS

CHIHUAHUA

Rio Grande

EL PASO

CHIHUAHUA

OKLAHOMA

TEXAS

COAHUILA

LEGEND

Kearny
Cooke
Graham

forms. Village leaders were persuaded to take an oath of allegiance to the United States and, so sworn, were continued in office. The legality of the oaths was questioned by Edwards who wrote: "If compulsatory [*sic*] oaths are illegal, this oath of course is of no effect, for these poor creatures were evidently compelled to take it for fear of giving offense to our army."[13] In addition to apparently winning the loyalty of the villagers, Kearny had another reason for satisfaction in this early phase of the bloodless conquest. At Las Vegas, he received the news that he had been promoted to Brigadier-general.

Though rumors continued to swirl about the column as it penetrated ever deeper into enemy territory, the Mexican defenders proved to be phantoms. American cavalry and infantry, supported by artillery, bravely charged into a pass near Las Vegas which they thought to be fortified. It was empty. The villages of Tecolote, where Cooke rejoined the column, and San Miguel del Vado were entered peacefully. The ceremonies first performed at Las Vegas were repeated. As at Las Vegas, the townspeople appeared not too disturbed with the turn of events. At San Miguel, Kearny was told that Armijo had fortified a pass on the road ahead just fifteen miles from Santa Fé. But, said the informant, when the officers argued over who was to command, the defending force melted away. The auxiliaries were sent home, and Armijo fled southward with his regulars. By this time, the Americans were wary of rumors, but when they arrived at the pass, today's Apache Pass, they found that they had been told the truth. The defile, which could have been defended easily by a small force, even against an army, was empty.[14]

[13] Edwards, "Journal," 155.

[14] George Rutledge Gibson, a Missouri volunteer and newspaper publisher, wrote in his journal: "Cannon at the mouth [of the narrow canyon] can sweep the whole road, as it is almost impossible even for infantry to ascend the precipitous sides of

The road to Santa Fé was open.

How successful the Cooke-Magoffin mission was in persuading the Mexicans not to fight is speculative. There is no official or first-hand record of the conversations. It appears that Armijo was convinced of the futility of resisting. Magoffin was not so successful with Colonel Diego Archuleta, Armijo's patriotic second in command. But Archuleta was also a personally ambitious young man, so the story goes, and was won over with the argument that he might secure western New Mexico for himself with a pronunciamiento since Kearny had no designs on that region. So persuaded, Armijo withdrew the regular troops and the militia was dissolved.

Whatever the reasons for the withdrawal of the Mexican forces, the capital was entered by August 18 and occupied by the Army of the West without firing a shot in anger. A salute was discharged by a battery of American cannon on a nearby hill as the stars and stripes was run up the flag pole in the town square. General Kearny was welcomed by the acting governor, Juan B. Vigil, in Armijo's absence. The general set up his residence and headquarters in the palace of the governor.

Many of the Santa Fé citizens feared the worst when the Americans entered the town. Some fled to the mountains. A number of the people expected to be branded on their cheeks with the letters "U.S." and covered their faces, sobbing, in anticipation.[15] When they found that their fears were for nothing, they talked freely with the Americans,

---

the mountain and attack in the rear, the only way to dislodge troops determined to hold their ground." George Rutledge Gibson, *Journal of a Soldier Under Kearny and Doniphan: 1864-1847*, ed. by Ralph Bieber (Glendale, 1935), 203.

[15] Edwards, "Journal," 159. According to Hughes, Indians had been told by priests that they would suffer the same fate if taken by the Americans. *Doniphan's Expedition,* 40.

cursing Armijo and calling him a coward for running. But they did not seem to mind that he was gone and, indeed, did not appear greatly disturbed by the change of sovereignty from Mexico to the United States.[16] For many years, the ties between New Mexico and Mexico City had been eroding.

American impressions of the vanquished province and its people were mixed. To some, the villages looked like enormous brick-yards, the flat-roofed houses presenting a "mean" appearance on the outside, though neat and clean on the inside "when compared with the general appearance of its inmates."[17] One soldier probably summed up the views of most of the troops when he wrote:

> The appearance of [the] town was shabby, without either taste or a show of wealth – no gardens that deserved the name, the fields all unenclosed, the people poor and beggerly, and nothing to pay us for our long march.[18]

Though many Americans found Mexican women not unattractive, they spent few compliments on the male population.[19] The Americans resident in Santa Fé before the

---

[16] A number of diarists noted this fact. *See especially* Emory, *Notes,* 47.

[17] Edwards, "Journal," 162. The same diarist added that some of the wealthier citizens had brightened up their homes with glass panes in the window holes, but that all these were shaken out when the newly-arrived Colonel Price fired a salute with his largest cannon. *Ibid.,* 163.

[18] Gibson, *Journal,* 205-6.

[19] Some diarists conceded nothing. For example, Cooke referred to Mexicans as "mongrels," while calling Americans, in comparison, a "superior race." *Conquest,* 18, 20. Others, in their evaluations, discriminated between the sexes. Gibson noted that the Mexican women who attended a ball given by General Kearny were "good-looking if not handsome," and that their "forms" were much better than the women in the United States. *Journal,* 224. While Hughes did not agree that they were "handsome," he believed that the women "possess more intelligence than the men, and are infinitely their superiors in vivacity and gracefulness of demeanor." *Doniphan's Expedition,* 38.

White Americans typically have reserved the greater share of contempt for the males in a people thought to be inferior. Male black Americans of the mid-twentieth century could sympathize with male New Mexicans of the mid-nineteenth.

occupation made little better impression on the conquerors. Captain Henry Smith Turner, a member of Kearny's staff, concluded that a "truthful American is rarely seen here." [20]

As the townspeople became accustomed to the American presence, the civil and social life of Santa Fé returned to normal. The oath of allegiance was administered to Mexican government officials, and most remained in office.[21] Though at first retaining the governorship for himself, Kearny later appointed Charles Bent to that post. Captain David Waldo, the ex-associate of Ewing Young and David E. Jackson, and one of the few Americans in the capital who knew Spanish, was made responsible for translating the government's directives into the local language. Antoine Robidoux continued as Kearny's personal interpreter.

Word of the American occupation spread quickly to the surrounding countryside. In response, Indian deputations arrived almost daily in Santa Fé to ask about intentions toward them and, once assured, to swear allegiance to the United States. There was an interesting legend among the Navajos that was suggested as the reason for their submitting so readily to the Americans. It seems that Montezuma had lit a holy fire and had told his people that they must keep it burning until he returned to deliver them from the Spaniards' yoke. The legend held that Montezuma would reappear with the sun. Accordingly, the Navajos for generations tended the holy fire and mounted their rooftops each morning to look towards the east for their salvation. The Americans, coming to New Mexico from the east, had fulfilled that prophecy.[22] A simpler explanation is that the

---

[20] Turner, *Journals,* 73.

[21] Hughes, *Doniphan's Expedition,* 34. Reprinted in the same publication are Kearny's message to the citizens of Santa Fé on the occasion and a formal proclamation issued three days later to further explain the change in sovereignty. *Ibid.,* 34-36.

Indians, by aligning themselves with the Americans, made common cause against their traditional enemies, the Spaniards and their successors, the Mexicans. Even the Apaches, as we shall shortly see, sought alliances with the Americans.

There were persistent rumors during late August that Armijo was gathering an army of Mexican patriots and Indians to attempt the reconquest of New Mexico. To silence these rumors, or to meet the enemy, whichever the case might be, Kearny assembled a troop of about 725 mounted soldiers and rode out of Santa Fé with an air of expectancy. Alas for those who sought glory on the field of battle, the great enemy army did not materialize.

The circuit of the countryside south of Santa Fé was not without excitement. The general had been invited to visit the pueblo town of Santo Domingo on the Rio Grande, near the mouth of Galisteo Creek, and he took this opportunity to accept the invitation. Lieutenant Emory was in Kearny's escort on the occasion and described the reception prepared for them:

> When within a few miles of the town, we saw a cloud of dust rapidly advancing, and soon the air was rent with a terrible yell. . . The first object that caught my eye through the column of dust, was a fierce pair of buffalo horns, overlapped with long shaggy hair. As they

---

22 Gibson heard the tale in Santa Fé and apparently believed that the Navajos welcomed the Americans because of it. Gibson, *Journal,* 210. It seems that he had read Josiah Gregg's description of the legend for he refers to Gregg in his journal. Gibson neglected to notice that Gregg also pointed out that for some reason unknown to him, the sacred fire eventually had gone out. This catastrophe, said Gregg, had induced the Indians to abandon their villages and, presumably, their hope for deliverance from the East. *See* Gregg, *Commerce of the Prairies,* 189.

Captain Johnston's version differs from Gibson's or Gregg's. According to Johnston: "The vigils of the people in these super-human religious exercises had gradually thinned them out; and when they were driven . . . [from their homes by other Indians] . . . the remnant of them fled to the adjacent hills, where they still keep their sacred flame burning, looking for the return of Montezuma from the east." Johnston, "Journal, 1846," 103.

approached, the sturdy form of a naked Indian revealed itself beneath the horns, with shield and lance, dashing at full speed, on a white horse, which, like his own body, was painted all the colors of the rainbow; and then, one by one, his followers came on, painted to the eyes; their own heads and their horses covered with all the strange equipments that the brute creation could afford in the way of horns, skulls, tails, feathers, and claws.

As they passed us, one rank on each side, they fired a volley under our horses' bellies from the right and from the left. Our well-trained dragoons sat motionless on their horses, which went along without pricking an ear or showing any sign of excitement.

When the Indians had passed the soldiers, they wheeled about, raced by them again in two files, fighting a mock battle with each other all the while. Arriving at the steep cliff that dominated the village, the Indians rode up to the edge and halted there. "Their motionless forms projected against the clear blue sky above," wrote Emory, "formed studies for an artist." Thrilled with the display, he concluded: "This has been a great day." [23]

Viewing the spectacle from a distance of two or three miles, the Missouri volunteers with the main body of the army were not sure what sort of day this was to be. At first they thought Kearny's force had joined battle with the Indians. But when the troops accompanying the general made no move to meet the Indians' charge and the sound of cannon was not heard, they realized that it was only a sham battle. When Kearny's column and the Indians rode together toward the town, the volunteers concluded that "the general might drink his wine and puff his 'cigaritos' without our aid; so we moved onward." [24]

This last comment is indicative of a certain amount of

[23] Emory, *Notes,* 37-38. Captain Turner called the warlike maneuvers of the mounted braves "one of the most thrilling exhibitions ever witnessed." *Journals,* 76.
[24] Hughes, *Doniphan's Expedition,* 43.

resentment building toward General Kearny. At least, the resentment seems to have been common among the Missouri volunteers. Some condemned him, in private of course, for his policy of gentle pacification, claiming that he was too soft on the Mexicans. They had been infuriated on the departure of the column from Santa Fé to see riding beside Kearny an escort of fifty or sixty Mexican volunteers.[25]

The Missourians doubtless gained some satisfaction when the general was humbled by their own Captain Reid. Ever the professional, Kearny had ordered that all men wear their coats as a matter of military discipline, pointing out that the government had paid them liberally for their clothing. Reid's reply obviously was heated: His men had come here to fight, not to dress. Furthermore, his men had not received one dime since entering the service. What money of their own they had when they entered had long ago been spent for bread while they were on half rations, "owing to the neglect of your chief Commissary."[26] The general bit his lips and rode away without answering.

The southern extremity of the march was at Tomé, a Rio Grande valley town south of Albuquerque. No Mexican army had appeared, but the soldiers had enjoyed the fresh fruits and the entertainment at the villages along the way. The army returned to Santa Fé on September 13.

Convinced that New Mexicans were favorable to American sovereignty, Kearny turned to planning for the extension of the conquest. The column that would march to California was first set at 700 troops, but the number was pared in mid-September to a force of 300 dragoons under Major Sumner and Lt. Emory's mapping party of some-

25 *Ibid.*, 41.
26 *Ibid.*, 42. *Also see* Edwards, "Journal," 166-67.

thing over twelve.[27] The battalion of 500 Mormons would follow later. Colonel Doniphan was directed to hold his Missourians in Santa Fé until the arrival of Colonel Price with his battalion of Missouri volunteers. Price was expected to arrive from Fort Leavenworth in the first half of October. Thus relieved, Doniphan was to march south to Chihuahua to join forces with Brigadier-general Wool.

On the very eve of the departure of the Army of the West for California, Philip St. George Cooke confided to his diary sentiments that appear to have been shared by a majority of those who would take part:

> Tomorrow three hundred wilderness-worn dragoons, in shabby and patched clothing, who have long been on short allowance of food, set forth to conquer or "annex" a Pacific empire; to take a leap in the dark of a thousand miles of wild plains and mountains, only known in vague reports as unwatered, and with several deserts of two and three marches where a camel might starve if not perish of thirst.
>
> Our success — we never doubt it! [28]

Aware that fame belongs only to those who succeed in spite of great difficulties, Cooke saw the California conquest as an opportunity.[29]

The Army of the West marched out of Santa Fé on September 24, 1846, bound for California. The column's

---

[27] Turner, *Journals,* 75. Besides Emory, there were Lieutenant Warner of topographical engineers, a draftsman, an assistant, eight teamsters and assistants and an undesignated number of private servants of the two officers. Emory, *Notes,* 45.

[28] Cooke, *Conquest,* 36.

[29] At least, he was determined to make the best of it. He was still not convinced that he was in the right place. Though he could refer to the march to California as a "venturesome expedition," he continued to grieve over his absence from the center of conflict: "Nothing is heard of the war in Mexico; our position here has been unfortunate, irksome, disheartening – so far from the 'sabre clash' of the sunny South! Truly there is a 'Fortune of War' and the pedestal of the goddess is Opportunity! That a soldier should pass through a war without distinction I used to think – and does not the world? – is to be set down to his fault or want of merit." Cooke, *Conquest,* 35-36.

course was southward, along the Rio Grande. Expecting a difficult journey over rough, dry country, Kearny had sent his horses back to Fort Leavenworth and substituted mules and oxen. Before leaving Santa Fé, the general had heard that the route to California was suitable for wagons, and he planned to take his provisions wagons all the way. Nothing had been heard of the course of the war in California, and it was assumed that the province was still in Mexico's hand. Anticipating the need for early reinforcements, Kearny left orders in Santa Fé for Captain Hudson's 100 California Rangers to follow as soon as possible.[30]

The beginnings of the march were not auspicious. The country was so barren that it "would not feed one goose to the acre," according to Dr. John S. Griffin, one of the two doctors with the Army of the West.[31] Kearny had heard that Armijo had a map of New Mexico, which would be invaluable in assisting the army's march, but it could not be found.

Adding woe to his burden, Kearny received a message from Santa Fé, telling of the death of Lieutenant-colonel Allen at Fort Leavenworth. Allen had supervised the organization of the Mormon Battalion and was to have been its commander on the march to California. Kearny ordered Cooke to return immediately to Santa Fé and assume command of the battalion on its arrival there.

As the column advanced, Kearny continued his policy of wooing the Mexican people. Horses were traded for mules,

[30] Captain Hudson previously had headed the Laclede Rangers, a cavalry unit of 107 volunteers from St. Louis which had been attached to the dragoons. Following Kearny's instructions, Hudson relinquished this command to form the California Rangers from the various units at Santa Fé. Hughes, *Doniphan's Expedition*, 55, 77; Bancroft, *Arizona and New Mexico*, 410.

[31] John S. Griffin, *A Doctor Comes to California*, ed. by George Walcott Ames, Jr. (San Francisco, 1943), 17. The other physician with Kearny's column was a Dr. Simpson.

and mules were purchased. Occasionally when Mexicans would not agree to a reasonable price, the army seized the mules, but paid so liberally that the owners were delighted with the transactions. Griffin observed that the Mexicans were "for a conquered people . . . treated with a damn sight more courtesy than they deserve." The doctor also thought it unfair when Kearny forced soldiers to pay damages of twice the value when the soldiers' animals wandered into farmers' fields.[32] All of the troopers seemed especially upset when, traveling through arid country, they were forced to buy firewood to cook their meals. Kearny's benevolent policy toward the local inhabitants fed the growing anti-Mexican prejudice held by many of the soldiers. Troopers often compared Indians favorably with Mexicans.[33]

On October 6, a few miles below Socorro, the army met a party of about fifteen men on the trail. Their leader was Lieutenant Kit Carson who was carrying sealed dispatches from California to Washington.[34] California had fallen without a blow, said Carson, to the combined forces of Captain, later Commodore, Robert F. Stockton and Lieutenant-colonel John C. Fremont. The stars and stripes floated in every port, and the province was in the quiet possession of the armed forces of the United States. A civil government was being organized, and Fremont was to be the first governor.

Far from being pleased that they had thus escaped the

32 *Ibid.,* 18.

33 Philip Gooch Ferguson, "Diary of Philip Gooch Ferguson, 1847-1848," in *Marching with the Army of the West,* ed. by Bieber (Glendale, Ca., 1936), 323. Ferguson was with a column that marched from Fort Leavenworth to Santa Fé in 1847, but his comments are typical. Also *see* Griffin, *A Doctor Comes to California,* 18.

34 Carson received his orders on September 5. He was directed to reach Washington within sixty days, a feat, he wrote later, that he could have accomplished if General Kearny had not interfered. *Own Story,* 77-78.

prospect of a bloody encounter, the general reaction to Carson's news by the soldiers appears to have been disappointment. Most of the troops, said Griffin, "hoped when leaving Santa Fé – that we might have a little kick up with the good people of California but this blasted all our hopes, and reduced our expedition to one of mere escort duty." [35] Carson counseled the dejected dragoons not to expect a battle with the Californians in any case because, he said, they would not fight.

Kearny was pleased in a professional sense that the war was going well for the United States, but doubtless felt some personal regret at Carson's news. His orders to take California and set up a temporary civil government had already been completed, and he was still hundreds of miles away. Putting his personal feelings aside, he reorganized his command in light of the new developments. Since hostilities were not to be expected in California, the general reduced his command to two companies of dragoons with a total of about 100 men. He ordered the remaining three companies back to the settlements under the command of Major Sumner. There was a reshuffling of equipment, the best being requisitioned for the two companies that would continue the march to California. Straws were drawn to determine which of the two doctors would accompany Kearny. Dr. Griffin won, if, he mused, "it be said to be a gain to have such a march going and if we get there to have just such another returning." [36]

The Army of the West, thus reorganized, consisted of the following: General Kearny and his aides, Captains Turner and Johnston; Major Swords, the quartermaster; Dr. Griffin, surgeon; Lieutenant Emory and his party; two companies of fifty dragoons each, officered by Captain Ben-

---

[35] Griffin, *A Doctor Comes to California*, 20.   [36] *Ibid.*

jamin D. Moore and Lieutenants Thomas C. Hammond and John W. Davidson; a few hunters; Antoine Robidoux, guide and interpreter; and – Kit Carson. Each of the two companies of dragoons was assigned three wagons, each drawn by an eight-mule hitch. Lieutenant Davidson was delegated responsibility for the wheeled mountain howitzers.[37]

Carson was not at all happy with his change of assignment. He had been directed to deliver his dispatches to Washington personally. He had wanted very much to carry out these orders. He was not unaware of the honor that would fall to the man who notified the President that the long-admired California was now an American possession. Furthermore, Carson had been absent from his wife and family for a long time and had looked forward eagerly to seeing them. He objected when Kearny asked him to turn around to guide the army to California. The general insisted that he needed Carson because he knew the trail and, in fact, had just passed over it. Kearny assured the mountain man that he would relieve him of all responsibility for the dispatches. Carson finally agreed.[38] Thomas Fitzpatrick was given the messages and sent on his way to Washington.

Resuming the march, Kearny soon was forced to make a difficult decision. He had hoped to open a wagon road to California, but the country was getting rougher and the wagons were slowing his advance. A number of Apaches

[37] Emory, *Notes,* 53; Hughes, *Doniphan's Expedition,* 78-79; Bancroft, *Arizona and New Mexico,* 410.

[38] But he never forgave Kearny. His dislike for the general was perhaps matched by his admiration for Fremont. The friction later in California between Kearny and Fremont doubtless served to heighten Carson's attitudes toward the two men. When Cooke heard the details of Carson's reassignment, he agreed that Carson had been forced to swallow a bitter pill. *Conquest,* 44. Certainly, Cooke could sympathize with the disappointed mountain man, for he too had been diverted from what he considered a more desirable assignment to serve under Kearny.

who had joined the column as guides could advise no route that was practicable for wagons. Carson doubted that they could be taken through at all. The general hated the thought of leaving the wagons, but he wanted to get to California as quickly as possible, so he sent word to Major Sumner's encampment at Albuquerque to send packsaddles and take Kearny's six wagons back to his camp.[39]

The army settled down to wait for the packsaddles. The march thus far had been hard, but there were some compensations. The column had moved along the river bottoms occasionally, and the soldiers were able to supplement their short army rations on turtles and catfish taken from the river. Emory busied himself throughout, sketching and noting in detailed scientific terminology the strange plants he saw. Certainly, everyone enjoyed the four-day delay.

On October 13, the party from Albuquerque arrived, and the job of repacking began. The few Mexicans in camp were in much demand because most of the Americans knew absolutely nothing about loading packsaddles. In spite of a certain amount of apprehension, both animals and men adjusted well. Two or three mules balked at the packs and threw them off, damaging Dr. Griffin's kit slightly, but all soon settled down and fell in line.

As the party from Albuquerque set out on their return with Kearny's wagons, the army resumed the march southward. Packs were lighter, and the animals were in better

---

[39] Griffin, *A Doctor Comes to California,* 21-22; Turner, *Journals,* 80-81; Emory, *Notes,* 55. Emory was a step ahead of his commander. Perhaps anticipating difficulties with wagons, he had brought packsaddles with him. *Ibid. See also* Hughes, *Doniphan's Expedition,* 79. Hughes added, strangely, that during the four-day wait for Major Sumner's party to arrive, "Captain Cooke was employed in opening a road for the howitzers and pack animals." *Ibid.* He is mistaken since Cooke left Kearny's column on October 3 to return to Santa Fé where he assumed command of the Mormon Battalion on October 13. Perhaps Hughes meant Lieutenant Davidson who was responsible for the howitzers.

condition after grazing on the good bottom grasses. The only wheeled vehicles still with the column were the small howitzers. Each gun was mounted on wheels which were ten feet in circumference and which stood three feet apart. The cannon, it was said, could go anywhere a mule could go. The statement almost proved a prophecy. The howitzers were a constant annoyance throughout the journey and served as a source of great punishment to the mules. It was feared that they eventually would break down all the mules and have to be abandoned.

On October 15, the army turned southwestward, away from the Rio Grande, "the sight of which has become irksome to us," wrote Turner,[40] and set their course for the headwaters of the Gila River. They doubtless were following the well-trod trail from the Rio Grande to the copper mines. It was not long before Kearny and his officers were congratulating themselves on the decision to leave the wagons behind. On the very first day they left the river, they crossed ravines that the wagons could not possibly have negotiated. Even the pack animals had trouble and did not arrive in camp until an hour after dark. On this day also, Kearny sent word to Cooke, assigning him the task of opening a wagon road to the Pacific. Guides were detached to look farther southward for a road by which Cooke might skirt the mountains. Jean Baptiste Charbonneau was among those who eventually joined Cooke for guide duty.[41]

The column eventually arrived at the Santa Rita copper mines. The Americans were impressed with the richness and extent of the mines. Buildings were still standing and, for the most part, in good repair. Griffin went down into some of the shafts and found a piece of nearly pure metal. There

[40] Turner, *Journals,* 83.

[41] Charbonneau was the son of Toussaint Charbonneau and Sacajawea who contributed to the success of the Lewis and Clark Expedition.

also appeared to be a high gold content in the ore.[42] Apparently still valuable, the mines had been abandoned because of Apache depredations.

At the mines, Turner had a tiff with the general that might have had serious consequences. As soon as the army encamped at the mines, Turner promptly set out to examine the works, arriving there before anyone else. When Kearny heard of it, he gave Turner a dressing-down for going without his permission. Turner explained that he did not think permission was necessary and, feeling that he had been treated shabbily, asked Kearny for an explanation. When he did not receive a satisfactory answer, Turner submitted an official application for transfer to his old company, then in Mexico under General Wool.[43] Kearny did not take action on the request, and the tension of the moment passed.

While encamped at the mines, Kearny was visited by Mangas Coloradas – Red Sleeve, as the Americans called him – who promptly assured the general of the Apaches' friendship. When Kearny told the chief of his mission, Mangas offered to furnish guides and agreed to bring a trading party to the army's camp the following day. Kearny accepted the offer of guides and gave the Apaches an introductory letter to take to Cooke whose column they would then join. The letter explained that Charbonneau could probably communicate by signs with the Indians who did not understand Spanish.

---

[42] Griffin, *A Doctor Comes to California,* 24; Hughes, *Doniphan's Expedition,* 79.

[43] Turner, *Journals,* 85. Turner was in no mood for what he doubtless thought military nonsense. For days, he had worried over the news that his daughter was dangerously ill. In his concern for her, he yearned for his family and his home. He learned later that his daughter's health had improved, but that his wife had contracted a serious cough and that her financial condition was precarious. Contrasting his present condition with the joys of home and family, Turner had decided to leave the army at the end of the present campaign and become a farmer. *Ibid.,* 78-79, 81-82, 84.

The next day, the army broke camp and marched toward the Gila. That evening, Mangas and a party of Apaches came into camp for trading, as promised. The Indians had whips, rope, mescal and seem to have had a goodly number of mules, which the army bargainers especially wanted. The Americans were surprised to find the Indians shrewd traders. Turner was particularly annoyed at the Apache practice of raising the price after the buyer had agreed to the first price.[44] When Kearny threatened to leave, the Apaches became more reasonable and the serious trading began.

The interlude gave the soldiers an opportunity to look the Apaches over. Judging from their trappings, the Indians were in frequent and hostile contact with Mexicans. They sported Mexican saddles and wore sundry pieces of Mexican clothing. Emory thought they looked like "antique Grecian warriors," but in personal appearance and intelligence compared them unfavorably with the few Delawares in camp. Yet, he found them not unfeeling. Their gentleness in caring for a deformed Apache woman "made it hard for me to believe the tales of blood and vice told of these people."[45]

The Apaches reaffirmed their friendship for Americans and their hatred for Mexicans. One of the chiefs proposed to Kearny that the Americans and Apaches join forces against their common enemy:

> You have taken New Mexico, and will soon take California; go, then, and take Chihuahua, Durango and Sonora. We will help you. You fight for land; we care nothing for land; we fight for the laws of Montezuma and for food. The Mexicans are rascals; we hate and will kill them all.[46]

---

[44] Turner, *Journals*, 86-87.

[45] Emory, *Notes*, 52, 61. The Delawares, whose people had been living among whites for many generations, were probably the six who were in Kit Carson's party when he met the Army of the West on October 6.

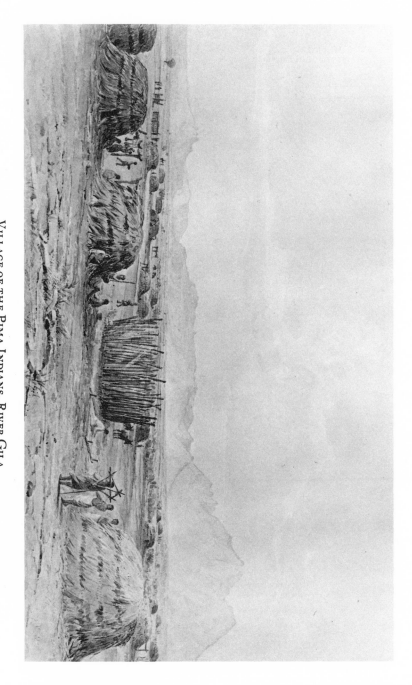

VILLAGE OF THE PIMA INDIANS, RIVER GILA
By Seth Eastman. On deposit in the John Carter Brown Library
from the Museum of the Rhode Island School of Design

KIT CARSON
About the age of 50. From a photograph, circa 1860.
Courtesy, State Historical Society of Colorado

Kearny declined the offer, but gave Mangas and two other chiefs papers which acknowledged their profession of perpetual friendship for Americans.[47] Carson's comment on the exchange was that he would not trust any of the Apaches.[48]

The trading finished, packs were made and the army was once more on the trail. That same day, October 20, the expedition struck the Gila. They found it a beautiful, clear stream, about thirty yards wide and bordered by stands of cottonwood trees. Fish were abundant and deer sign plentiful. Though the scenery was spectacular, the weary troopers soon tired of it as they began the difficult trek through the canyon of the Gila. Because the steep canyon walls were nearly at the edge of the water, the column had to cross the river every half mile or so. Carson pointed out to the grumblers that the trail was a turnpike compared to another they had considered. This hardly cheered the fatigued men, nor were they encouraged by his warning that the trail ahead was rougher. Nor by his casual remark that he had never known a party on the Gila that did not leave it starving.[49]

The country had different effects on the soldiers. Emory was fascinated with it, one day racing toward what appeared from a distance to be a great castle, only to find it a clay butte, another day examining the ruins of ancient villages and broken pottery strewn along the river bank. Turner's impression was exactly opposite. It depressed him. The sterile soil, he wrote, was best suited to producing cactus in great abundance and variety. Though he disagreed with

[46] *Ibid.*, 60. Hughes's version of the speech reads: "You have taken Santa Fé; let us go on and take Chihuahua and Sonora; we will go with you. You fight for the *soul;* we fight for *plunder;* so we will agree perfectly; their people are bad christians; let us chastise them as they deserve." Hughes, *Doniphan's Expedition,* 80. Emory's account appears the more likely.

[47] Hughes, *Doniphan's Expedition,* 80.   [48] Emory, *Notes,* 60.
[49] Griffin, *A Doctor Comes to California,* 25.

those who claimed that the country was needed for a highway to tie California with the United States, he found himself wishing that there already was a railroad through it so he could speed along at sixty miles an hour.[50] While hardly intending praise, Turner foresaw what eventually became one of the greatest attractions of the region: "The country is healthy to a degree far surpassing in this respect all parts of the United States and perhaps all other parts of the world – there never was a purer atmosphere than I am breathing at this moment." But, for Turner, yearning for his family, that was not enough:

> . . . [H]aving said this there is nothing more to be said in favor of the country. Invalids may live here when they might die in any other part of the world, but really the country is so unattractive and forbidding, that one would scarcely be willing to secure a long life at the cost of living in it. . .
>
> But for the climate of this desolate region, which is certainly unparalleled, 'twere better for it to be blotted out from the face of the earth.[51]

Few of the ranks at that moment would have disagreed with those sentiments.

On October 26, marching in a southwestward direction toward the present-day town of Solomon in eastern Arizona, the trail became more rugged. Deep gullies along the Gila forced the column away from the river and into the high mountains. It required eight and a half hours to travel a very difficult sixteen miles before the army was able to descend again to the river. This stretch of trail they named the "Devil's Turnpike." Emory thought the name entirely suitable:

> The whole way was a succession of steep ascents and descents, paved with sharp, angular fragments of basalt and trap. The metallic clink

---

[50] Turner, *Journals,* 94. [51] *Ibid.,* 89-92.

of spurs, and the rattling of the mule shoes, the high black peaks, the deep dark ravines, and the unearthly looking cactus, which stuck out from the rocks like the ears of Mephistopheles, all favored the idea that we were now treading on the verge of the regions below. Occasionally a mule gave up the ghost, and was left as a propitiatory tribute to the place. This day's journey cost us some twelve or fifteen mules.[52]

One of Emory's own mules tumbled over a sheer cliff, but to everyone's surprise, survived. That night a trooper, lost in the darkness, fell from a thirty-foot bluff, but escaped with slight injuries. Exhausted men were still straggling into camp after midnight. Some five or six did not get in at all and slept on the trail. Nor did the howitzers arrive that night. It was one of their worst days.

As the expedition continued to march alongside the Gila, contacts with Apaches became more frequent. The army crossed raiders' trails leading from Sonora that were covered with fresh tracks of horses and mules. Though this traffic was deplored by the Americans, they seized every opportunity to trade with the Apaches for the stolen animals. Near the mouth of the San Francisco, a small tributary of the Gila, Captain Moore and Carson tried to persuade two Indians to come to the army's camp for trading. The Indians refused. It seems that they had not forgotten what had happened not many years before to their now legendary chieftain, Juan José. On another occasion, a small party of Indians declined to enter the expedition's camp for the same reason until they were told that the Americans were at war with the Mexicans and were persuaded of the Americans' friendly intentions. The Apaches agreed to return to the army's camp the following day.

The trading the next day was disappointing, but once again the soldiers were given the chance to observe the

[52] Emory, *Notes*, 65-66.

Indians at close range. Turner declared them "a worthless, squalid looking set," yet with "countenances for the most part pleasant."[53] Griffin described the Indians as "fine formed, active healthy looking fellows," but added that they were, "as usual among Indians," great beggars. The chief, a fine-looking man of about thirty years dressed in beaver skins, he called the greatest beggar among them.[54] When he did not succeed in his "begging," or in his attempt to sell his mule for more than Major Swords was prepared to pay, he mounted his horse and the trading ended.

Continuing down the rugged course of the Gila, frequently crossing the river, sometimes forced to leave the river on dry marches, the punishment began to show on man and beast. The animals especially suffered on the waterless trails. Grass sometimes was poor, but it is significant to note that at only three camps since leaving Santa Fé had there been any want of an adequate supply.[55] Nevertheless, the brutal labor required of the mules was wearing them down, and the beef cattle were becoming poorer and poorer. The cows would soon be gone, and everyone anticipated with some humor the prospect, indeed the certainty, of mule soup.

The expedition eventually reached a point that was less than a three-day ride from Tucson, the nearest Mexican settlement. There was some fear that if the Mexicans knew about the wretched condition of the column, they might mount an attack, if for no other reason than to capture General Kearny who they might trade for General R. Díaz de la Vega whom the Americans had taken at Resaca de la Palma early in the war.[56] But no attack came, and the army

---

[53] Turner, *Journals*, 101.					[54] Griffin, *A Doctor Comes to California*, 29-30.
[55] Emory, *Notes*, 74.					[56] Griffin, *A Doctor Comes to California*, 31.

continued to plod along, its want increasing daily and still hundreds of miles from its destination.

On November 5, 1846, the column camped on the Gila a mile or two above the mouth of the San Pedro River. Camp was not moved the next day to permit the ever-straggling howitzers to catch up. During the enforced rest, Emory rode and walked about the countryside, looking for seeds and geological specimens. Impressed with the strangeness of the country, his

> . . . thoughts went back to the States, and when I turned from my momentary aberrations, I was struck most forcibly with the fact that not one object in the whole view, animal, vegetable, or mineral, had any thing in common with the products of any State in the Union, with the single exception of the cottonwood, which is found in the western States, and seems to grow wherever water flows.[57]

One can almost imagine Emory, amidst the grumblings of those who thought themselves at the very end of the earth, wandering about, taking notes and sketching, as if at a natural science display prepared especially for him.

The next night, after an uneventful march, still crossing and recrossing the river frequently, the army camped at the mouth of a stream emptying into the Gila on the north side. Emory named the stream Mineral Creek because of the abundant mineral signs he saw in the vicinity. He predicted that a few years hence there would be flat boats descending the Gila from this point, carrying gold and copper ores. That same evening, three Apaches were persuaded to enter the camp and, after a good meal, agreed to bring in cattle, mules and horses to trade. They left the next morning and

---

[57] Emory, *Notes,* 77. I have made no attempt to detail Emory's extensive observations on vegetation, animals, insects and geological and mineralogical phenomena. He has filled his *Notes* with data, and the interested reader should consult that publication.

were never seen again. No one was particularly surprised. By then, the troopers had come not to trust the word of the roving Apaches.[58]

For days in early November, cloudy skies foretold rain. Turner's dark and pessimistic mood mirrored the weather signs:

> November 3, Tuesday. It is really cloudy this evening, and were I in a country where it had ever rained, I should expect a steady rain before morning.
>
> November 4, Wednesday. The heavens have been overcast today, looking like rain, but we do not expect it.
>
> November 7, Saturday. It is quite cloudy this evening, threatening rain, but it won't – I know it won't – it cannot rain in this country.
>
> November 8, Sunday. Had quite a rain last night.[59]

The half-hour thunderstorm was the first rain of any consequence since leaving Santa Fé. The soldiers had been so long without rain, they neglected to prepare for it. As a result, blankets and other gear were soaked.

The army finally emerged – at last – from the last canyon into flat country. The soldiers were overjoyed to be through with the mountains. Because they had endured so much privation there, they believed that the hardest part of the journey was behind them. Their elation was cut short as Carson told them what to expect ahead. In leaving the mountains, they also left grass. Henceforth, their poor mules must subsist by browsing on cottonwood and willow and the long green ephedra. The soldiers knew too well that their suffering would be multiplied if the beasts could not survive on such thin fare. And there was the desert. And the Mexican garrison at Tucson was still only about three days' march away. In the end, it appeared that only the howitzers,

---

[58] Griffin, *A Doctor Comes to California,* 32; Turner, *Journals,* 105; Emory, *Notes,* 78.   [59] Turner, *Journals,* 102-3, 105.

which by this time had had every piece of their running gear broken, repaired, broken again and re-repaired, would benefit from the flat terrain.

The column wended its way down the valley of the Gila, passing extensive ancient ruins where broken pottery was strewn about. On November 10, the Americans saw the Casa Grande. The magnificent structure was a ruin when Father Kino said mass there in 1694 and probably was visited by Marcos de Niza and Coronado in 1539-1540. The expedition camped that night a few miles upstream from the Pima villages.

That evening, some Pimas visited the army's camp to learn the identity and intention of the strangers. When they found that they were Americans, they were delighted and hurried back to their villages. Within three hours, the camp was filled with a throng of Pimas, eager to trade or just to visit. The Indians offered watermelons, sweet corn, shelled corn, beans, honey, dried pumpkins, molasses made from prickly pear, pepper and other goods. The quartermaster obtained an ample supply of provisions while the Pimas desired in return mostly white beads and red cloth.

The next day, the expedition camped adjacent to the Pima villages. For the rest of the day, and part of the following, trading and visiting continued. To Major Sword's dismay, he could find no mules or horses for sale and only two or three cows. The few cattle owned by the Indians were used for plowing. Riding animals also were highly prized. Emory described an attempt to purchase an Indian's mount:

> One dashing young fellow, with ivory teeth and flowing hair, was seen coming into our camp at full speed, on a wild unruly horse, that flew from side to side as he approached, . . . The Maricopa . . . was without saddle or stirrups, and balanced himself to the right or left with such ease and grace as to appear part of his horse.

He succeeded in bringing his fiery nag into the very heart of the camp. He was immediately offered a very advantageous trade by some young officer. He stretched himself on his horse's neck, caressed it tenderly, at the same time shutting his eyes, meaning thereby that no offer could tempt him to part with his charger.[60]

Most of the Americans were favorably impressed with the Pimas. They appeared to be healthy and in fine physical condition, a people who enjoyed life and who wished to live in peace and harmony with everyone. Turner saw traits in them that he had not seen in other southwestern Indians. "The men," he wrote, "generally have kind, amiable expressions," and added:

. . . [N]ever did I look upon a more benevolent face than that of the old chief – he is a man of about 60 years of age – spare & tall, & exhibits more of human kindness in his face, air & manner than I have ever seen in any other single individual.[61]

All agreed they were exceptionally honest. During all the time the Pimas came and went in the army's camps, not a single item was lost to thievery. The Indians expected no less from the Americans; they freely left their packs unattended in the camp while visiting. They also left their belongings unwatched in their villages, with no fear of losing anything.

Of their industry, no one doubted. Their fields were neat, fenced, and well tended. The crops were irrigated by canals running to the fields from the Gila and, wasting nothing, the unused water was returned to the river. In addition to growing all the food they could use, including an ample supply for trading, they grew cotton which they spun into thread and then manufactured their own clothing. Emory perhaps summed up the overall impression the Americans gained of their hosts:

---

[60] Emory, *Notes,* 84.   [61] Turner, *Journals,* 109.

To us it was a rare sight to be thrown in the midst of a large nation of what is termed wild Indians, surpassing many of the christian nations in agriculture, little behind them in the useful arts, and immeasurably before them in honesty and virtue.[62]

It should not be presumed, because the Pimas were kindly and peace-loving, that they were weak and defenseless. They displayed no fear of the American soldiers, unlike the mountain Indians. They were generally well-mounted and well-armed, and they were formidable fighters. As in Kino's and Garcés' days, they held their own against the Apaches. Shortly before the arrival of Kearny's force, a Pima war party had conducted a successful punitive raid into Apache country. They had returned with eleven scalps and thirteen prisoners.[63] The prisoners customarily were sold as slaves to Mexicans.

Before leaving the Pimas, General Kearny gave "Governor" Juan Antonio Lunas a letter, certifying that he was a "good man," and ordering all United States forces that might pass this way to respect him, his people and their property.[64] Ten or eleven broken-down mules and two bales of goods also were left with Lunas to be turned over to Cooke on his arrival.

The expedition set out once more down the course of the Gila. To cut off the great bend of the river, the column soon left the Gila and did not visit the Maricopa villages down-

---

[62] Emory, *Notes*, 84.

[63] Though they fought well when war was forced upon them, the Pimas' nature remained essentially nonagressive. They continued to place a high value on human life. A warrior who returned from battle carrying an enemy scalp (or four scalp hairs which served as a trophy) was required to submit to a ritualistic 16-day treatment for insanity. Pima war speeches all closed with an admonition: "You may think this over, my relatives. The taking of life brings serious thoughts of the waste; the celebration of victory may become unpleasantly riotous." William Brandon, *The American Heritage Book of Indians* (New York, 1961), 112.

[64] Emory, *Notes*, 84. Lunas held office by appointment of the Mexican governor of California, according to Emory. *Ibid.*, 87.

stream from the Pimas. The Maricopas were disappointed, but assured the Americans of their friendship and brought their trade goods to the expedition's camp. Though a separate tribe from the Pimas, the Maricopas lived in perfect harmony with them and exhibited like virtues. In addition to offering the same products as the Pimas, the Maricopas had salt which they collected by skimming the surface of sinks. Before the Maricopas left the camp, a chief told Kearny that, while trading was good, if the army had entered his country hungry and poor, their wants nevertheless would have been filled with no thought of payment.[65]

The two-day march to cut off the bend of the Gila was an ordeal. The strain began to tell even on Emory who, absorbed in the strangeness of the country, rarely complained. He was especially distressed by the pitiful noises made by the mules at night after an unusually hard day's march without grass or water. Indeed, Carson warned that there would be no more grass for the animals until they reached the mouth of the Gila. Adding to the gloomy prospects, local Indians told them they would find no grass until the Mexican settlements in California – 300 miles distant. The animals, the Indians said, would have to subsist on seeds and willows along the banks of the Gila. After crossing the Colorado, there would be only sand.

The second day of the jornada began at 3:00 a.m. when the moon rose. At sunrise, the column passed the summit of the range they were crossing and began the descent to the Gila. Emory's mind wandered:

> As the sun mounted, the mirage only seen once before since leaving
> the plains of the Arkansas, now began to distort the distant mountains,

---

[65] Hughes, *Doniphan's Expedition,* 83. Kit Carson would have verified this sentiment. On a previous trip, when he asked Pimas for provisions, he was told: "Bread is to eat, not to sell – take what you want." *Ibid.,* 82.

which everywhere bounded on the horizon, into many fantastic shapes. The morning was sharp and bracing, and I was excessively hungry, having given my breakfast, consisting of two biscuits, to my still more hungry mule. I was describing to Mr. Warner how much more pleasant it would be to be jogging into Washington after a fox hunt, with the prospect of a hot breakfast, when up rose to our astonished view, on the north side of the Gila, a perfect representation of the capitol, with dome, wings, and portico, all complete. It remained for full twenty minutes with its proportions and outline perfect, when it dwindled down into a distant butte.[66]

As predicted, neither grass nor water was found during the two-day march, and the riding animals suffered grievously.

The Gila was struck again on November 14 and, to their relief, they found grass. The happy discovery, however, was not enough to lift the clouds of gloom that had settled about the army. The jornada had cost them six or eight mules. Lieutenant Davidson had been forced to hitch his private mules to the howitzers which continued to take a fearful toll of the animals. Without nourishment or water during the tortuous forty-five mile journey, the beasts that survived appeared to be near death. To save the mules, the general ordered a one-day halt to take advantage of the good grass.

[66] Emory, *Notes,* 88. Benjamin Butler Harris, traveling the Gila route to the California mines in 1849, saw a similar mirage "resembling the city of Washington, showing the Capitol, White House, and other features identified by those who had visited that city . . ." Harris, *The Gila Trail,* 85.

It is unfortunate that the diarists of the Army of the West said so little about their "social" life during the march. Perhaps the rigorous demands of the trail and caring for the animals left little energy for anything but sleeping and eating. One of the rare comments made in a journal about another member of the army was Turner's reference to the comparative merits of Emory and Warner:

"A strange man this Lt. Emory, beset with one mania, a greediness for immortality – in other respects a clever enough sort of man. I am disappointed in not finding him an agreeable person to be associated with – his assistant Lt. Warner is just the reverse – good natured and sociable." Turner, *Journals,* 94. Whether Turner's comment indicates Emory's shortcomings or his own, we can only guess. It is interesting that while we condemn the gossip of our contemporaries, we are delighted to find it in historical sources.

Further, he directed that on resumption of the march, half the dragoons be dismounted in order to free animals for packing.

By the time the army neared the Colorado, most of the men were afoot. Even the general's horse failed, and he was forced to ride his mule. The animals had subsisted mostly by browsing on cane and mesquite twigs with an occasional treat of rough weeds, none of which provided much nourishment, and were on the verge of collapse. The only break in the monotony of the journey was the discovery of Indian hieroglyphics scratched into the stone hillsides. Some of the carvings, representations of the sun, moon, stars, horned frogs and humans appearing most often, seemed to be very old, some more recent. The dragoons also saw a flat rock on which were inscribed the names of several American trappers. Unfortunately, none of the expedition's chroniclers bothered to list the names in his journal. Turner wrote only that he saw the names of "Hacher, Maxwell etc." [67] Some of the members of Carson's recent eastbound party also had carved their names there.

Approaching the confluence of the Gila with the Colorado, the column came upon a fresh trail that was deeply marked with the hooves of hundreds of animals. After considerable speculation, it was generally agreed that the prints had been made by a large force of Mexicans, probably recruited in Sonora and led by General José Castro who had fled California at the opening of hostilities there. His force must now be camped at the Colorado crossing, en route to California to recover that province from the American invaders. Kearny decided that his command was too small to be attacked, therefore he determined to attack the Mexicans that very night, counting on the darkness to add terror to surprise.

---

[67] Turner, *Journals,* 114.

Pitching camp about a mile and a half south of the mouth of the Gila, preparations for the engagement began. Speculation, perhaps hopefully, began again. Perhaps it was not a Mexican army after all. Maybe the tracks were made by a large band of Indians who had just returned from a successful stock raid in Sonora and California. That possibility was promptly discarded when the dragoons saw a Mexican horseman appear on a nearby hill. After surveying the expedition's camp, he disappeared.

The mystery was soon solved. A small party of Mexicans and Californians, under one José Maria Leguna, a Mexican army colonel, was driving a herd of 500 horses and mules from California to Sonora for General Castro's use. Questioned about the conditions in California, they replied that the citizens of Los Angeles had rebelled and recovered that part of the country while the Americans were still in control of San Diego and the coastal areas. This shocking news was confirmed when a lone Mexican rider was brought into camp and searched. He proved to be a courier with messages from California for General Castro. When the letters were opened and read, there was no doubt now that the conquest had been upset.[68]

Expecting that they would find no grass during the crossing of the Colorado Desert, Kearny ordered a layover to allow the jaded army mounts to recuperate and the dragoons time to select remounts from the Mexican herd. Much to the Californians' surprise, they were paid well for the horses and mules seized by the Americans.[69]

---

[68] Emory, *Notes,* 94-96. Hughes wrote that Captain Turner resealed the letters after their contents had been noted and returned them to the messenger who was then sent on his way. *Doniphan's Expedition,* 84. Turner does not mention this unlikely courtesy.

[69] Turner says that the army paid "a fair compensation in poor mules and money." *Journals,* 118. According to Griffin, $12.00 per head was paid for the animals. *A Doctor Comes to California,* 38.

During the interlude, Emory took the opportunity to explore. With Warner and another, he rode to the confluence of the two rivers where the "sea-green" waters of the Gila "were lost in the chrome colored hue of the Colorado." Emory speculated that the Colorado should be navigable at all times by steamboats and that the Gila probably would be navigable by small boats at all stages of water.[70] Near the junction of the rivers, they saw the ruins of Purísima Concepción mission. Emory wrongly stated that the mission had been built at the beginning of the seventeenth century by Father Kino.[71] Actually, it was built largely through the efforts of Father Garcés in the latter part of the eighteenth century. Emory can be excused the error. Few others who passed this way for years after would be even remotely aware of the Spanish past of the country.

The first day of march following the layover was a short trek down the Colorado to the fording place about nine or ten miles below the mouth of the Gila. The trek was uneventful except for the kicking and bucking of the new mounts. The expedition's numbers had been augmented by some of the Mexicans who had been detained or persuaded to guide the army to California over the trail which they had just covered. The rest of the Mexicans were released to go their own way with the remainder of the herd.

The next day, November 25, the expedition crossed the mighty Colorado. The river at the ford was about 1,500 feet wide and four feet in depth at its deepest part. The rate of flow was a mile and a half per hour. The banks at the ford were low, about four feet high. With its reddish waters and sandy islands, the Colorado reminded some of the

---

[70] Emory, *Notes,* 95. Two days before reaching the junction, Turner had noted that the Gila was "assuming a much more river like appearance – it has attained the width from 100 to 150 yards – and is in average depth about 4 feet – quite deep enough to float a steamboat." *Journals,* 115.   [71] Emory, *Notes, 95.*

soldiers of the Arkansas River, except that the Colorado was wider and the valley of the Arkansas more heavily wooded.

The column apparently had no difficulty with the crossing, in spite of the circuitous and narrow ford. A step two or three feet to the right or left of the path left one in deeper water, an unpleasant sensation which Emory experienced when his horse stepped off the ford and was set afloat. There were no Indians at the river that day. Their assistance had helped the Spaniards immeasurably in crossing the Colorado, but they had long since changed their habitation. They would return to the ford later to assist, and plague, future travelers.

The river behind them, the army entered the dreaded Colorado Desert. Heeding Carson's repeated warning that they would find no grass in the desert, every man before leaving the Colorado's banks gathered grass and tied it in a bundle behind him on his saddle. The troopers soon found that Carson was right. Before the end of the three-day trek, even the stoutest mules and horses were staggering. The animals were reduced to eating twigs and poor shrubs. Many of the beasts did not make it across the desert and were left along the trail to perish. Men as well as animals suffered severely from thirst.

On November 28, the column reached Carrizo Creek and the end of the desert. The spring, twenty or thirty feet in diameter, was located in a gap in the mountains that was visible for four days. There they found plenty of water for men and animals and cane for the stock. More than one exhausted beast was brought up to the spring by one soldier pulling at the halter rope and another pushing from behind. Dr. Griffin might have summed up the feelings of the entire column when he wrote: "I have seen the Elephant and I hope I shall never be compelled to cross it again." [72]

---

[72] Griffin, *A Doctor Comes to California*, 39.

Though the desert was left behind, the army's suffering was not at an end. The country was still barren, and hunger and fatigue increased as the weather varied from hot to the cold dampness of dense fog. Greatcoats were broken out for the first time since leaving Fort Leavenworth as snow began to fall in the nearby mountains. Wolves followed close on the track of the column, feasting on the fallen animals which, bloated on water and cane, gave out by dozens. The army's provisions were almost gone, and horse and mule flesh were tasted by many for the first time.[73]

This inhospitable land was not the California the Americans had expected. "We are still to look for the glowing pictures drawn of California," Emory wrote. "As yet, barrenness and desolation hold their reign. We longed to stumble upon the rancherias, with their flocks of fat sheep and cattle."[74] All expected relief at Warner's Ranch.[75]

General Kearny led the column in to Warner's on December 2, 1846. Warner was absent, but Edward Stokes, an Englishman who lived nearby at Santa Ysabel, confirmed that the Mexicans indeed had successfully risen at Los Angeles and the Americans were concentrated in San Diego where Commodore Stockton's fleet lay. Hearing that a Mexican force was positioned between the ranch and San

---

[73] Apparently, there had been no need to kill mules or horses for food until the final stages of the journey. In fact, one is struck by the few times that the diarists mention the lack of rations. Perhaps, being officers, they did not have to endure want as the common soldiers might have. Emory does mention a number of times that a mule or horse was slaughtered for food. Nearing the end of the journey, Major Swords was distressed to find one of his best pack mules killed secretly by some hungry troopers. Emory, *Notes,* 103. As late as two days before reaching Warner's Ranch, Turner noted that a horse was killed for food and that the men who tasted the flesh pronounced it good. *Journals,* 122-23.

[74] Emory, *Notes,* 105.

[75] Jonathan Trumbull (later Juan José) Warner settled in California after arriving in 1831 with the David E. Jackson expedition of that year. *See above,* pp. 185, 191.

Diego, Kearny sent a message to Stockton, asking for reinforcements and guides. Seizing some mounts from a nearby herd of horses and mules believed to be the property of Don Mariana Flores, the commander of Mexican forces, the army set out for San Diego. At the same time, a party of Mexicans was dispatched to meet Cooke at the Pima villages whence they would guide the Mormon Battalion to the California settlements.

Before reaching San Diego, the Army of the West, reinforced by a detachment sent by Stockton, was battered by the Californians on the plain of San Pascual. Forced to a hilltop refuge, the Americans remained for four days, subsisting on the flesh of their animals until a unit of 200 men from San Diego came to their assistance. The army resumed the march and arrived in San Diego on December 12, 1846.

In spite of its disastrous arrival in California, some significance can be attached to the march of the Army of the West across northern Mexico, shortly to become the United States Southwest. Reduced before leaving New Mexico to little more than an escort force, the little army successfully brought the military governor to California, though even this accomplishment almost was nullified at San Pascual where General Kearny was among the wounded. Perhaps the most important contributions of the Army of the West for the American people in 1846 lay in its example of courage and human endurance and in demonstrating that the early part of the route which it followed was exceedingly difficult. The army's trail from the Rio Grande to the Pima villages never became a popular route among later travelers.

CHAPTER VII

For God and Country

> I must ask pardon for thinking or saying that they may all go to hell together. I will see them (meaning the whole United States) in hell before I will fire one shot against a foreigner for them   those who have mobbed, robbed, plundered and destroyed us all the day long and now seek to enslave us to fight for them.

So wrote John Steele, a Mormon, when he heard in June 1846 that a call had gone out for the formation of a battalion of his brethren to fight in the war against Mexico.[1] Other Mormons expressed similar sentiments, but they eventually were overruled and a fighting force of Mormon volunteers was organized.

The decision to establish a Mormon Battalion was not a hasty one, nor was it a surprise to Mormon leaders. Rather it was a culmination in the attempts of some of those leaders to secure some sort of assistance from the United States government in the westward migration of the Mormons from Nauvoo, Illinois, from which they had recently been expelled. Responding particularly to the visits of a Mormon representative named Jesse Little during the spring and summer of 1846, President Polk expressed his friendship for the Mormons and promised that he would not forget that he had received Mormon votes.[2] As a form of assistance,

---

[1] John Steele, "Extracts from the Journal of John Steele," *Utah Hist. Qtly.,* VI (Jan. 1933), 6-7. Born in Ireland in 1821, Steele emigrated first to Scotland where he became a Mormon, then to the United States in 1845. He arrived in Nauvoo in time for the expulsion of the Mormons. *Ibid.,* 3-6.

[2] Brigham Henry Roberts, *The Mormon Battalion* (Salt Lake City, 1919), 8-11, citing numerous passages from Little's Report (to Brigham Young), History of

the President suggested that Mormons be taken into the military service.

Instructions eventually were issued to then Colonel Kearny to enlist Mormons into the Army of the West, a task the commander delegated to Captain James Allen of the First Dragoons. Allen met the Mormon migration at Council Bluffs, Iowa, and presented the government's offer: enlistment for one year, at the end of which the men would keep their guns and equipment. The Mormons were anything but receptive at first. They were reluctant to leave their families at the very start of the migration, and they hated the thought of serving a country that did not love them.[3]

Mormon leaders intervened in the discussions and declared that the battalion would be raised. Brigham Young pointed out that the pay of the enlistees would speed the migration along, their families would be cared for while they were away, and their weapons would be useful to the community when they returned. Besides, he added, not a single volunteer would fall to enemy bullets.[4] Thus assured,

Brigham Young, MS. Bk. 2. It has been suggested that the policy of the government toward the Mormons at this time also was influenced by a desire to woo them from any thought of joining with the British in the Pacific Northwest. Robert W. Whitworth, "From the Mississippi to the Pacific: An Englishman in the Mormon Battalion," ed. by David B. Gracy II and Helen J. H. Rugeley, *Ariz. and the West,* VII (Summer 1965), 128. Whitworth was one of two Englishmen who served in the Mormon Battalion. He and his companion had only recently arrived in the United States from England and enlisted on a whim. Whitworth's diary is especially interesting because he noticed and noted many things that would not have impressed an American, even an American from the east coast. Furthermore, the diary contains insight into the march of this strongly religious group since the diarist, judging from the lack of religious sentiments expressed in the journal, was not a Mormon. *See Ibid.,* 129-34, for comments on Whitworth's experiences during his journey from England to Fort Leavenworth where he joined the battalion. There was at least one other non-Mormon in the battalion, a man named John Allen.

3 For the reaction of one of those who eventually, but reluctantly, enlisted, *see* Henry W. Bigler, "Extracts from the Journal of Henry W. Bigler," ed. by Adelbert Bigler, *Utah Hist. Qtly.,* v (April 1932), 36.

4 Their only fighting, Young said, would be with wild beasts. He added that there

volunteers stepped forward, though not without lingering doubts, and the enrollment was completed on July 16, 1846.

The Mormon Battalion of 513 men departed the Mormon encampment on July 20 and arrived at Fort Leavenworth on August 1. Accompanying them were about twenty wives who were permitted to travel with their husbands as laundresses, four for each of the five companies.[5] The gear for each company was carried in two wagons, a total of ten for the battalion.

The layover at Fort Leavenworth was short. Here each recruit received his personal equipment and his clothing allowance of $42.00, most of which was sent back to families and to Elders who were en route to missions in England.[6] It is unlikely that the volunteers spent much of the clothing allowance on clothing for themselves.

Soon after leaving Fort Leavenworth, the battalion faced its first crisis. Newly-promoted Lieutenant-colonel Allen had remained behind at the fort due to illness, but promised that he would catch the column as quickly as possible. On the trail one day short of Council Grove, news of Allen's

would be fewer bullets whistling around their ears than there had been around those of Dr. Willard Richards in Carthage jail. Daniel Tyler, *A Concise History of the Mormon Battalion in the Mexican War, 1846-1847* (Salt Lake City, 1881), 118. (Tyler was a volunteer in the battalion.) According to Bigler, it was Richards, one of President Young's councilors, who said: "If we . . . [are] . . . faithful in keeping the Commandments of God, . . . not a man shall fall by an enemy." Bigler, "Journal," 36. The prophecy, so far as the Mormon Battalion was concerned, was literally fulfilled.

[5] John W. Hess was one of those lucky men who had his wife with him. He drove one of his company's wagons and so was able to make his wife as comfortable in the wagon as a couch of kettles and tent poles can be. Hess confided in his journal that "for this and other reasons that I will not mention, I was glad that I was a teamster." John W. Hess, "John W. Hess, With the Mormon Battalion," extracts from his journal by Miss Wanda Wood, *Utah Hist. Qtly.,* IV (April 1931), 49.

[6] Henry Standage, "Journal of Henry Standage," in *The March of the Mormon Battalion from Council Bluffs to California,* by Frank Alfred Golder in collaboration with Thomas A. Bailey and J. Lyman Smith (New York, 1928), 138-39; Bigler, "Journal," 37.

death saddened the Mormons for he had won their respect and affection.[7] Allen had promised that command would pass to the next ranking officer, a Mormon, if he, Allen, became disabled for any reason. At Council Grove, Captain Jefferson Hunt, commander of A Company, was duly elected to the position of battalion commandant. The election was voided by the arrival of a regular army officer, Lieutenant Andrew Jackson Smith, from Fort Leavenworth to assume command of the battalion.[8] After considerable discussion among themselves, the Mormons reluctantly accepted Smith.

Doubtless, the Lieutenant was offended, and this perhaps influenced his relationship with his charges. It was not so much that he brought them under strict military discipline as that he was completely incapable of command. At least, so the record seems to indicate. The story of the Mormon Battalion would have turned out quite differently had Smith not eventually been succeeded by Philip St. George Cooke, for while Allen won the respect and the hearts of the volunteers and Cooke their respect, Smith earned neither. The Mormons were equally unhappy with Dr. George Sanderson, brought by Smith from Fort Leavenworth to serve the battalion.[9]

It must have seemed to the Mormons that Smith and

---

[7] Diarists were unanimous in their expression of grief. Standage wrote that Allen "was much beloved by the Battalion and his loss severely felt by all." "Journal," 149. See also Tyler, Mormon Battalion, 141; Roberts, Mormon Battalion, 27; and Bigler, "Journal," 37.

[8] Andrew J. Smith, a Pennsylvania native and an 1838 graduate of the United States Military Academy, had served with Kearny the previous year in his expedition to South Pass. Ralph P. Bieber and Averam Bender, eds., Exploring Southwestern Trails (Glendale, 1938), 68, n. 141.

[9] Dr. Sanderson, an English-born Missourian, was mustered into the army at Fort Leavenworth on August 20, 1846, just about the time the Mormon Battalion was leaving there. He resigned from the army the following August after returning from California. Bieber and Bender, eds., Exploring Southwestern Trails, 68, n. 143.

Sanderson were out to do them in. The Mormons refused to take the medicines perscribed by the doctor, known to them as a "Missouri mobber" who reportedly had said that "he did not care a damn whether he killed or cured [Mormons]" [10] and "would send as many to hell as he could." [11] Smith insisted that the volunteers take the doctor's medicine and threatened those that did not with severe punishment.[12] When Smith heard that some of the men refused the medicine on religious grounds, he asked the battalion adjutant, George P. Dykes, himself a Mormon, if there were religious teachings against taking medicines. Dykes replied in the negative, and the dosing continued.[13] Though an Elder of the church, Dykes became increasingly unpopular with his brethren.

The march of the battalion during the first few weeks was marked by hunger and thirst and not a little adventure for the recruits. The weather was so hot and water was found so infrequently that the Mormons could drink from pools of rain water fouled with buffalo dung and urine and pronounce it a blessing.[14] Great herds of antelope and buffalo were seen on the treeless plains. The buffalo served the volunteers as they served all whites who ventured into their range, as food, fuel and sport.

The Mormons were not immune to that inexplicable compulsion that seized white men when they first came face to face with live buffalo. More of the beasts were killed

---

[10] Bigler, "Journal," 38.   [11] Standage, "Journal," 163.

[12] On one occasion, Smith promised to cut the throat of anyone who disobeyed his orders. Another day, he threatened to tie an offender behind a wagon and drag him for a day. *Ibid.*

[13] Brigham Young, in fact, had cautioned the volunteers against taking medicine. In a letter dated August 19, 1846, addressed to the battalion at Fort Leavenworth, Young had urged: "If you are sick, live by faith, and let surgeon's medicine alone if you want to live." Quoted in Tyler, *Mormon Battalion*, 146.

[14] Standage, "Journal," 166.

than could possibly be used. The carnage distressed Henry Standage. "This brought to mind the word of the Lord," he wrote, "and the woe pronounced on those of the Saints who sheddeth blood, wasteth flesh and hath no need."[15]

In mid-September, the battalion passed Bent's Fort. During a pause, Lieutenant Smith detached Captain Nelson V. Higgins of Company D to escort a number of families to Pueblo, upstream from Bent's Fort on the Arkansas River. A temporary settlement was soon constructed there as winter quarters for the families. The rest of the battalion continued toward Santa Fé. With a march of over three weeks ahead of them, only ten days' rations on hand and the buffalo herds now behind them, hard times were expected. The firm of Thompson and Campbell, which had contracted with the government to supply beef to the army, was following with 1,400 cattle, but they were too many days behind to be of any help.[16] Shortly after crossing the Arkansas River, the battalion overtook another unit of the Army of the West, the second regiment of Missouri Volunteers under Colonel Sterling Price.[17] The Mormons lost no love on Price. He was remembered as the leader of the "mob militia" in Missouri in 1838 when the Mormons were attacked at Far West.[18]

---

[15] *Ibid.*, 160.   [16] Hughes, *Doniphan's Expedition*, 54.

[17] Price, a member of Congress from Missouri, resigned his seat in the early summer of 1846. He applied for the command of the new volunteer force and received the appointment from President Polk. The second regiment of Missouri volunteers included about 1,200 men. *Ibid.*, 52.

[18] Christopher Layton, *Autobiography of Christopher Layton*, ed. by John Q. Cannon (Salt Lake City, 1911), 50. It should be noted that Layton's *Autobiography*, written after 1898 and published in 1911, and Tyler's *Mormon Battalion*, published in 1881, contain a number of verbatim passages.

Colonel Doniphan was an officer of militia in Missouri and a prominent lawyer who called the 1838 court martial sentence of Joseph Smith and others to be shot in the presence of their families an act of cold-blooded murder. He declared at the time that neither he nor his militia regiment would witness the execution. When the

On October 3, an express was received from General Kearny, saying that if the battalion was not in Santa Fé by October 10, he would reject it. Battalion officers decided to push forward at maximum speed with the strongest men and teams. The rest of the train was left to come up as quickly as it could. About 250 men made up the advance unit. Two days later, the group again was split. A detachment of the sixty-five strongest men set out on a forced march for Santa Fé, determined to make Kearny's deadline. The exhausted troopers entered the capital late in the afternoon of October 9 in the middle of a raging storm of rain and hail.[19]

The remainder of the battalion continued to plod on toward Santa Fé. Approaching Las Vegas, Steele made a strange entry in his journal:

> From the top of this hill, our faded ranks could be seen straggling along for nearly the whole 30 miles as teams and men were nearly gave out. The Spaniards could see our command for all this distance, and as they had a fort built of logs and trees, at the end of a long lane of road where their cannon could rake us for nearly four miles. (They had nine pieces.) But when they saw our dust for such a distance they thought it was an overwhelming army, and so they left their fortifications, and fled some 200 miles from there.[20]

It was then early October. General Kearny had entered Santa Fé on August 18. It is not likely that there were Mexican military units still active seven weeks later. Whatever the explanation, the column encountered no resistance. Indeed, the volunteers were welcomed. Steele found the Mexicans at Las Vegas very kind and generous. On the other hand, it is not surprising that Robert W. Whitworth,

---

Mormon Battalion marched into Santa Fé, Colonel Doniphan ordered a salute of 100 guns fired in their honor. Colonel Price and his Missouri volunteers were not so received. Tyler, *Mormon Battalion,* 164-65.

[19] Bigler, "Journal," 41; Steele, "Journal," 8; Whitworth, "Englishman in the Mormon Battalion," 142.   [20] Steele, "Journal," 9.

an Englishman and unaccustomed to frontier life, described the inhabitants as "half civilized people."[21] The last straggling groups of the Mormon Battalion finally arrived in Santa Fé on October 11[22] and 12, 1846.

Colonel Philip St. George Cooke, who had been waiting in Santa Fé since October 7, assumed command of the battalion on October 13. He found the unit riddled with sickness, encumbered by women and children and the animals poor. Cooke took prompt action to put the battalion in order. He appointed Lieutenant Smith assistant commissary of subsistence, Lieutenant George Stoneman assistant quartermaster and Doctor Sanderson assistant surgeon. Doctor Stephen C. Foster was selected as interpreter. A civilian observer was Willard P. Hall. Prominent in Missouri politics and law, Hall had served as an enlisted man in the Army of the West and, at Kearny's request, figured prominently in the writing of a code of laws for the new American province of New Mexico. Notified at Santa Fé that he had been elected to Congress, Hall was released from the army, but nevertheless expressed a desire to accompany Cooke to California.[23]

Cooke directed that women and children and the sick be detached from the battalion and sent to winter at the Mormon settlement at Pueblo near Bent's Fort. Dr. Sanderson pointed out that the sick persons could be discharged for reasons of disability, but Cooke said that he would retain them in the service. Able-bodied men were ordered to make

---

[21] Whitworth, "Englishman in the Mormon Battalion," 143.

[22] Thomas Fitzpatrick also arrived at the capital this day en route to Washington with the dispatches from California which Kit Carson had carried as far as his meeting with General Kearny. *See above,* p. 216.

[23] William Elsey Connelley, *Doniphan's Expedition and the Conquest of New Mexico and California* (Kansas City, Mo., 1907), 238-40, n. 51. After arriving in California, Hall returned to Missouri in the spring and by winter had taken his seat in Congress. *Ibid.,* 240.

ready for the march to California. Some of these able-bodied men were husbands of the women who now were directed to leave the battalion. The commander's order did not set well with the husbands because they had been led to understand that their wives would accompany them all the way to California. Following some remonstrances, Cooke reversed himself and permitted all husbands who wished to do so to return to Pueblo with their wives.[24] The detachment of eighty-five to 100 persons under the command of Captain James Brown of Company C departed Santa Fé on October 18 and reached Pueblo on November 17.[25]

The difficulties Cooke faced in preparing the battalion for the trek to California were not slight. Army paymasters in Santa Fé had almost no specie, so the Mormons had to be paid with treasury drafts.[26] Funds were not available for the purchase of provisions, equipment or better riding and draft animals. For this reason also, Colonel Doniphan, com-

---

[24] There are some differences of opinion over the genesis of this last order. At least two husbands claim credit for persuading Cooke to permit the husbands to remain with their wives. *See* Steele, "Journal," 11-12, and Hess, "With the Mormon Battalion," 50-51. *See also* Cooke's account in Philip St. George Cooke, "Report of Lieut. Col. P. St. George Cooke of His March From Santa Fé, New Mexico, to San Diego, Upper California," ed. by Hamilton Gardner, *Utah Hist. Qtly.*, XXII (Jan. 1954), 19, and the editorial comment, 18, n. 9.

[25] The parting was especially hard for Henry Bigler, who remained in Santa Fé with the battalion. He wrote: "In that detachment I had a dear sister and brother-in-law, John W. Hess. I felt lonesome after they left for I liked their company very much." Bigler, "Journal," 41. The journey of the unit from Santa Fé as far as Bent's Fort was marked by great suffering. The Mormons buried two of their number along the trail. The Pueblo contingent eventually was discharged at Salt Lake Valley in Utah on July 28, 1847. Hess, "With the Mormon Battalion," 53; Steele, "Journal," 12-13.

[26] Thereby adding to the hardships of the volunteers' families and friends in winter quarters in Iowa. The volunteers scraped up as much money as they could spare and sent it to Council Bluffs by John D. Lee, Howard Egan, Samuel Gully and Roswell Stevens. Steele, "Journal," 12. At the same time, the battalion officers wrote a letter to Brigham Young dated October 18, 1846, expressing regret that they could not send more and hope that they would be able to send money from California. Standage, "Journal," 179.

mander of all United States forces in New Mexico, ordered the disbanding of Captain Hudson's unit of California Rangers, which had been formed at Kearny's orders and which was to have been attached to Cooke's command.[27] In spite of these setbacks, the battalion was soon ready.

Shortly before the scheduled departure date from the capital, Cooke received Lieutenant Love of the First Dragoons, en route to the east with messages from General Kearny. A letter for Cooke notified him that the Army of the West had abandoned its wagons and it was now left up to Cooke and the Mormon Battalion to pioneer a wagon road to California. Cooke was skeptical because of the poor condition of his mules – he estimated that half his animals were in no shape for even a routine march – but immediately determined that he would succeed.[28]

The Mormon Battalion marched out of Santa Fé on October 19, 1846. On that same day, General Kearny and the Army of the West were one day short of striking the Gila. Cooke's train included eighteen government wagons, twelve drawn by mules – three to each of the four companies – and six ox-drawn. There also were four or five private wagons and teams belonging to the two captains and three sergeants who had secured Cooke's permission to take their wives at their own expense.[29]

Provisions were hopelessly inadequate. Embarking on a

27 Cooke, "Report," 17. Doniphan might also have been influenced by the news that California had already fallen to the Americans, thereby reducing the need for more troops. Hughes, *Doniphan's Expedition,* 55.

28 Philip St. George Cooke, "Cooke's Journal of the March of the Mormon Battalion, 1846-1847," in *Exploring Southwestern Trails, 1846-1854,* ed. by Ralph P. Bieber in collaboration with Averam Bender (Glendale, 1938), 69. Cooke's "Journal" and his "Report" are different documents. The "Journal" is a daily record which Cooke maintained during the journey. The "Report" is his resume of the trip which he submitted to General Kearny shortly after the arrival of the Mormon Battalion in California.

29 Cooke, "Report," 19; Cooke, "Journal," 67.

journey estimated to require 120 days of hard labor, there were rations for but sixty days, consisting of beef and mutton on the hoof, flour, salt, sugar and coffee. In addition, there were thirty days' supplies of pickled pork and soap for twenty days. The arduous march of the Mormons was literally begun on insufficient rations. The day following the departure from Santa Fé, Whitworth noted that the "Col. made a speech and shortened our rations."[30] By the end of the month, the volunteers were on half rations, and before seeing the Pacific Ocean, they would be on quarter rations.[31] The deprivation was not the result of national poverty, merely proof of faulty army logistics.

Marching southward along the Rio Grande, the battalion followed Kearny's route. Indeed, the tracks of the Army of the West were still visible in places. The general had ordered Cooke to follow his trail all the way to California, but early in the journey Cooke would find this impossible. Kearny doubtless would have agreed to the deviation from his route. He had issued the order to follow his trail before his column hit the rough country that proved impassable for wagons.

In planning his route, Cooke was influenced by the guides sent by General Kearny. The general had met the trapper, Pauline (Powell) Weaver, on the Gila River, coming from California and persuaded him to join Cooke's force.[32] Charbonneau, following Kearny's orders, had scouted the countryside and reported to Cooke that he had found a better

---

[30] Whitworth, "Englishman in the Mormon Battalion," 144.

[31] Bigler, "Journal," 41.

[32] According to Stephen C. Foster, Weaver came from California with Kit Carson. "Reminiscences," 48. The son of an English father and Cherokee mother, Weaver originally had hunted and trapped for the Hudson's Bay Company. He left the cold North for the milder climate of the Southwest where he trapped the Gila and Colorado, becoming acquainted in the meantime with the Apaches.

way to the copper mines than that taken by Kearny. It would require descending the Rio Grande south of the point at which the general had left the river, then following a road that ran from El Paso to the mines. Cooke was encouraged, but continued to worry about the route that he should follow between the mines and the Gila.[33]

Selection of a route was only one of Cooke's concerns. He worried about his animals. Poor at the start, their condition worsened on a diet of too little grass and too hard tasks, and they broke down in alarming numbers. When the battalion marched in settled country, Cooke was able to get a few indifferent beasts on two-for-one trades or by purchase.

Not the least of Cooke's problems were the Mormons themselves. The volunteers were just not accustomed to the sort of ordered existence that their commander required of them. Burdened as he was with his other concerns, and being unwell himself,[34] it is understandable that he was annoyed at the lack of discipline. At the end of a particularly trying day, Cooke wrote:

> It took me until half past nine o'clock to make . . . [certain] . . . arrangements, which I had repeatedly ordered eighteen hours before, and then had to do it myself. A dumb spirit has possessed all for the last twenty-four hours, and not one in ten of my orders has been understood and obeyed. All the vexations and troubles of any other three days in my life have not equalled those of the said twenty-four hours. . . .
>   . . . There is a wonderful amount of stolidity, ignorance, negligence, and obstinacy which I have to contend against.[35]

Cooke nevertheless was patient with his troopers, and the Mormons found him a firm and impartial disciplinarian. While he punished two enlisted men for neglecting to salute

---

[33] Cooke, "Journal," 74-75.

[34] Near Albuquerque, he wrote: "I have not one minute of time unoccupied and am unwell." Cooke, "Journal," 74.   [35] *Ibid.,* 83-84.

Lieutenant Dykes by tying them behind an ox wagon and making them march thus, he also required an officer to march in the rear of the column for disobeying orders.[36] The morale of the volunteers was immeasurably improved on November 1 when Lieutenant Dykes resigned his position as adjutant.[37] The new adjutant was P. C. Merrill.[38]

At the point where the battalion was supposed to leave the Rio Grande to head west, Cooke paused to assess the strength of his force and its prospects for success. A group of guides, sent by Kearny, described the rough country and hard marches ahead. Antoine Leroux,[39] one of their number in whom Cooke apparently had some faith, gave the commander the distressing report that the distance from the Rio Grande to the Gila, assuming a route south of Kearny's to avoid the mountains, was 400 miles. The country in that direction was mostly unexplored and unknown to any of the guides who had been refreshing themselves in a Mexican village instead of exploring, as directed by Kearny.[40] Dead

[36] Tyler, *Mormon Battalion*, 177, 187.

[37] By that time, he had become so odious to the Mormons that they dubbed him "the accuser of the brethren." Tyler, *Mormon Battalion*, 187. Standage was "[v]ery glad of this change, for Lieu. Dykes had been working against the interest of the Battalion all the way." "Journal," 181. Mormon officers of the battalion already had reported their dislike of Dykes to Brigham Young, who originally had appointed Dykes to his position, in a letter dated October 18, 1846 from Santa Fé. *Ibid.,* 178.

[38] Bancroft, *Arizona and New Mexico*, 410.

[39] Leroux was a French-Canadian trapper who had come to the Southwest in the 1820s, became a Mexican citizen and trapped widely in the region.

[40] On the other hand, there is some evidence that both Leroux and Weaver were with David E. Jackson in 1831 when he led his party of eleven men from Santa Fé to California on a mule-buying venture. *See* D. W. Hayes, "David E. Jackson," in LeRoy R. Hafen, ed., *The Mountain Men and the Fur Trade of the Far West*, IX, 232-35. If Leroux and Weaver were with Jackson, then they were not totally unfamiliar with the region, though the route taken by Cooke was not identical to Jackson's. Certainly, the column would see no more guide posts such as that seen on November 2, a simple board sign with the words, "Mormon Trail," undoubtedly left by someone in Kearny's column to mark the trail. Robert S. Bliss, "The Journal of Robert S. Bliss, with the Mormon Battalion," *Utah Hist. Qtly.,* IV (July 1931), 76.

and worn-out mules were being left almost daily beside the trail. The remaining draft animals were in poor condition. A number of the troopers were sick and were being carried in the already overloaded wagons. Provisions were dwindling.

Cooke decided that he must strengthen his force, or all was lost. A group of fifty-five men [41] who were too ill to continue the march were detached from the battalion and, under the command of Lieutenant William S. Willis, were sent back up the trail to the camp of Captain John K. Burgwin. Burgwin's unit was part of the force under Major Sumner which Kearny had detached after Kit Carson brought news of the fall of California to the Americans. Presumably, Willis's detachment was to travel with Burgwin to Santa Fé, thence to Pueblo where they would winter at the Mormon camp there. [42] Cooke was satisfied that he had strengthened the battalion, but he concluded that even "[a]fter these two weedings of the old, the feeble and sickly, from the battalion, lads and old gray-headed men still remained." [43]

The column's load was lightened when Cooke gave orders to leave two ox wagons and superfluous gear. The wagons were left in the care of some trappers who planned to be in

The middle section of the Bliss journal is written in red, while the sections at the beginning and end are written in blue and black ink. Bliss ran out of ink during the journey, but continued his journal with blood he obtained by pricking his arm with a pin. *Ibid.,* 68.

[41] Cooke, "Journal," 95. Cooke says fifty-eight in his "Report," 21. I wonder, however, whether he is not erroneously repeating the figure for the distance from his present position to Major Burgwin's camp, fifty-eight miles, which distance appears in the next line of the "Report." Or, the duplication could be a typographical error in the published document.

[42] Bigler, "Journal," 42.

[43] Cooke, "Report," 21. By "two weedings," Cooke was referring to the group he had just detached under Lieutenant Willis and the party sent to Pueblo from Santa Fé under Captain Brown.

the vicinity a few days, and word was sent back to an army unit to recover the wagons. The strongest animals were hitched to the remaining wagons while the weakest oxen and mules were fitted with individual packs. By these efficiencies in equipment and manpower, Cooke estimated that the battalion's load was reduced twenty per cent and that the rations – at a half-ration rate – of the remaining troops were increased by eight days. The day's work left him encouraged that he might yet reach California with his wagons.[44]

Though still early in the journey, the suffering of the volunteers was considerable. As long as they marched through Mexican settlements, they traded old clothing and spent the little cash they had for fruits, vegetables and meats. One mess felt extremely fortunate to get a beaver from the trappers with whom Cooke left the wagons. Rations often were reduced to a soup made from a sprinkling of flour and the gelatinous flesh of oxen that had collapsed in their harnesses. Oxen were never killed until they could no longer pull their loads. For most of the march, noted Whitworth, the volunteers had "empty bellies and Sharp Appetites."[45]

Yet, the spirits of the Mormons seem not to have been low. They were in surprisingly good physical condition and kept their sense of humor. Their spare time was used to advantage, for example in the discussions of a debating club formed by some of the men to occupy their evenings.[46] Perhaps the Mormons' state of mind, an appreciation of hard reality laced with a tranquil resignation, was best caught by Robert L. Bliss, a volunteer, who wrote on November 6, shortly before the battalion turned westward from the Rio Grande:

---

44 Cooke, "Journal," 97; Cooke, "Report," 21.
45 Whitworth, "Englishman in the Mormon Battalion," 146.
46 Bigler, "Journal," 43.

.   .   . [W]e are now on half rations & [have] only 60 days
Rations from Santa Fee   .   .   . & [w]e expect it will take us at least
120 days to go to the Pacific Ocian or Bay of San Francisco   our
teams are tiring out & we expect a hard time [even] if we are not
intercepted by an Enemy; we are cheerful & happy notwithstanding
we have to carry our Guns accoutrements Napsacks Canteen haver-
sacks & Push our Waggons all day over hills which are not few nor
far between & we expect still greater difficulties when we leave this
River to cross the Mountains.[47]

On November 13, at a point about fifteen miles northeast
of the present-day town of Rincon, the battalion left the
Rio Grande. Within a few days, they were traveling a road
that even the trapper and Mexican guides did not know.
Whitworth wrote, erroneously, that they were on the Old
Spanish Trail to California. "[I]t must have been very
old," he added, "for we did not see much sign of it." [48]
Cooke tentatively planned to march southwestward to hit
the San Pedro River, then go downstream – northward – to
the Gila. He consulted maps of the area, but found them
contradictory and virtually useless.[49] He would have to rely
on his guides and his own judgment.

On a typical day, Leroux and five to seven other guides
would be out miles ahead of the column, sometimes a day in
advance, searching for water. As soon as any sort of water
was found – a spring, a seep, even a puddle in rocks or mud
– Leroux sent one man back to lead the battalion to the

---

[47] Bliss, "Journal," 76-77. Bliss's reference to the possibility of enemy action might
have been prompted by a persistent rumor the past few days that a Mexican army
was approaching, bent on attacking the column. When the enemy force did not
materialize, Bliss remarked that "we returned thanks to our protector &c &c." *Ibid.,*
76. The only person in the battalion endangered by rifle fire to this point was Cooke
himself. A trooper, while dismounting, accidentally discharged his carbine, and the
ball almost hit Cooke. Cooke, "Journal," 90.

[48] Whitworth, "Englishman in the Mormon Battalion," 146-47.

[49] He mentioned two maps, those of Mitchell and Tanner, both published in 1846.
He noted, for example, that they disagreed two degrees of longitude in the relative
positions of Santa Fé and San Diego. Cooke, "Journal," 107.

water. The remainder of the guides continued their explorations. When another source of water was located, another
man was sent back who then became the guide. This process
continued until Leroux ran out of men to send back or until
the party of scouts was reduced to an unsafe number. Then
all returned to the column, regrouped, and set out together
again. Meanwhile, each day a work crew was some distance
ahead of the column, improving the road so that it would
be passable for the wagons. On a good day, the wagons
would not have to wait for the completion of a piece of road
work.[50]

When the road was sandy, trail was broken for the tired
teams by soldiers walking in front of the wagons in two files,
spaced just far enough apart for the wagon wheels to roll in
their tracks. At the end of an hour, the men and wagons of
the leading company stopped and took up the rear. In this
way, the burden of breaking trail fell equally on all the
companies. "It was much like tramping snow – very hard
on the men," wrote volunteer Daniel Tyler, "especially
those who took the lead, as we had no road or trail to follow." [51] A variation of this routine had each of the companies
and the staff taking turns, on a daily basis, driving their
teams in the lead to break trail.

Loose stock and pack animals also had places in the order
of march. The cattle were driven by a corporal and three
butchers who slaughtered at camp each night. Sheep were
tended by two shepherds. The herds were last to leave camp
each morning with the rear guard. Some mules, it seems,
were driven loose, but each company had twelve packsaddles which probably were used in difficult places to take

---

[50] Cooke, "Report," 22; Cooke, "Journal," 100; Foster, "Reminiscences," 48. By
this time, Foster was serving with the guides at his own request, there being no
need for an interpreter until Mexican settlements were reached. *Ibid.*

[51] Tyler, *Mormon Battalion,* 207.

some of the weight from the wagons. The packed mules followed the advance guard and pioneers so they could be unpacked and put out to graze each evening before the main column reached camp.[52]

Though sufficient water was found at the Ojo de Vaca or Cow Springs, about twenty-six miles south of the copper mines, the guides brought news that ahead lay a stretch of 100 miles where water would be extremely scarce, if there was any at all. Failing to learn anything of the country from local Indians or Mexicans, Cooke reluctantly agreed to the guides' advice to skirt the dry tableland ahead by turning south toward the Mexican settlements. Though unhappy about adding days to the journey to the Pacific, Cooke's new plan was to march to Janos[53] in Chihuahua, then travel westward to Fronteras and northwestward to Tucson on an old road originally built to connect these frontier presidios.[54] Cooke rationalized that mules and provisions could be procured in the settlements and that the detour would add only four days' travel time.

Most of the Mormons were disturbed at news of the detour. They were afraid that the change in direction would lead them to a clash with Mexican forces, and they were anxious to get to California as quickly as possible where they expected to be discharged and eventually to rejoin their families. Not all of the volunteers were of the same mind. When the battalion began the march toward Janos, Whitworth wrote that "[e]very man was in high spirits for we were very willing to fight for something to eat."[55] Nathaniel

---

[52] Cooke, "Journal," 192.

[53] The presidio at Janos, around which the town grew, was established in 1690 on an Apache raiding trail. It was one of the few frontier presidios that were not relocated in Oconor's reorganization of 1776. *See above*, pp. 55-56, and Christiansen, "Presidio and the Borderlands," 32.

[54] Cooke, "Report," 23.

[55] Whitworth, "Englishman in the Mormon Battalion," 147.

V. Jones, the orderly sergeant of Company D, estimated that one-third of the battalion shared Whitworth's sentiments.[56]

Cooke shortly reversed his decision. After only a mile or two on the road to Janos, the trail turned not to the southwest, as the guides had predicted, but to the southeast! Cooke pondered a moment, then ordered a turn to the right, that is, to the west. He declared aloud that he did not want to get under General Wool in northern Mexico, nor did he wish to circle the world to get to California. "God bless the Colonel!" shouted Father David Pettigrew, whom Brigham Young had appointed as spiritual advisor to the battalion's young men.[57] Many of the Mormons had prayed that Cooke would change his mind, and his order to the west seemed an answer to their prayers.[58] Whitworth, who had welcomed the march to Janos, was disappointed. Perhaps reflecting the minority view, he declared that "our Colonel, not being half starved like the rest of us or else wanting courage, altered our course, so that we avoided the main settlements."[59]

The Mormons' joy in their western course was short-lived as the guides' assessment of the country they now entered proved all too accurate. Little water was found the first day. In the blistering heat, a mirage danced almost constantly before them, appearing at times as a river, at others as a sea or lake. It was the second night on the prairie before enough water for both men and animals was found on the marshy shore of a dry lake bed.[60]

---

[56] Nathaniel V. Jones, "The Journal of Nathaniel V. Jones, with the Mormon Battalion," *Utah Hist. Qtly.,* IV (Jan. 1931), 7.

[57] Quoted in Tyler, *Mormon Battalion,* 207.

[58] Bigler wrote that "thanks to God was in every soldiers heart, their prayers were answered." "Journal," 45. Nathaniel Jones declared that "some unforeseen power intercepted our course." "Journal," 7.

[59] Whitworth, "Englishman in the Mormon Battalion," 147. Whitworth was alone among volunteer diarists in registering displeasure at the new course and virtually alone in not recognizing divine intervention in the affair. This appears to be further evidence that the Englishman was not a Mormon.

Provisions diminished until the volunteers were reduced to roasting the entrails and raw hides left over after butchering the poor cattle that had been driven all the way from Missouri. Some troopers stole a piece of pork from an officer who himself had stolen it from a commissary wagon. A hapless volunteer was tied to a wagon wheel for six hours at Cooke's order for buying a piece of pork from a black servant of Lieutenant Smith.[61] When the short rations were supplemented briefly with some dried meat purchased from some passing New Mexicans, the volunteers for the first time in a great while ate their fill, "a great era in our lives," noted Whitworth.[62] Though the oily meat was assumed to be horse, no one was bothered, trooper Henry W. Bigler pronouncing it "the sweetest meat I ever tasted." [63] Cooke also purchased twenty-one mules from the New Mexicans and hired one of the men to take Leroux to Apaches from whom he hoped to secure a guide as well as mules and corn.

By late November, the battalion's suffering was relieved somewhat by changes of diet and landscape. Leaving the dry, treeless plain behind them, the column, wrote Bliss,

---

[60] Playas Lake, a few miles southeast of the town of Animas in the southwestern corner of New Mexico.

[61] Bigler, "Journal," 43; Bliss, "Journal," 79; Jones, "Journal," 7. It is not clear whether the black man was an employed servant or a slave, though probably the latter as Jones noted that he belonged to Smith.

[62] Whitworth, "Englishman in the Mormon Battalion," 147-48. Whitworth was a keen observer and had an active, dry sense of humor. He often noted the plants he saw and their uses, if any. For example, he wrote that the ". . . musqueet [mesquite] is a very prickly bush, bearing a sort of bean which the Indians make into bread. When it is baked it has much the appearance of a piece of granite, tastes sweet and rather sickly. It is very binding for people who have not leather Stomachs. Musscrew is a bush much the same as above, but the fruit is very different, being of a brown color and in a sort of small ringlet or screw. I do not know whether the name was taken from the peculiar form of the Fruit, or the faculty of Screwing the Stomach of the Person who eats it. We ground it in Coffee mills and mixed it with our Flour. It has a sweet sickly taste. Our Doctor made a fearful hole in his purging Medicines in this place." *Ibid.,* 148.

[63] Bigler, "Journal," 46.

passed through the "most beautiful valleys I ever saw, with
here & there Groves of beautiful Oack Timber Ever
Green." [64] The troopers' meager rations were multiplied
when hunters brought in antelope, deer, bear and other
game.

During the last days of November, the battalion was
engaged in crossing the continental divide. A trail was found
that appeared to run between Janos, on the east of the divide,
and the ruined San Bernardino Ranch, once the headquarters of a vast cattle ranching enterprise, on the western slope.
The trail soon narrowed to a mule track amidst tumbled
boulders and precipitous, rocky peaks. Prospects for finding
a wagon road bed down and through the scenic chaos seemed
remote, but Cooke would not be dissuaded though his companions decided that the country was impassable for wagons.

During the transit of the high country, an Apache chieftain named Manuelita came into camp with Leroux. It
seems that the lesson of Juan José was still remembered
throughout Apacheria, and Manuelita had been persuaded
only with great difficulty to visit the encampment. Cooke
assured the chief of the Americans' friendship, at the same
time urging that Apaches and Americans ally themselves in
the war against the Mexicans, their common enemy. At
Cooke's request, Manuelita promised to bring mules to the
battalion's camp for trading.

As the road crew continued its work, the wagons were
unloaded and their contents packed on mules six to twelve
miles down the mountain to the next camp. This business
continued for two days. Then the empty wagons were taken
down. At places where the mules could not haul the wagons,
the wagons were lifted and carried by the men. On more
than one occasion, the vehicles had to be let down over ledges

---

[64] Bliss, "Journal," 78.

with long ropes. A number of wagons were damaged. One broke loose and was smashed on the rocks. Another was abandoned. The portage almost completed, Dr. Foster, the interpreter, came in with the astonishing news that he had found the bed of an old wagon road crossing Cooke's road! Cooke investigated Foster's find and was "mortified" to find "indications and even tracks of a wagon" in the rough country.[65] Foster had stumbled upon Guadalupe Pass, an easier trail across the mountains that would be used by later travelers on Cooke's road.

A march of a day or two brought the column down from the pass to the San Bernardino Ranch.[66] The ruins were found in a beautiful, well-watered valley with grass two feet high. Antelope were sighted as well as cattle, now gone wild. As arranged, Manuelita and some companions soon appeared. Cooke gave the Indians gifts and spoke again of the Americans' friendship for the Apaches. He explained that as long as the Indians remained friendly, American traders would supply their wants and the United States government would give them annual presents. The Apaches replied with protestations of undying friendship and, according to Bliss, promised that they would "never lift the hatchet against us till the sun & moon should fall." [67] Trading was not very productive. Cooke got at least one mule; the Apaches wanted only blankets. Though Cooke forbade

---

[65] Cooke, "Journal," 125.

[66] John Russell Bartlett described the ranch in his *Personal Narrative of Explorations and Incidents in Texas, New Mexico, California, Sonora and Chihuahua* (2 vols.; New York, 1854), I, pp. 255-56. The ruins of the adobe buildings covered about two acres, evidence of the extent of the enterprise. But the high, bastioned wall which enclosed the buildings, was not sufficient to protect the ranch from Apache depredations. The ranch was abandoned around 1830, and stray cattle were left to multiply and grow wild. Bliss heard a curious anecdote about San Bernardino: "Strange is the Tale of this Town, the Opachees [Apaches] killed 700 Spaniards & took their wives prisoners & their squaws became jealous & killed all the Spanish women." "Journal," 79.   [67] Bliss, "Journal," 79.

the traffic, the volunteers bought roasted mescal from the Apaches.[68]

Cooke, it might be added, had a low opinion of the Apaches. He described them in his journal as dirty and ugly and whose language was "by far the most brutal grunt that I have ever heard."[69] Some of the volunteers disagreed with their commander's assessments. Bliss referred to the Indians as "Noble looking fellows,"[70] while Whitworth added that the women were "very good looking, plump pieces of baggage."[71]

Following a one-day layover at San Bernardino to rest and feast on fresh beef, the battalion took up its march westward. Cooke's Apache guide refused to go more than about twenty miles, fearing the solitary return to his own country, but described the remainder of the trail to the San Pedro River. The column crossed a wagon road which Cooke assumed led to the Mexican frontier outpost of Fronteras, about fourteen miles to the south.[72] Though the terrain was not difficult, at times a path had to be hacked through the dense thickets of mesquite and other thorny growth.

The guard doubtless thought that their commander wished to add to their hardship as he ordered them to shoulder their weapons and carry their knapsacks and blankets. When

[68] The mescal in this case was the Apache food of that name rather than the alcoholic, hallucinatory beverage that is generally associated with the term. The mescal plant was to Apaches what the buffalo was to plains Indians. It provided them a staple food that could be stored as long as six months, an intoxicating beverage, thread, clothing, and other items. The Apache food was not new to the volunteers at San Bernardino Ranch. They had bought it from the Mexican traders near Playas Lake in New Mexico. On that occasion, Whitworth had written that the soldiers, then in great want, would be much better off if the column could delay long enough to cook the root. Whitworth, "Englishman in the Mormon Battalion," 148.

[69] Cooke, "Journal," 129-30.   [70] Bliss, "Journal," 79.

[71] Whitworth, "Englishman in the Mormon Battalion," 149.

[72] Cooke, "Report," 25. The distance was thirty miles according to Cooke, "Journal," 134.

reminded that some of the companies had private wagons to carry such gear, Cooke, according to Bigler, replied that he "did not care a damn, you shall carry them." [73] Discipline had become slack during the San Bernardino repose, and Cooke, it seems, wished to restore order in the ranks. The order to carry arms should have seemed reasonable enough since the column was within easy striking distance of the Mexican garrisons at Fronteras and Tucson. To add further to the volunteers' discomfort, the weather turned cold, and snow fell briefly.

Striking the San Pedro River and turning north, the battalion was threatened by wild cattle which, first seen at San Bernardino Ranch, had become more numerous and increasingly aggressive. Cattle were being shot every day along the trail for fresh beef and for drying as insurance against leaner days ahead. The fierce cattle often charged the hunters and were hard to kill. At San Bernardino, a bull that repeatedly charged two hunters was hit six times, any one of which should have been fatal, before it expired. [74] Since then, a number of men had been wounded while stalking the wild bulls. Marching along the course of the San Pedro, Cooke noted that there "is not on the open prairies of Clay county, Missouri, so many traces of the passage of cattle and horses as we see every day." [75]

Finally on December 10, the soldiers fought a regular battle with the wild cattle in the vicinity of the deserted ranch of San Pedro, a satellite of San Bernardino. Some hunters inadvertently had driven a group of bulls toward the column. Some of the animals were shot, and this appeared to enrage the others. Cooke saw what was coming and ordered the volunteers to load their muskets to protect them-

[73] Bigler, "Journal," 47.

[74] Tyler, *Mormon Battalion*, 212.   [75] Cooke, "Journal," 142.

selves. Then the bulls charged. Cooke described the engagement:

> One [bull] ran on a man [Private Amos Cox of D Company], caught him in the thigh, and threw him clear over his body lengthwise; then it charged on a team, ran his head under the first mule, tore out the entrails of the one beyond, and threw them both over. Another ran against a sergeant, who escaped with severe bruises, as the horns went each side of him. A third ran at a horse tied to a wagon, and, as it escaped, its great momentum forced the hind part of the wagon from the road. I saw one rush at some pack mules and gore one so that its entrails came out broken. I also saw an immense coalblack bull charge on Corporal [Lafayette N.] Frost of Company A. He stood his ground while the animal rushed on for one hundred yards. I was close by and believed the man in great danger to his life and spoke to him. He aimed his musket very deliberately and only fired when the beast was within ten paces; and it fell headlong, almost at his feet. One man, when charged on, threw himself flat on the ground, and the bull jumped over him and passed on. I have seen the heart of a bull with two balls through it, that ran on a man with those wounds, and two others through the lungs! [76]

Tyler, who saw the whole affair, claimed that the "coal-black bull" was charging Cooke and that Frost stood his ground in order to protect his commander.[77] Whatever the truth, Cooke considered Frost a very brave man. Lieutenant Stoneman, in the excitement, almost shot off his own thumb. The sergeant, who was lucky to escape a fatal goring, suffered some broken ribs, but declined Dr. Sanderson's treatment. Private Cox had his wounds sewn up by the doctor and eventually recovered, though he could not walk for several weeks. The two gored mules died, but the remainder of the stock seem not to have been injured in the melee. Reforming and resuming the march, the column presently crossed a stream which Cooke appropriately named "Bull Run."

[76] *Ibid.,* 143.   [77] Tyler, *Mormon Battalion,* 220.

Continuing down the course of the San Pedro River, Cooke pondered the best route to the Gila. The road that followed the San Pedro to its confluence with the Gila was rough and crossed the river several times. If, instead, the battalion left the San Pedro on a known road and marched via Tucson directly to the Pima villages, the distance was almost 100 miles shorter and the road better. He had heard, however, that the Mexican garrison at Tucson might resist. While he did not wish to do battle if it could be avoided,[78] Cooke knew that his troops were in no condition to walk an unnecessary hundred miles on a bad or good road and decided to follow the advice of his guides who recommended the Tucson route. He also realized that the future road to California inevitably would follow the easier route and pass through Tucson.

Before the expedition left the San Pedro for the march toward Tucson, a scouting party returned. While looking for water, they had come upon a group of Mexican dragoons and some Apache families – a strange gathering – making mescal whiskey at a watering place. The Indians told the Americans that the garrison at Tucson included about 200 soldiers with some artillery. It seems that all of the small frontier outposts in the neighborhood had concentrated there. The Apaches also told Leroux that the Army of the West had passed the Pima villages just twenty days before. This was the first news of Kearny's column in weeks. When the Mexican soldiers questioned Leroux about his party, he replied that they were trappers. The dragoons

---

[78] Nor did the Mormons wish to fight. Learning that an engagement at Tucson was a possibility, Bliss wrote that "we hope the Lord will deliver us from all enemys & we dont wish to shed blood." "Journal," 80. This should not be read as an implication that the Mormons would not and could not fight. They had proved to the contrary. It does, however, illustrate a distinct difference in the attitudes of the troopers of the Mormon Battalion and those of Kearny's force, who seemed always to be spoiling for a fight.

appeared unconvinced, so Foster returned with them to
Tucson to give substance to the lie.[79]

The next day, December 13, Cooke prepared the battalion
for the battle he hoped to avoid. The volunteers were drilled
and ammunition was issued. To the assembled force, he had
the following order read. It is an interesting statement for it
gives some insight into Cooke's personality as well as his
strategy:

ORDER NUMBER 19
Headquarters Mormon Battalion
Camp on the San Pedro, December 13, 1846

Thus far on our course to California we have followed the guides
furnished by the general. These guides now point to Tucson, a gar-
risoned town, as our road, and they assert that any other course is a
hundred miles out of the way, and over a trackless wilderness of
mountains and river hills. We will march then to Tucson. We came
not to make war against Sonora, and less still to destroy an unimportant
outpost of defense against Indians. But we will take the straight course
before us and overcome all resistance. But shall I remind you that the
American soldier ever shows justice and kindness to the unarmed and
unresisting? The property of individuals you will hold sacred. The
people of Sonora are not our enemies.[80]

Cooke's reference to not wishing to wage war on Sonora will
be clarified shortly. The attitude displayed toward the civilian population of Sonora was certainly an enlightened one.
The document also reveals an unfortunate trait. Cooke's
desire not to destroy this outpost of defense against the
Indians runs directly counter to the sentiments expressed
earlier to Manuelita, the Apache chieftain. In his talks with
the Apaches, Cooke had encouraged them to continue their
attacks on Mexicans, even to the point of leading the
Apaches to expect American support. He had not, in his
exhortation, excluded Sonorans from Apache ravaging.

79 Cooke, "Report," 26; Cooke, "Journal," 145-46.   80 Cooke, "Journal," 147.

On the following day, the battalion set out for Tucson. At the watering place visited recently by Leroux's party, Cooke found some Mexican soldiers. A sergeant gave Cooke a message from the commander of the Tucson garrison, Antonio Comaduran. The Mexicans had not been fooled by Leroux and Foster. The commandant respectfully requested that the United States commander not approach the town, but that he pass on either side of it. The note explained that he had orders to hold the town, but that he could not, outnumbered as he was.[81] Cooke promptly sent word back to assure the inhabitants that the Americans were friends, not enemies, who only wanted to purchase flour and other provisions from them. He told the messenger that if the garrison indeed was weak, he probably would not molest it.[82]

Resuming the march the next morning, December 15, the column fell in with some Mexican soldiers, who seemed friendly or indifferent to the war. Beginning to fear for Dr. Foster, who had not returned from Tucson, Cooke had three of the Mexicans held as hostages. A fourth was sent to the garrison commandant to inform him that the hostages would be released as soon as Foster, who Cooke now assumed was being detained, returned to the battalion camp.

About midnight Foster appeared, accompanied by a party of soldiers. One of the Mexicans presented Comaduran's offer of truce. The terms were simply that the Americans pass the town and make no communication with the citizens. Cooke rejected the terms and made his own offer. The garrison must surrender and agree not to serve against the

---

[81] Indian informants had greatly exaggerated the size of the American force. Tyler, *Mormon Battalion*, 225.

[82] Cooke, "Journal," 149. On this day, December 14, Cooke also received confirmation that Kearny had passed the Pima villages twenty-five or twenty-six days previously, leaving some Indian goods and some papers for him with a Pima chief. *Ibid.*

United States in the war. The Americans were to have free access to Tucson to relax and trade. The Mexican officer methodically recorded Cooke's offer, had him sign it, promised him that it would be delivered promptly to the garrison commander, and assured him that it would not be accepted.[83]

As predicted, Comaduran rejected the American peace offer. A Mexican dragoon delivered his commandant's answer to Cooke when the battalion was but five miles from Tucson. Cooke told the soldier that there was no reply, and the dragoon rode away. Cooke then ordered preparations for an engagement. These were stopped short when two townspeople rode up with the news that Comaduran had abandoned the town, taking his garrison with him. Other citizens came out as if to welcome the Americans and, so accompanied, Cooke marched the battalion through the town and camped on its west side.

The short occupation of Tucson was peaceful and pleasant. Wary at first, the townspeople became friendly and open when they realized that neither their persons nor their property was endangered. Some of the inhabitants who had departed with the Mexican soldiers returned. The fleeing garrison apparently had tried unsuccessfully to force the entire population to abandon the town. The garrison had succeeded in removing all portable public property except 5,000 paper cigars, for which the Americans had no use, and about 1,500 to 2,000 bushels of wheat, which was a godsend. Cooke ordered an immediate issue of two quarts for each three men and took twenty-five bushels to be fed to the mules during the march to the Gila, having heard that grass was scarce on the route.

The next day, the trail-weary volunteers enjoyed a welcome rest. "It looked good," wrote Bigler, "to see young

[83] Cooke, "Report," 26-27.

green wheat patches and fruit trees and to see hogs and fowls running about and it was music to our ears to hear the crowing of the cocks." [84] The soldiers got along well with the citizens of Tucson. Bliss thought them the friendliest and most intelligent "Spaniards" he had yet seen. [85] Townspeople came to the battalion's camp and offered a variety of products for sale, beans, tobacco, meal, quinces, but the Mexicans were sharp traders and the volunteers had little money. The members of one mess contented themselves with the purchase of a small quantity of beans and flour in exchange for some of their clothing.

Cooke spent his day leading sixty volunteers in pursuit of the Mexican garrison. After marching ten miles into an increasingly dense mesquite forest, Cooke and his officers all agreed that the setting was perfect for an ambush. That said, the chase was abandoned and the unit returned to Tucson. [86]

The battalion's second night in Tucson was anything but restful. A strong guard was posted throughout the town that evening. Perhaps the fear of an ambush earlier in the day had left the Americans with a feeling that the Mexican dragoons might be lurking about. In any case, at midnight the quiet was shattered by a call to arms. Cooke was awakened by a breathless sentry who informed him that a large Mexican force was advancing on the camp. To Cooke, this "high-sounding announcement only aroused dreamy thoughts of events of historical importance." [87]

---

[84] Bigler, "Journal," 49.   [85] Bliss, "Journal," 81.

[86] Cooke, "Journal," 154. Cooke's account of the abortive march in his "Report" is different. There, he somewhat ambiguously wrote: ". . . [T]o cover some small parties of mule hunters, I made a reconnoissance, with about sixty men, marching half way to an Indian village, ten miles off, where the enemy were stationed. (I intended attacking him under favorable circumstances.)" "Report," 27-28. Nathaniel Jones told an even different story. He explained that Cooke's purpose was to capture the arms carried by the Mexican soldiers. "Journal," 9.

[87] Cooke, "Journal," 160. Cooke was an unembarrassed romantic militarist. In his book, *Scenes and Adventures in the Army* (Philadelphia, 1857), he describes his army experiences with a romantic flair and a flambuoyant style.

PHILIP ST. GEORGE COOKE

Tucson, Sonora

By John Russell Bartlett in his *Personal Narrative of Explorations*, vol. II.
Courtesy, John Carter Brown Library, Brown University

Cooke dispatched a party to search the town, then soon was compelled to send another party to search for the first. But it turned out to be a false alarm, perhaps to the commander's disappointment. A thorough scouring of the area revealed no enemy force. The only shots fired came from some soldiers on guard duty who had leveled on the troops that had assembled at the first alarm. There were no casualties.[88]

Assuming that Comaduran would return his garrison to Tucson after the departure of the Americans, Cooke sent him a note by a citizen of Tucson. In it, he explained that he had taken some of the public wheat, but had destroyed or wasted none and that no other public property was taken. He also requested the commandant to forward an attached letter to Don Manuel Gándara, the governor of Sonora. The letter to the governor, who Cooke believed to be favorable to the United States,[89] is interesting as is another statement, along with the Order Number 19 issued at the San Pedro camp, of his strategy:

> Camp at Tucson, Sonora, December 18, 1846
>
> . . . I have found it necessary to take this *presidio* [Tucson] in my route to the Gila. Be assured that I did not come as an enemy of the people whom you govern. . . Sonora refused to contribute to the support of the present war against my country, alleging the excellent reasons that all her resources were necessary to her defence from the incessant attacks of savages, [and] that the central government gave her no protection and was therefore entitled to no support. To this might have been added that Mexico supports a war upon Sonora. For I have seen New Mexicans within her boundary trading for the spoil of her people, taken by murderous, cowardly Indians who attack

---

[88] Cooke, "Journal," 160; Whitworth, "Englishman in the Mormon Battalion," 151; Jones, "Journal," 9; Bliss, "Journal," 81. It is interesting that Cooke does not mention the incident at all in his "Report."

[89] Indeed, Cooke gained the impression during his stay in Tucson that if he would march toward the Sonoran capital, enough malcontents would join his force to constitute a revolution. Cooke, "Report," 28.

only to lay waste, rob, and fly to the mountains. . . . Thus one part
of Mexico allies itself against another. The unity of Sonora with the
. . . [United States] . . . is necessary effectually to subdue
these Parthian Apache. Meanwhile, I make a wagon road from the
streams of the Atlantic to the Pacific ocean, through the valuable
plains and mountains (rich with minerals) of Sonora. This, I trust,
will prove useful to the citizens of either republic, who, if not more
closely [tied], may unite in the pursuits of a highly beneficial commerce.[90]

Thus Cooke attempted to encourage separatist views in
Sonora and to show the reasonableness of political union
with the United States or, at the least, close commercial ties.
Cooke's sincerity must be doubted, however, if for no other
reason than that of the conscious contradictions in dealing
with Manuelita and Governor Gándara. With Manuelita,
he urged an alliance between Apaches and Americans
against their common enemy, the Mexicans. A few days
later, he was explaining to Gándara the necessity for Americans and Mexicans to unite to defeat the Apaches. The
sentiment implicit in Cooke's relations with the Apaches —
that Indians cannot be trusted, therefore one need not be
frank with them — was commonly held by Americans. Furthermore, Cooke's strategy of appearing to make common
cause with each side in the perpetual war between Mexicans
and Apaches was excellent from a military point of view.
Neither fact renders Cooke's actions less dishonest.

The Mormon Battalion set out from Tucson on Decem-

---

[90] Cooke, "Journal," 159-60. Cooke apparently was more familiar with current
politics than with the history of northern Sonora. In his "Journal," 153, he wrote:
"We saw . . . a very large stone church built by Jesuits: it is at a large pueblo
about ten miles" from Tucson. If he had known anything about San Xavier del
Bac, surely he would have noted the name.

After departing Tucson for the Gila, Cooke received a message from the commandant of the Tucson garrison, acknowledging Cooke's message and promising to
forward the letter to the governor. *Ibid.*, 166-67.

ber 18,[91] bound for the Gila. For the most part, the terrain
was level and the road good. But it was the driest stretch
since leaving Santa Fé, and men and animals suffered con-
siderably. Cooke was proud of his troops:" They are almost
barefooted, carry their muskets, knapsacks . . . and do
not grumble." [92] Other than the constant search for water
and grass, which had long ago become part of the daily
routine, little happened to break the monotony of the three-
day march. There was one light moment that indicated that
the Mormons, at least, had not lost their sense of humor.
The account is Bigler's:

Sunday 20th. This morning I was detailed to be the Colonel's
orderly for the day. On going to his marquee to report myself I found
him feeding his mule some wheat he had brought from Tucson. There
was another mule determined to share with the Colonel's. He had
driven it away several times but as soon as his back was turned the
mule would march boldly up for another morsel of wheat until at last
the Colonel turned around and said, "Orderly is your gun loaded"?
I replied, "No sir", he then said, "Load your gun and I will shoot that
G. d. mule," and walked into his tent. I knew it was not one of Uncle
Sam's for it did not have the U.S. on it and therefore it must be a
private mule belonging to some of our men. All of a sudden a thought
came into my mind not to cause the mule to be killed and I took from
my cartridge box a cartridge, clapped it in my mouth and with my
teeth tore off the bullet end and put the ball in my pocket and emptied
the powder into my musket and rammed the paper on top of it. Pretty
soon out came the Colonel walking up to me, seized my gun and ran
up within ten feet of the mule, standing broadside and fired. The
moment he saw the mule was not hurt he dropped the musket and with
an oath said, "You did not load that gun right." His bugler and others
who saw the trick nearly split their sides with laughter, the Colonel

---

[91] Battalion diarists differ often on dates. Cooke differs even in his two accounts.
For example, Cooke indicates a departure date of December 18 in his "Journal,"
164. But in his "Report," 28, he has the battalion twenty-four miles from Tucson on
the road to the Gila on the night of December 17. I have generally followed the
"Journal" for dates.   [92] Cooke, "Journal," 166.

walked into his tent and I have wondered how it was he did not punish me for disobeying his order.[93]

No other joke succeeds in the military like one pulled off on the "old man," especially when the commander is a stiff-backed, no-nonsense, do-it-by-the-book professional. It seems that Cooke realized this, for there is no indication that he ever took punitive action against Bigler. In his canvas sanctuary, perhaps he realized also the foolishness of the vengeful attack on the strange mule. Certainly the act was out of character. Perhaps the incident illustrates nothing more than that the desert sun bakes the brains of commanders as well as those of the ranks.

The battalion reached the Gila on December 21 at a point just west of the present town of Florence. Crossing the still-recognizable trail of Kearny's column, the battalion camped in reasonably good grass about eight miles from the Pima villages. Pimas appeared almost immediately with trade goods and letters from General Kearny and Major Swords. The next day, the battalion moved down the river and encamped at the villages.

As usual, the Pimas were hospitable and friendly and made quite a favorable impression on the Americans. "The poison of the civilized asp is unknown among them," Tyler wrote, "and our American and European cities would do well to take lessons in virtue and morality from these native tribes."[94] Several diarists noted the handsomeness of the Pimas. Jones thought them the healthiest people he had ever seen.[95] Cooke was attracted to "this friendly, guileless and singularly innocent and cheerful people, the Pimos." Riding into the village in advance of the main column, Cooke came upon a group of men, women and girls:

[93] Bigler, "Journal," 50-51.
[94] Tyler, *Mormon Battalion,* 234.   [95] Jones, "Journal," 9-10.

These last, naked above the hips, were of every age and pretty. It was a gladdening sight, of so much cheerfulness and happiness. One little girl particularly, by a fancied resemblance, excited much interest with me. She was so joyous that she seemed very innocent and pretty. I could not resist tying a red silk handkerchief on her head for a turban; then, if perfect happiness ever momentarily dwells on earth, it seemed that it was with her.[96]

The incident had not gone unnoticed among the volunteers. In Tyler's view, "[k]indness to the natives, by military officers, as manifested in several instances by Colonel Cooke, is so rare in this age, that this circumstance may be mentioned, as one of the noteworthy events of our journey." [97]

The Pimas proved equal to the trust that Kearny had placed in them. Though the general had left only ten or eleven worn-out mules with the Pimas to be turned over to Cooke, they had thirteen. Apparently, the additional animals had been abandoned by the Army of the West along the Gila and were later retrieved by the Pimas. The two bales of goods left by Kearny also were delivered to Cooke. Cooke learned that a detachment of twenty-five Mexican soldiers had visited the villages since the passing of the Army of the West and had demanded that the animals and goods be surrendered to them. The Pimas had refused and replied defiantly that they would hold the property by force if necessary. The Mexicans had departed, empty-handed, and passed Tucson while the Mormon Battalion was resting there.[98]

Trading with the Indians seems to have been satisfactory. The Pimas had little to offer since Kearny's force had been there only six weeks before, but the Maricopas, whose vil-

---

[96] Cooke, "Journal," 170. The "fancied resemblance" of the Pima child was to Cooke's own youngest daughter, according to Otis E. Young, *The West of Philip St. George Cooke, 1809-1895* (Glendale, 1955), 215.

[97] Tyler, *Mormon Battalion,* 235.   [98] Cooke, "Report," 28.

lages Kearny did not visit, had ample food stocks to sell. With his Indian goods and every piece of public property he could spare, Cooke bought provisions: beans, meal, and especially corn which was fed to the nearly spent mules. The volunteers also traded directly with the Indians, though Cooke unsuccessfully forbade the traffic. Standage traded a button for a cake [99] while Whitworth traded his last shirt, other than the one he wore, for corn. "[W]e all thought more of the Belly than the Back," he explained.[100] During their short sojourn among the Pimas and Maricopas, the troopers relished such delicacies as hominy, boiled beans, molasses, pumpkin, and wonder of wonders at the Christmas season: watermelon.

Cooke visited with Pima and Maricopa chiefs and assured them of the friendship of the United States. He told one Pima leader that in all his travels he had found no Indian nation happier than the Pimas. Desiring to add to their comfort and industry, he gave the chief three ewes with lambs. To a Maricopa chieftain who said that his people would rather live under the Americans than the Mexicans, Cooke gave a commendatory letter, granting him the authority to retrieve abandoned United States army mules to hold for later recovery by the army. Indeed, Cooke was so impressed by the Gila River Indians that he spoke to two senior Mormon captains about planting a Mormon settlement in the region. The Mormons appeared favorable to the suggestion, and Captain Hunt took the initiative to speak to a chief about it.[101]

During the halt at the Indian villages, Cooke received three messengers with letters from General Kearny and Captain Turner sent from Warner's Ranch. Cooke was

99 Standage, "Journal," 199.
100 Whitworth, "Englishman in the Mormon Battalion," 152.
101 Cooke, "Journal," 168.

delighted to learn that he was thirty days ahead of schedule, but the rest of the news was bad. The Californians had risen in a "counter-revolution." The conquest was in trouble. Haste was in order, and the Mormon Battalion commander prepared his troops to march.

Surveying the expedition as preparations were made for departure, Cooke was dismayed. In spite of the layover at the villages, the volunteers and the animals still were not strong, certainly in no condition for a forced march.[102] Provisions, especially pork, were in seriously short supply, a shortage that Cooke attributed to mismanagement by the companies.[103]

To speed the battalion's pace, Cooke lightened the expedition's load. He ordered over 200 sheepskins sold and abandoned 140 packsaddles. He further commanded that private provisions of persons who were drawing government rations, presumably excluding wives and servants, were not to be carried in the wagons. This last order did not set well with men who literally had sold the shirts off their backs for food to supplement the short government rations. The volunteers, however, had not become such obedient soldiers that they had lost their resourcefulness. Through the conniv-

---

102 Cooke makes an odd comment in his "Report," 29, concerning the condition of his animals at this point. Addressing General Kearny, Cooke wrote: "I have good reason to believe that, even with pack mules, better time can be made on my route than yours; and the *mules kept in good order,* for mine improved on the greater part of it." The reference to his mules improving during the trek surely was an exaggeration to convince Kearny, and perhaps whoever else might read the report, that Cooke's wagon road was the better route. As late as January 15, 1847, in the middle of the Colorado Desert, Jones wrote that the expedition's mules had "had no grass from the San Pedro to this place, a distance of four-hundred miles." "Journal," 11. Jones also was exaggerating, but no more so than Cooke who had frequently noted in his daily journal the scarcity of grass and water and the poor condition of his mules.

103 "One company," wrote Cooke, "which should have, without wastage, twenty-six days' [rations], has eight! What can a commander do with a people who act and manage thus?" Cooke, "Journal," 174.

ance of a Mormon officer, in at least one case, private provisions were carried along "and no thanks to . . . the colonel," added a soldier who had traded clothes for some meal and beans.[104]

Cooke, it seems, had the same problem shared by many modern military commanders: the failure to convince the lower ranks of the reasonableness of orders. Almost alone in a battalion of volunteers who had little use for strict military discipline, Cooke's task was more difficult than that of most other commanders.

With the hardest part of the journey to California still to come, the battalion set out, not yet in desperate straits, but ill prepared for the ordeal ahead.[105] Cooke decided to cut off the great bend of the Gila by marching overland.[106] The trek challenged the endurance of all, men and animals. A single journal entry of Whitworth's says it all: "December 25: Marched 43 miles without water. Found water after dark – a Merry Christmas." [107]

Again striking the Gila, the battalion soon was marching in deep sand. Expecting no more stony trails on the route to San Diego, Cooke had the mules' shoes removed to relieve

---

104 Jones, "Journal," 10.

105 Shortly before leaving the Pima-Maricopa country, Cooke ended his map-making. His compass by that time was not reliable and since he was now on the same trail as that followed by the Army of the West and the topographical engineers, who would be mapping the remainder of the road to California, he had decided that there was no need for him to continue. Cooke, "Journal," 174.

Cooke's sketch map of the march of the Mormon Battalion can be found in a number of publications, for example, in Cooke, *Conquest*. Emory incorporated Cooke's map into his own of the route followed by the Army of the West. *See* Emory's map in Emory, *Notes,* and Griffin, *A Doctor Comes to California.*

106 From this point forward, Cooke's selection of a trail undoubtedly was influenced by a Mexican named Francisco who Kearny had sent to guide the battalion to California. Francisco, who had marched with the Army of the West all the way from New Mexico to California, was one of the couriers who had brought Kearny's letters to Cooke at the Indian villages.

107 Whitworth, "Englishman in the Mormon Battalion," 152.

them of the weight. The shoes, 150 pairs, and approximately sixty pounds of nails were cached along the trail.[108]

On December 28, Cooke decided to send his "useless guides" – Leroux, Charbonneau and three others – ahead. Willard Hall accompanied them. They were directed to observe any movements of Mexican troops on the route and to notify Cooke of their locations. If they came upon Mexican parties driving horses or mules from California without proper passports, they were to seize the animals and bring them to Cooke, leaving one or two guides to continue on to California. They were entrusted with a letter to deliver to Kearny. If the general was found at San Diego, one or two of the guides were to examine the road between Warner's Ranch and San Diego, then to return to Warner's by January 21 to guide the battalion over the road. Finally, they were to locate in the vicinity of Warner's and bring back to the advancing column from twenty to seventy fresh mules and eight or ten beef cattle. The stock were to be rounded up and driven with the assistance of locally hired men.[109] Quite a large order to be required of five "useless guides." To be fair to Cooke, reference to the guides as "useless" might simply have meant that he no longer needed them, since the battalion was now following Kearny's track.

Cooke became increasingly concerned about the fate of the battalion and its mission. He considered taking a picked force of 200 men on a forced march to aid Kearny, but abandoned the thought, fearing that the rest of the train would be helpless with the loss of his guidance and the battalion's best men. In an attempt to lighten the load of the weary mules and accelerate the battalion's advance, Cooke experimented with floating supplies down the Gila in a

---

108 Obviously, it was Cooke's intention to have the cache recovered, and perhaps it was, but I have seen no record of its recovery.

109 Cooke, "Journal," 179-80; Cooke, "Report," 30.

makeshift boat. Made of two excess wagons joined end to end between two cottonwood logs, the boat was loaded with road tools, corn and some of the rations.[110] The Mormons, already on short rations, were not enthusiastic about the risky project.

Their fears were fully realized, for after five days the experiment proved a costly failure. Though some flour was recovered where Lieutenant Stoneman had beached the boat, everything else was lost. Cooke was reluctant to take full responsibility for the fiasco and attempted to shift at least some of the blame on Stoneman, the officer in charge of the pontoon-boat.[111]

The earlier prediction of quarter-rations before the end of the trip appeared more likely than ever now. After the boating losses, there was left but nine days of largely-rotten half-rations to reach the California settlements, estimated to be twelve days distant. Bigler and his messmates tried to stretch their provisions with a half-and-half mixture of mesquite and flour. They abandoned the experiment when the concoction caused constipation "to an alarming extent." [112]

In their want, the Mormons were sustained as much by their sense of humor and their faith as their scant provisions. On the same day they learned about the boating losses, they held a "weighing frolic." Jones weighed 128 pounds. His weight at the time of his enlistment was 198 pounds.[113] In spite of the weight loss, Jones seems to have remained in relatively good spirits and health throughout the trip. There

---

110 Jones noted that they "made boats of two wagon beds and put about twelve oxen in each boat and started down the river." "Journal," 10. Surely Jones is wrong. Cooke says nothing about putting oxen in the boat, an act that hardly would have lightened the load on the mules.

111 Cooke,"Journal," 194-95.

112 Bigler, "Journal," 53.   113 Jones, "Journal," 198.

is no reason to believe that his case was unusual. Robert Bliss indicated the extent of their deprivation and something of the spirit that strengthened the Mormons when he wrote:

> We are now reduced very low for provisions & those of the poorest kind; we drew 9 oz. of meal last night for a day   we left waggons, harness, chains &c &c &c because of the failure of our mules   we leave something of value daily that we cannot carry & it is as much as some of the men can do to get into camp at night although we are favoured remarkable with health in the Army   we have been preserved in that way that all must acknowledge the hand of God in it.[114]

The battalion reached the Colorado River on January 8, 1847. It was a welcome sight, if only to indicate some progress on the road to California. Resting a day on the eastern bank to allow the animals to graze, the Colorado was crossed on January 10 and 11 in the vicinity of present-day Algodones, Baja California. The Army of the West had crossed at the same ford on November 25. Cooke's wagonboat, which had been floated empty down the Gila, was used in the battalion's crossing to ferry men and provisions to the far side.[115]

The crossing was not made without some friction between commander and troops. Cooke undoubtedly was concerned about the safety of men and animals and became irritated when things did not seem to go smoothly. On the far side, where Kearny had found grass for his animals, Cooke found none. Cooke did not delay and set out on January 11 on the trail westward, even while part of the train was in mid-

---

[114] Bliss, "Journal," 83.

[115] After it had served its purpose, the wagon-boat was abandoned. Perhaps this was the same derelict that was recovered and used as a ferry in 1848 by John Glanton of Texas and his party of scalp hunters. One of the party was Samuel Emery Chamberlain, a wagon master who deserted from Major Lawrence P. Graham's expedition which shortly before had crossed the Colorado River on a march from Chihuahua to California. Samuel Emery Chamberlain, *My Confession*, ed. by Roger Butterfield (New York, 1956), 287-88. Also *see below*, pp. 288-89.

stream and the sheep and rear guard yet to wet their feet.

The battalion now began what Cooke later called the most difficult part of the entire journey from Santa Fé.[116] Grass was almost nonexistent, and mules wore out regularly. Kearny's wells were found, but more often than not, they yielded too little water. Cooke had some anxious moments in the desert. He knew that the lives of his men and his own military future depended on the water seekers. Cooke realized also that his reputation as a wagon-road builder was in jeopardy. As the mules failed in alarming numbers, more wagons had to be left behind.

On the second day in the desert, a tragedy appeared to be reaching its climax. Insufficient water was found. More wagons were abandoned. The march became less orderly as men stumbled along. The column lengthened, eventually stretching to fifteen or twenty miles. Many of the volunteers were shoeless in the scorching sand. Some protected their feet by wrapping old clothes around them. Others fashioned crude boots of rawhide cut from dead oxen. Provisions were almost exhausted. The few remaining cattle and sheep were very poor and on the point of failing. The track from the Colorado was marked with dead and dying mules.

For days, Cooke and the volunteers had searched the horizon for some sign of the guides returning from the California settlements. Bliss recorded their arrival:

> Frid. 15th   Started at Sun Rise & continued our slow march over the plains with poor prospects for we have not had any word from our Express yet; our men have not half enough to eat & what we do eat is poor but we are kept from starving so far we look to Him who is

---

116 Cooke, "Journal," 224. In the "Report," 34, however, he identified the worst stretch of the road as that opposite the upper and middle parts of the Jornado del Muerto, which lay east of the Rio Grande, near the present-day Elephant Butte and Caballo Reservoirs.

able to help us in this time of Want; traveled 10 miles to Wells of poor water but what was our joy to meet here our Express with 12 beef cattle & 40 mules for our relief; thus again we are preserved by Him who watches over us all the time by night & by day.[117]

The animals and news of Kearny's defeat at San Pascual set the battalion in motion. Cooke was equally concerned about the safety of his own men and the future of the conquest, but he decided that the battalion must push on as quickly as possible. He ordered a beef killed for a meal – hardly enough for an entire battalion of hungry men – and had the half-wild new mules hitched side-by-side with the harness-wise mules. "After we had got a fair start," wrote Whitworth, "our heavy waggons bowled over the plains with the Speed of Stage Coaches – for our new mules felt very frisky."[118] That was quite a feat for animals that had had but little water for about thirty-six hours.

The battalion reached Carrizo Creek on January 17 or 18.[119] Cooke ordered a one-day layover at this camp to give the men a chance to rest and prepare themselves for the battle that now appeared to be imminent. Weapons were cleaned and clothes mended. In spite of their hunger and fatigue, the volunteers' spirits rose. The weather was "clear and nice," wrote Bigler, "frogs are singing." The camp took on the air of a holiday outing:

---

[117] Bliss, "Journal," 84. Cooke says that Leroux sent back fifty-seven mules, but that the incompetent hired herders had lost twenty of them. "Report," 31.

[118] Whitworth, "Englishman in the Mormon Battalion," 154.

[119] Here, Cooke wrote, a party of nine Mexicans overtook the column: "To two principal ones I gave permission at Tucson to follow me. I believe they are poor men seeking to better themselves by moving to California. They are nearly starved, have been living on our dead mules, etc. I have directed that two sheep be given to them. . . At the crossing of the Colorado they were a day behind us and met a large war party of Indians. One of the Mexicans left Tucson eight days after me but brings no news. He says the military did not return for three or four days after my departure." Cooke, "Journal," 216-17.

Some of the boys went to the top of a mountain south of our camp and amused themselves by rolling large boulders down the mountain making a noise like peals of thunder, fairly shaking the earth like an earthquake, while others in camp sang songs, fiddled and danced; this got away with the Colonel and he swore that he did not see how it was when the men could hardly keep up with the command but when they got into camp, by G. d. the fiddle was going and the men dancing.[120]

That evening, Cooke received a letter notifying him that Kearny had marched the Army of the West to Los Angeles.

The next day, the battalion, now somewhat refreshed, took the trail in orthodox military fashion with the scouts ahead and the wagons at the rear. There were still five government wagons and three private ones. The column advanced but a few miles when it halted. Within a few miles of Warner's Ranch, it appeared that the remaining wagons would have to be abandoned. The trail ran through a ravine with rock walls that were a foot narrower than the wagons. Nor could the wagons be taken over the ridge through which the ravine ran. Others declared the situation hopeless, but Cooke would not admit defeat. He was determined to take the wagons through. Cooke picked up a tool and attacked the stone wall. The Mormons followed his example, and by nightfall the battalion encamped at the summit. It was a rough passage they had carved. At particularly bad places, the wagons had to be unloaded and their contents packed while the men carried the wagons. Two wagons had to be dismantled and carried through in pieces.[121]

---

[120] Bigler, "Journal," 54-55. Cooke had indeed referred to "the poor men staggering, utterly exhausted, into camp." Cooke, "Report," 32. Certainly by this time, Cooke was aware of the Mormons' love of music and as Wallace Stegner wrote, their "habit of dancing away troubles in a cotillion." For a description of the dance on the occasion of the Battalion's departure from Council Bluffs, see Stegner's, *The Gathering of Zion: The Story of the Mormon Trail* (New York, 1964), 80-82.

[121] Cooke, "Report," 32; Cooke, "Journal," 220; Bigler, "Journal," 55; Tyler, *Mormon Battalion*, 246, 248. Tyler says that all but two light wagons had to be dismantled or carried through.

For the next two days, the battalion made its way down the mountain toward Warner's Ranch. The volunteers were cheered by the spectacle of live oak trees and green grass along the course of a small stream and gloried in the view from the trail overlooking the valley of Agua Caliente. At San Felipe, one of the guides sent ahead earlier reported to Cooke. He had just come from San Diego, but he had no news. On January 21, 1847, the column arrived at Warner's.

The battalion did not move the next day to give the men the opportunity to rest "before commencing," wrote Cooke, "as I hoped, active operations." [122] The commander procured cattle and ordered that each man should have four and a half pounds of fresh beef daily. The heretofore half-starved Bigler, the Compleat Soldier, grumbled that it was "flat eating without bread or salt." [123]

Since Kearny now was marching northward to Los Angeles, Cooke decided to alter his course from San Diego. His intelligence reported that Fremont was advancing on the pueblo from the north. Cooke then would approach from the east. The battalion left Warner's on January 23.

Marching toward Los Angeles, the volunteers were lashed by high winds and drenched in a torrential rain for the most part of two days. At Temecula Valley, Cooke received a letter from General Kearny notifying him that hostilities had ended and ordering him to march to San Diego. The battalion accordingly moved off in that direction. En route, another message was received at San Luis Rey directing Cooke to the San Diego Mission.

The column arrived at the mission on January 29. That same evening, Cooke rode to San Diego by moonlight to report to General Kearny, thus symbolizing the end of the

---

[122] Cooke, "Report," 33.   [123] Bigler, "Journal," 55.

march of the Mormon Battalion. The next day, Cooke
issued the following order:

ORDER NUMBER 1
Headquarters Mormon Battalion,
Mission of San Diego, January 30, 1847

The lieutenant-colonel commanding congratulates the battalion on
their safe arrival on the shore of the Pacific ocean, and the conclusion
of the march of over two thousand miles. History may be searched in
vain for an equal march of infantry. Nine-tenths of it has been through
a wilderness where nothing but savages and wild beasts are found, or
deserts where, for want of water, there is no living creature. There,
with almost hopeless labor, we have dug deep wells which the future
traveler will enjoy. Without a guide who had traversed them, we have
ventured into trackless prairies where water was not found for several
marches. With crowbar and pick and ax in hand we have worked our
way over mountains which seemed to defy aught save the wild goat,
and hewed a passage through a chasm of living rock more narrow than
our wagons. . . Thus, marching half naked and half fed, and living upon wild animals, we have discovered and made a road of great
value to our country. . .[124]

At the end of the reading of the order, the volunteers sent
up a cheer. It was a fitting end to a memorable march.

In his report submitted to General Kearny on February 5,
Cooke included a resume of his journey and an evaluation
of the Mormon Battalion and the road which together they
had pioneered. He explained that he could have arrived in
California sooner had he not been required to bring the
wagons with him. But, as a point of honor, since the general
had wished it, he brought them through. He pointed out the
value of the road to future travelers and expressed his conviction that the lands along the Gila and Colorado would
soon be settled by Americans. Of the volunteers, Cooke
reported that

---

124 Cooke, "Journal," 238-40.

. . . much credit is due to the battalion for the cheerful and faithful manner in which they have accomplished the great labors of this march, and submitted to its exposures and privations. They would have preferred to lighten and abridge them, by leaving the wagons; but, without previous discipline, all was accomplished with unity and determination of spirit.

In the concluding paragraph of the report, Cooke loosed a parting shot to remind the general that he had not forgiven him for removing him from the center of conflict and glory:

Thus, general, whilst fortune was conducting *you* to battles and victories, I was fated to devote my best energies to more humble labors. . . But it is passed! and I must be content with having done my duty in the task which you assigned to me. . .[125]

But Cooke was not content. He chafed to join his old regiment in Mexico before the fighting there ended. After a number of rebuffs, Kearny relented and agreed to release Cooke from his command of the Mormon Battalion. Cooke eventually returned to the United States with Kearny's party which left Los Angeles in May 1847 and arrived at Fort Leavenworth in August. Cooke finally received his long-awaited orders to Mexico and arrived there in time to serve at Vera Cruz and Mexico City in the closing battles of the war. Ironically, while Cooke never forgave Kearny for snatching him from battle and honor in Mexico, history remembers him for his service in the United States Southwest and neglects to notice his part in the campaigns of southern Mexico.

The story of the Mormon Battalion after its arrival at San Diego is anticlimactic. The volunteers were discharged at Los Angeles on July 16, 1847, the anniversary of the establishment of the battalion at Council Bluffs. While

---

[125] Cooke, "Report," 34-36.

Cooke and the Mormons had had their differences they parted on cordial terms, and that relationship seems never to have changed thereafter.[126] The volunteers looked back on their service in the battalion with bittersweet memories, and the march now has passed into the history and folklore of the Mormons and the American West.[127]

Cooke's wagon route was improved shortly after the passage of the Mormon Battalion. In 1848, following the end of the war with Mexico, Major Lawrence P. Graham led a battalion of United States dragoons from Chihuahua to California. Marching through Janos, the column crossed the mountains at or near the Guadalupe Pass. Beyond San Bernardino Ranch, Graham, who apparently was drunk for most of the march, forded the San Pedro River and continued traveling westward until he reached the presidio of Santa Cruz. From there, he followed the course of the Santa Cruz River to Tucson. Graham's march thereafter essentially followed Cooke's road.[128]

---

[126] By a twist of irony, Cooke later faced many of these same men in a potentially explosive situation. In the spring of 1858, he commanded a regiment of dragoons in the Utah Expedition which had been sent to Utah Territory to put down any possible resistance to President Buchanan's appointment of civil officials. Ex-Mormon Battalion volunteers were among the militia force poised to meet the army units. Hostilities were averted, and the Mormons' generally warm regard for Cooke was not altered. For a full account of the Utah Expedition, *see* LeRoy R. Hafen and Ann W. Hafen, *The Utah Expedition* (Glendale, 1958).

When Cooke died, Mormons requested that he be interred in the New Zion. Though the petition was not granted, Mormons continued to honor Cooke's memory, notably on the Mormon Battalion Monument on the state capitol grounds at Salt Lake City. Young, *The West of Philip St. George Cooke,* 193.

[127] An interesting contribution to the story of the Mormon Battalion is a song written by a Mormon poet, Levi Hancock. Dubbed the "camp singer" by the volunteers, he often led the entertainment around the campfire. A testimony of the hardships borne by the Mormons, the song is printed in Tyler, *Mormon Battalion,* 182-83.

[128] At the Gila River, Lieutenant Cave Johnson Couts recorded that the Pimas, like countless generations of their ancestors, "were exceedingly anxious to see the white men come and live amongst them, . . . How long before they are coming? How many moons? and such questions." *Hepah California! The Journal of Cave Johnson Couts,* ed. by Henry F. Dobyns (Tucson, 1961), 67.

While Major Graham, dubbed "whiskey"[129] by Cave
Johnson Couts, a junior officer of his command, could hardly
be called a pathfinder, he did make two detours from Cooke's
route that were followed by most southern-route emigrants
during the gold rush and after. Cooke had not passed
through Janos. Graham and most travelers who came that
way in later years did. With the war ended, there was no
reason not to go through that frontier outpost. Perhaps for
the same reason, Graham marched from San Bernardino to
Santa Cruz rather than down the San Pedro and then west
to Tucson as Cooke had done.[130] There was no reason now
not to pass through Santa Cruz and the remnants of imperial
Spain – Tumacacori Mission, the Tubac presidio and San
Xavier del Bac – that lay on the road to Tucson. Later,
argonauts and emigrants arrived at Janos from many directions, but most of them traveled from that point to California over Cooke's road with the exception of the detour
through Santa Cruz.[131]

---

[129] Couts, *Hepah California!*, 35. The Major, wrote Lieutenant Couts near Janos,
"is now drunk and will leave here drunk, and will be drunk as long as mules last
to haul the sutler's . . . whiskey." (p. 45.) Later, on the Gila River, when the
command was forced to abandon eleven wagons and reduce all teams, the indignant
Couts noted that the Major nevertheless retained "a fine six mule team to haul his
bed and *whore!*" (p. 70).

Graham was not the only member of the command who enjoyed more than the
ordinary soldier's comforts. Samuel Chamberlain, a wagon master, shared his tent
with an eighteen-year-old blond beauty who wanted to go to California. Early in
the journey, Chamberlain agreed to release her from the "Scotch marriage" so she
could accept a legitimate offer of marriage from another wagon master in the
column. Too late, Chamberlain realized his loss but found some solace in liquor, of
which he always had a good supply in his wagon. Chamberlain, *My Confession*,
240, 253-54, 257.

[130] Though Graham's detour from Cooke's route later would prove the better
road, some of Graham's troopers thought it a foolish move. Couts was disgusted:
". . . scorning to follow *Cook's trail, Cook's wagon route!* we must have a
'Major Graham's wagon route!' " Couts, *Hepah California!*, 53.

[131] Cooke and Graham share the credit for traveling the route first, but Father
Garcés thought of it first. Graham's route all the way from Chihuahua to the Colorado River is exactly the same as that suggested by Garcés in 1777 for the purpose

Philip St. George Cooke and the Mormon Battalion hardly opened a highway. But they did take wagons from Fort Leavenworth to the Pacific Ocean. They proved that it could be done over a southern route. They opened a track which, with Graham's modifications, became the most heavily traveled road to California across the present United States Southwest.

---

of supplying proposed missions on the Gila and Colorado rivers. *See above,* p. 104.

Evidence that Graham's Santa Cruz detour became the accepted road is furnished by the diarist of the Fremont Association which traveled in 1849 through Apache Pass in southeastern Arizona and crossed the San Pedro River almost due east of Tucson. Beyond the river, the Americans struck "Colonel Cooke's trail, which the guide says has not been travelled since Cooke went over it, the emmigrants taking another route going around the mountains." Robert Eccleston, *Overland to California on the Southwestern Trail, 1849,* ed. by George P. Hammond and Edward H. Howes (Berkeley, 1950), 196. The other route to which the guide referred was Graham's detour via the town of Santa Cruz and the Santa Cruz River.

CHAPTER VIII

End and Beginning

There continued to be alternate paths to California through the American Southwest after 1848, but Cooke's feat may be seen as a culmination in 300 years of pathmaking in the region and 150 years of deliberate searching for a practical southern route. Though Spaniards and later Mexicans had opened and maintained a tenuous overland route to California, desires for land and souls in the north and fears of foreign encroachment were not sufficient to convince authorities to develop the route. On the occasions when officials were persuaded, resources either were not available or were inadequately committed. It remained for a United States army of conquest to accomplish in the midst of war what could not be done or was not done during 150 years of relative peace.

The war between the United States and Mexico had hardly ended when the western trails were flooded with emigrants. President James K. Polk in December 1848, confirmed the discovery of gold in the foothills of the Sierra Nevada, and the rush was on for California.

Considering the hardships suffered by argonauts who traveled Cooke's road and variations, one might question why the gold-seekers did not follow the long-established, sure and comparatively safe Santa Fé Trail and Old Spanish Trail. The Santa Fé Trail was well-known in the United States, and surely those Americans who had any thought of going west would have learned something of the Old Spanish Trail in the course of inquiring about routes.

A combination of these two trails would seem to have been ready-made for those who had no need to take wagons to California. Of course, the route would not have been practicable during the winter of 1848-1849. The Old Spanish Trail ran too far to the north and had too many passes. But for the other three seasons, the only possible explanation for the argonauts' failure to use the route is that it was just too long, and they were just too impatient. They were willing to risk the deserts and Indians of the lower route to get to California a few days faster.

Almost all of the southern-route travelers in 1849 and the 1850s were seeing the southwestern country for the first time. Hardly any party had a guide who knew any more about the country than its most ignorant member. While mountain men who had trapped the streams of northern Mexico served as guides for the Army of the West and the Mormon Battalion, they seem not to have been so employed by emigrants to the same extent that their compatriots were on northern trails.

Many of the emigrants carried guidebooks which were generally either woefully insufficient or dangerously misleading. Among the more reputable guidebooks consulted were the journals of Emory, Cooke and others which had been published as government documents. Yet, these volumes, though reasonably accurate, first-hand narratives, had never been intended for use as guides, and also proved inadequate. The military journals were more useful in later years to army engineers. Cooke's and Emory's reports especially were studied by officials who were responsible for locating new wagon roads and railroads to meet the transportation needs of a growing number of settlers in the Southwest and an exploding population in California.

The argonauts' prospect of entering a country about which they knew next to nothing was an old story in the Southwest. For 300 years, each generation had failed to benefit from the successes and failures of its predecessors. Kino had crossed, re-crossed and criss-crossed the Pimería Alta. He knew the locations of Indian trails, watering places, villages, and the haunts and habits of both friendly and hostile Indians. He wrote at length about all these things, as well as detailing his own itineraries, in his journals. The same can be said for Garcés, Sedelmayr, Anza and many others. It might appear, then, that nineteenth-century travelers should have had an easy time of it by gleaning information from the Spanish journals. That they could not do, simply because the journals written by Spanish explorers were lost to public view for generations, hidden away in closets or unclassified archives. Precious knowledge of the frontier regions and its peoples gained through years of toil appeared to die with the explorers. In an age not yet attuned to classification of archives and publication of historically-valuable documents, the loss of the travel narratives perhaps was inevitable. Fortunately, many documents were only temporarily lost, to be recovered years later by researchers.

Trails, like journals, often were abandoned and forgotten. A pathfinder in the Spanish or Mexican period often "opened" a route which had been well-traveled a few decades previously, as if the country had never before been visited by non-Indians. In the 1820s, American trappers thought they were the first white men ever to see the Gila River. As late as 1853, Lieutenant Williamson of the United States Army, while exploring in southern California in search of a railroad route, "discovered" the San Gorgonio Pass. Of the region, Williamson wrote: "Nothing is known of the country. I have never heard of a white man who penetrated it."[1] In fact, the region had been known and the pass used for many years.[2]

The same failure to build on the knowledge of successive generations of explorers is evidenced in mapmaking. Nineteenth-century American cartographers did not have access to the narratives of Spanish mapmakers and apparently did not consult their maps, if indeed they were available. The American Antiquarian Society, for example, published an 1836 map by Albert Gallatin which showed the Gila River and Colorado River flowing independently into the Gulf of California. Spaniards knew that the Gila flowed into the Colorado which then emptied into the gulf, and their maps showed it: Kino's of 1701; Venegas' of 1757; Font's of 1777, and others.[3] Unfortunately, Gallatin could not or did not consult any of the dozens of American trappers who by that time could have verified many of the details of the Spanish maps.

The greatest failure in the story of the southern route is in the tragic relationships between Indians and whites. Nowhere else in the present United States were Indians so

---

[1] Quoted in Bean, *Romero Expeditions,* xvi.

[2] There is rather persuasive evidence that the pass was used frequently during the 1820s, 1830s and 1840s. Romero definitely traveled over the pass in 1824-1825, and Pedro Fages probably crossed it as early as 1772. Indeed, Johnston's article, "San Gorgonio Pass," is an attempt to show, in his words, that "San Gorgonio Pass saw more settlement and use by travelers than has hitherto been believed" (p. 125).

[3] Gallatin's map is reproduced in Dale L. Morgan and Carl I. Wheat, *Jedediah Smith and his Maps of the American West* (San Francisco, 1954), facing p. 20. An excellent cartographic history of the United States Southwest is in Volumes I-III of Carl I. Wheat, *Mapping the Trans-Mississippi West* (5 vols.; San Francisco, 1957). Volume I describes and illustrates maps prepared by early Spanish explorers as well as fanciful – and delightful – maps drawn by Europeans who had never seen the region. The volume covers map-making for the period 1540-1804. The second volume, for the years 1804-1845, is especially interesting for maps of the Southwest by Pike, Jedediah Smith and Fremont. Volume III, covering the years 1846-1854, contains the output of a flurry of map-making, mostly of the Southwest, to which attention was focused at that time because of the Mexican War. Emory's map is included.

receptive, and in some cases, eager, for prolonged contact with whites, at least during the early Spanish period. The padres planted a seed that might have borne fruit. Whether the fruit would have grown bitter or sweet can only be speculative, for delay and betrayal gradually alienated the Indians and the ties were broken, or at the best, severely strained. By the time Mexico established its sovereignty, the estrangement was well-advanced.

Peace in northern Mexico was disrupted most often by the Apaches. The threat to travel was posed most often by that tribe. The Apaches seem not to have particularly disliked the Spanish. When they attacked Spanish towns or travelers, they were merely doing what they had done for generations. They lived by raiding. Whether they plundered a Pima village or a Sonoran mission seemed immaterial to them. By the second quarter of the nineteenth century, however, following the establishment of the Republic of Mexico, a new dimension of hate was added to the conflict as outrage was matched by outrage. No single event so enraged the Apaches as the treacherous killing of the Apache chieftain, Juan José.

Though Juan José's murderer was an American, the Americans nevertheless benefitted from this bitter enmity between Apache and Mexican. The repeated declarations of friendship for the Americans by Mangas Coloradas typifies the opportunity presented. Certainly, there were bands of Apaches other than those who adhered to Mangas and his policy of friendship and association with the Americans. In this relationship, nevertheless, there also was a seed that might have been cultivated.[4] That it was not is well-known.

---

[4] Mangas continued after 1847 to show his esteem for Americans. During the gold rush, when hundreds of argonauts were seen in Apache country, Mangas could still say, according to Benjamin Butler Harris, that he "loved Americans." Harris, *The Gila Trail*, 70. In the early 1850s, Mangas and his band often visited

The history of the southern route to California can never be told completely since there are no written Indian sources to consult. That void in the documentary record can never be filled by chance discoveries in dusty archives. There are no Indian journals, no diaries, no archives. What stories might have been told by chroniclers of the tribes that figured so much in the history of the trails: Yumas, Pimas, Maricopas, Cocomaricopas, Mojaves, Hopis, Apaches, Navajos! What insights might have come from the quills of Palma and Mangas!

Though there are no Indian written records, there are documents – Spanish, Mexican and American – from which one can glean glimpses of the Indians, the way they lived and their part in the development of the trails to California. Unfortunately, until recent years historians generally have been content to herald the feats of white explorers without adequately acknowledging that most of them had Indian guides most of the time.

It cannot be denied, nevertheless, that the generations of pathmakers in the Southwest left a rich legacy. Spaniards found the first overland route to California through the combined efforts of Kino, Garcés and Anza. Kino pioneered the trail as far as the Colorado River. Garcés crossed the

the camps of the United States boundary survey party where they strolled about with complete freedom. Bartlett and Mangas talked about Kearny, Cooke and the outcome of the war with Mexico. Bartlett often had Mangas and other Apache chiefs dine with him. "On these occasions," the commissioner wrote, "their conduct was marked with as much decorum as though they had been used to civilized society all their lives." Bartlett, *Personal Narrative*, I, pp. 300-2, 317-20.

Though he eventually turned hostile to the Americans, Mangas remained a man of honor. In 1863, the old chief, then about seventy years old, voluntarily entered a United States army camp under a white flag, expecting to talk peace. There he was captured, tortured, murdered, scalped, decapitated. The official report of his demise stated that he was taken in battle and was killed while attempting to escape. His death served, as his leadership already had served, to inspire Apache resistance for many years to follow.

river and the desert beyond. Anza, with the assistance of Garcés and Tarabal, made it across the mountains to the heartland of California. Though the trail was hard and dangerous, it did serve as a link between New Spain and Upper California. The road seems to have been most valuable as a communications link than otherwise, for neither Spain nor Mexico was able to use it to strengthen its position in California to any significant extent. Ironically, the greatest exodus from Mexico to California came neither in the Spanish period nor the Mexican, but shortly after the Americans took control of the province. Sonorans were among the earliest arrivals in the California gold fields.

The direct link between New Mexico and California, while long sought by Spanish explorers, was forged finally through the separate efforts of Mexicans, notably the Armijo expedition, and Americans, especially the Wolfskill party. The Old Spanish Trail served as a useful commercial route until it was superseded finally by Cooke's road.

The final chapter in the development of the southern overland route was written by a combination of mountain men, Mormons and soldiers. American trappers did not go into the wilderness for the purpose of pioneering roads, but they did get to know the country as they traveled between New Mexico and California almost at will. When the United States Army needed to reach California as quickly as possible, mountain men led the Army of the West over the trails they knew best.

General Kearny promptly found that a path that was quite satisfactory for trappers was certainly not a wagon road and was terribly hard on troopers. The principal effect of the Army of the West's ordeal indeed was in demonstrating to future southwestern travelers that the path paralleling the Gila River from its headwaters to the Pima

villages was to be avoided. If there ever was a "Gila Trail,"
this was the biggest part of it, and when the last dusty strag-
gler of the Army of the West entered the oasis that was the
Pima vilages, that part of the trail was little used again.

It was Cooke's road, which skirted the Gila for most
of its length, that essentially completed the search for a
southern route. Graham's detour following the end of the
Mexican War was but a refinement. A long era which saw
northern Mexico opened and trails found through it to
California had ended.

Since the Cooke-Graham route became the most popular
road to California through the Southwest, some historians
eventually began to refer to it as "the" southwestern trail
to California. Argonauts and emigrants who used the road
either called it by no particular name or correctly labeled
it "Cooke's route" or "Cooke's wagon road" or something
similar. Some western historians found these names unsatis-
factory and began titling Cooke's route the "Gila Trail."
Confusion was added when other writers applied the term
"Gila Trail" to routes other than Cooke's road. The mis-
nomer became the myth of the Gila Trail – that there was
a single southwestern trail to California by that name.

By sheer coincidence, the year that saw the completion of
the first all-season wagon road from the United States to the
west coast, 1848, also witnessed the event that would send
tens of thousands of emigrants to California. It seemed as if
the pathmakers from Kino to Graham had been building
toward this moment. There were many ways to get to California during the gold rush, but the quickest, most practical
route that first winter of 1848-1849 appeared to be through
northern Mexico. The most impatient argonauts hurried to
Texas and Mexico to head west for El Dorado. The padres,
explorers, trappers and soldiers had pointed the way and

mapped the trails for the Forty-Niners. The adventures of this army of single-minded individuals is another story.[5]

Following the California gold discovery, there was a transportation boom of sorts in the Southwest. The Cooke-Graham route was improved. Surveys were made and new roads opened. Stagecoach travel was inaugurated, and the Butterfield Overland Mail ran a scheduled passenger and mail service to California. The Gadsden Purchase in 1853 acquired sufficient land from Mexico to plan for a south-western railroad to California, thereby avoiding both the Rocky Mountains and the Sierra Nevada. A flurry of rail-road building in the 1870s and 1880s and the completion of a line that spanned the Southwest signalled the end of the long haul by wagon over the old trails. But more roads to California were built, some of steel, some of concrete, and travel over the southern route continued unabated. Though the long haul by wagon ended, the lure of that golden land did not die with the trails.

---

[5] For an account of the gold rush over the southern route, *see* Ferol Egan, *The El Dorado Trail*.

Bibliography
and Index

Bibliography

A. Diaries and Other Personal Documents

This listing includes the principal diaries and other personal documents that were consulted for this study. Some of the items are books. Others are articles from scholarly journals, and some are articles from published collections of documents. In the last case, especially when more than one article was used from the same publication, it appeared desirable to list the collection by editor and then to cross-reference from the diarist's name to that of the editor. For example, to locate a diary written by Anza, the reader is referred to a publication edited by Bolton which includes the Anza journal. Annotations are added to a few listings to further identify them or to distinguish them from other similar publications.

Abert, James W. *Western America in 1846-1847: The Original Travel Diary of Lieutenant J. W. Abert.* Ed. by John Galvin. San Francisco: John Howell-Books, 1966.

Anza, Juan Bautista de. *See* Bolton, *Anza's California Expeditions,* section B, below.

Armijo, Antonio. "Armijo's New Mexico-California Diary, 1829-1830." *Southwest on the Turquoise Trail.* Overland to the Pacific Series. Vol. ii. Ed. by Archer Butler Hulbert. Denver: The Stewart Commission of Colorado College and the Denver Public Library, 1933.

Bartlett, John Russell. *Personal Narrative of Explorations and Incidents in Texas, New Mexico, California, Sonora and Chihuahua, Connected with the United States and Mexican Boundary Commission, during the Years 1850, '51, '52, '53.* 2 vols. New York: D. Appleton & Co., 1854.

Bigler, Henry W. "Extracts from the Journal of Henry W. Bigler." Ed. by Adelbert Bigler. *Utah Hist. Qtly.,* v (April 1932), 35-64.

Bliss, Robert S. "The Journal of Robert S. Bliss, with the Mormon Battalion." *Utah Hist. Qtly.,* iv (July 1931), 67-96.

Carson, Christopher. *Kit Carson's Autobiography.* Ed. by Milo Milton Quaife. Lincoln: University of Nebraska Press, n.d. A reprint of the original edition, Chicago, 1935.

——. *Kit Carson's Own Story of His Life.* Ed. by Blanche C. Grant. Taos: privately published, 1926. The book is reportedly based on Carson's own dictation.

——. *See* Camp, "Kit Carson in California," section B.

Castañeda, Pedro de. *See* Hammond and Rey, *Narratives of the Coronado Expedition 1540-1542,* section B.

Chamberlain, Samuel Emery. *My Confession.* Edited by Roger Butterfield. New York: Harper and Brothers, 1956.

Cooke, Philip St. George. *The Conquest of New Mexico and California.* Oakland: Biobooks, 1952.

A reprint of the original publication, 1878. This account of Cooke's southwestern experiences is not as detailed as his earlier accounts, but is more personal.

——. "Cooke's Journal of the March of the Mormon Battalion, 1846-1847." *Exploring Southwestern Trails 1846-1854.* Ed. by Ralph P. Bieber in collaboration with Averam B. Bender. Glendale: The Arthur H. Clark Co., 1938.

The editors used the original manuscript copy of Cooke's journal. The journal was originally published as S. Ex. Doc. No. 2, 31st Cong., Spec. sess. (1849). The government publication, however, is not considered an accurate reproduction of the original journal.

——. "Report of Lieut. Col. P. St. George Cooke of His March From Santa Fé, New Mexico, to San Diego, Upper California." Ed. by Hamilton Gardner. *Utah Hist. Qtly.,* XXII (Jan. 1954), 14-40.

A reprint of the government document of the same name originally published as H.R. Doc. No. 41, Serial 517, 30th Cong., 1st Sess. (1848). Cooke's "Report" and his "Journal" (see above) are not the same document. The "Journal" was maintained by Cooke as a daily record during the march. He prepared the "Report," a resume rather than a daily record, for submission to General Kearny in San Diego at the end of the march.

——. *Scenes and Adventures in the Army: or Romance of Military Life.* Philadelphia: Lindsay and Blakiston, 1857.

Coronado, Francisco Vázquez. *See* Hammond and Rey, *Narratives of the Coronado Expedition 1540-1542,* section B.

Couts, Cave Johnson. *Hepah California! The Journal of Cave Johnson Couts from Monterey, Nuevo Leon, Mexico, to Los Angeles, California, during the Years 1848-1849.* Ed. by Henry F. Dobyns. Tucson: Arizona Pioneers' Hist. Soc., 1961.

Díaz, Juan. *See* Bolton, *Anza's California Expeditions,* section B.

Dye, Job Francis. *Recollections of a Pioneer, 1830-1852: Rocky Mountains, New Mexico, California.* Los Angeles: Glen Dawson, 1951.

Edwards, Marcellus Ball. "Journal of Marcellus Ball Edwards, 1846-1847." *See* Bieber, *Marching with the Army of the West,* section B.

Eixarch, Tomás. *See* Bolton, *Anza's California Expeditions,* section B.

Emory, William H. *Notes of a Military Reconnoissance from Fort Leavenworth, in Missouri, to San Diego, in California, including parts of the Arkansas, Del Norte, and Gila Rivers.* H.R. Doc. No. 41, 30th Cong., 1st Sess. (1848).

This edition transmitted Emory's journal to the House of Representatives. Another, S. Ex. Doc. No. 7, 30th Cong., 1st Sess. (1848), transmitted the journal to the Senate. The latter edition includes Emory's large fold-out map which traces the routes of both the Army of the West and the Mormon Battalion.

Escobar, Francisco de. "Father Escobar's Relation of the Oñate Expedition to California." Ed. by Herbert Eugene Bolton. *The Catholic Hist. Rev.,* v (April 1919), 19-41.

Fages, Pedro. "The Colorado River Campaign, 1781-1782; The Diary of Pedro Fages." Ed. by Herbert Ingram Priestley. *Acad. of Pac. Coast Hist.,* III (May 1913), 133-233.

Ferguson, Philip Gooch. "Diary of Philip Gooch Ferguson, 1847-1848." *See* Bieber, *Marching with the Army of the West,* section B.

Font, Pedro. *See* Bolton, *Anza's California Expeditions,* section B.

Foster, Stephen C. "A Sketch of Some of the Earliest Kentucky Pioneers of Los Angeles." *Hist. Soc. of So. Cal. Ann.* (1887), 30-35.

Garcés, Francisco Tomás. *On the Trail of a Spanish Pioneer: The Diary and Itinerary of Francisco Garcés.* Ed. by Elliott Coues. 2 vols. New York: Francis P. Harper, 1900.

———. *A Record of Travels in Arizona and California, 1775-1776.* Ed. by John Galvin. San Francisco: John Howell-Books, 1967.

———. *See* Bolton, *Anza's California Expeditions,* section B.

Gibson, George Rutledge. *Journal of a Soldier under Kearny and Doniphan: 1846-1847.* Ed. by Ralph P. Bieber. The Southwest Hist. Ser., III. Glendale: The Arthur H. Clark Co., 1935.

Gregg, Josiah. *Commerce of the Prairies.* Ed. by Max L. Moorhead. Norman: Univ. of Ok. Press, 1954.

Griffin, John S. *A Doctor Comes to California: The Diary of John S. Griffin, Assistant Surgeon with Kearny's Dragoons, 1846-1847.* Intro. and notes by George Walcott Ames, Jr. and foreword by George D. Lyman. San Francisco: Cal. Hist. Soc., 1943.

Harris, Benjamin Butler. *The Gila Trail: The Texas Argonauts and the California Gold Rush.* Ed. by Richard H. Dillon. Norman: Univ. of Ok. Press, 1960.

Hess, John W. "John W. Hess, With the Mormon Battalion." Ed. by Wanda Wood. *Utah Hist. Qtly.,* IV (April 1931), 47-55.

Hughes, John T. *Doniphan's Expedition; Containing an Account of the Conquest of New Mexico; General Kearney's Overland Expedition to California; Doniphan's Campaign against the Navajos; His Unparalleled March upon Chihuahua and Durango; and the Operations of General Price at Santa Fé: With a Sketch of the Life of Col. Doniphan.* Cincinnati: J. A. & U. P. James, 1849.

Originally published in 1847 by the same company, it was later issued as S. Doc. No. 608, 63d Cong., 2d Sess. (1914).

Jaramillo, Juan. *See* Hammond and Rey, *Narratives of the Coronado Expedition 1540-1542,* section B.

Johnston, Abraham Robinson. "Journal of Abraham Robinson Johnston, 1846." *See* Bieber, *Marching with the Army of the West,* section B.

Jones, Nathaniel V. "The Journal of Nathaniel V. Jones, with the Mormon Battalion." *Utah Hist. Qtly.,* IV (Jan. 1931), 6-24.

———. *See* Jones, "Extracts from the Life Sketch of Nathaniel V. Jones," section B.

Kino, Eusebio Francisco. *Father Kino in Arizona.* Ed. by Fay Jackson Smith, John L. Kessell and Francis J. Fox. Phoenix: Arizona Hist. Assoc. 1966. Kino's 1698 journal.

———. *Kino's Historical Memoir of Pimería Alta.* Trans. and ed. by Herbert Eugene Bolton. 2 vols. Berkeley: University of California Press, 1948. Original edition, Cleveland: The Arthur H. Clark Co., 1919.

————. *Kino's Plan for the Development of Primería Alta, Arizona and Upper California.* Translated and annotated by Ernest J. Burrus. Tucson: Arizona Pioneers' Hist. Soc., 1961.

Lafora, Nicolás de. *The Frontiers of New Spain: Nicolás de Lafora's Description 1766-1768.* Ed. by Lawrence Kinnaird. Quivira Soc. Pubs., XIII. Berkeley: The Quivira Society, 1958.

Layton, Christopher. *Autobiography of Christopher Layton.* Ed. by John Q. Cannon. Salt Lake City: The Deseret News, 1911.

Magoffin, Susan Shelby. *Down the Santa Fé Trail and into Mexico: The Diary of Susan Shelby Magoffin, 1846-1847.* Ed. by Stella M. Drumm. New Haven: Yale University Press, 1962.

Marcos de Niza. *Discovery of the Seven Cities of Cibola.* Trans. and ed. by Percy M. Baldwin. Pub. in History, I. Albuquerque: Hist. Soc. of N.M., 1926.
    A translation of Marcos de Niza's Relación, telling about his journey and the report which he made to his superiors upon his return.

————. *See* Nuñez Cabeza de Vaca, *Journey,* as follows:

Nuñez Cabeza de Vaca, Alvar. *The Journey of Alvar Nuñez Cabeza de Vaca and His Companions from Florida to the Pacific, 1528-1536.* Trans. by Fanny Bandelier and ed. by A. F. Bandelier. New York: A. S. Barnes & Company, 1905. Includes the report of Marcos de Niza and a letter from Viceroy Mendoza.

Pattie, James Ohio. *Pattie's Personal Narrative of a Voyage to the Pacific and in Mexico: June 20, 1824-August 30, 1830.* Ed. by Reuben Gold Thwaites. *Early Western Travels Series,* XVIII. Cleveland: The Arthur H. Clark Co., 1905.
    A reprint of the original edition of Pattie's journal which was edited by Timothy Flint, Cincinnati, 1831.

Pérez de Luxán, Diego. *Expedition into New Mexico by Antonio de Espejo, 1528-1583.* Trans., with an intro. and notes by George Peter Hammond and Agapito Rey. Los Angeles: The Quivira Society, 1929. Pérez de Luxán was a member of the Espejo party.

Romero, José. *See* Bean and Mason, *Diaries and Accounts of the Romero Expeditions in Arizona and California 1823-1826,* section B.

Salmerón, Zárate. *Relaciones.* Trans. by Alicia Ronstadt Milich. Albuquerque: Horn and Wallace, Pubs., 1966.

Sedelmayr, Jacobo. *Jacobo Sedelmayr.* Trans. and annot. by Peter Masten Dunne. Tucson: Arizona Pioneers' Hist. Soc., 1955.
Four original manuscript narratives covering the years 1744-1751.

Simpson, James H. *Navaho Expedition: Journal of a Military Reconnaissance from Santa Fe, New Mexico, to the Navaho Country . . . in 1849.* Ed. by Frank McNitt. Norman: Univ. of Ok. Press, 1964.

Smith, Jedediah S. *The Southwest Expedition of Jedediah S. Smith: his personal account of the journey to California, 1826-1827.* Ed. and Intro. by George R. Brooks. Glendale, Ca: The Arthur H. Clark Co., 1977.

Standage, Henry. "Journal of Henry Standage." *The March of the Mormon Battalion from Council Bluffs to California.* Ed. by Frank Alfred Golder in collaboration with Thomas A. Bailey and J. Lyman Smith. N.Y: The Century Co., 1928.

Steele, John, "Extracts from the Journal of John Steele." *Utah Hist. Qtly.,* vi (Jan. 1933), 3-28.

Turner, Henry Smith. *The Original Journals of Henry Smith Turner: With Stephen Watts Kearny to New Mexico and California 1846-1847.* Ed., with an Intro. by Dwight L. Clarke. Norman: Univ. of Ok. Press, 1966.

Tyler, Daniel. *A Concise History of the Mormon Battalion in the Mexican War, 1846-1847.* Salt Lake City: n.p., 1881. Tyler was a volunteer in the Mormon Battalion.

Vélez de Escalante, Silvestre. *Pageant in the Wilderness.* Trans. and annot. by Herbert Eugene Bolton. Salt Lake City: Utah State Hist. Soc., 1960.
Escalante's journal of his 1776 expedition into the Great Basin.

Warner, J.J. "Reminiscences of Early California from 1831 to 1846." *Ann. Pub. of the Hist. Soc. of So. Cal.,* vol. vii, parts ii-iii (1907-1908), 176-93.

Whitworth, Robert W. "From the Mississippi to the Pacific: An Englishman in the Mormon Battalion." Ed. by David B. Gracy ii and Helen J. H. Rugeley. *Arizona and the West,* vii (Summer 1965), 127-60.

Williams, Isaac. "The Record Book of the Rancho Santa Ana del Chino." Ed. by Lyndley Bynum. *Hist. Soc. of So. Cal. Ann.,* xvi (1934), 1-55.

Wilson, Benjamin David. "Benjamin David Wilson's Observations on Early Days in California and New Mexico." Foreword by Arthur Woodward. *Hist. Soc. of So. Cal. Ann.,* xvi (1934), 74-150.

Yount, George C. *See* Camp, "The Chronicles of Yount," section B.

B. SECONDARY SOURCES

Bancroft, Hubert Howe. *History of Arizona and New Mexico, 1530-1888.* Vol. XVII of *The Works of Hubert Howe Bancroft.* 39 vols. San Francisco: A. L. Bancroft and Co. and The History Co., Pubs., 1882-1890.

Bandelier, Adolph P. *Contributions to the History of the Southwestern Portion of the United States.* Papers of Archaeol. Inst. of America, American Series, v. Cambridge: John Wilson and Son, 1890.

Bean, Lowell John, and Mason, William Marvin, eds. *Diaries and Accounts of the Romero Expeditions in Arizona and California 1823-1826.* Palm Springs: Palm Springs Desert Mus., 1962.

Beattie, George William. "Development of Travel between Southern Arizona and Los Angeles as it Related to the San Bernardino Valley." *Hist. Soc. of So. Cal. Ann.,* VII (1925), 228-57.

––––––. "Reopening the Anza Road." *Pac. Hist. Rev.,* II (March 1933), 52-71.

Beck, Warren A. *New Mexico: A History of Four Centuries.* Norman: Univ. of Ok., Press, 1962.

Benton, Thomas Hart. *Thirty Years' View; A History of the Working of the American Government for Thirty Years, From 1820 to 1850.* N.Y: D. Appleton and Co., 1856.

Bieber, Ralph P., ed. *Marching with the Army of the West.* Vol. IV of Southwest Hist. Ser. Glendale: The Arthur H. Clark Co., 1936.

––––––, and Bender, Averam, eds. *Exploring Southwestern Trails.* Vol. VII of Southwest Hist. Ser. Glendale: The Arthur H. Clark Co., 1938.

Bolton, Herbert Eugene. *Anza's California Expeditions.* 5 vols. Berkeley: Univ. of Cal. Press, 1930. This publication is frequently cited in the present work. The contents of the five volumes are:
Vol. I: *An Outpost of Empire.* Bolton's narrative of Anza's two expeditions.
Vol. II: *Opening a Land Route to California.*
Anza's Complete Diary, 1774; Anza's Diary from Tubac to San Gabriel, 1774; Anza's Return Diary, 1774; Díaz's Diary from Tubac to San Gabriel, 1774; Díaz's Return Diary, 1774; Garcés's Diary from Tubac to San Gabriel, 1774; Garcés's Brief Account, 1774; Garcés's Diary of His Detour to the Jalchedunes, 1774; Palóu's Diary of the Expedition to San Francisco Bay, 1774.

Bolton. *Anza's Expeditions* (contin.)

Vol. III: *The San Francisco Colony.*

Anza's Diary of the Second Anza Expedition, 1775-1776; Font's Short Diary of the Second Anza Expedition, 1775-1776; Eixarch's Diary of His Winter on the Colorado, 1775-1776; Palóu's Account of the Founding of San Francisco, 1776; Moraga's Account of the Founding of San Francisco, 1776.

Vol. IV: *Font's Complete Diary.* Font's more detailed diary of the second Anza expedition.

Vol. V: *Correspondence.* Letters, memoranda and reports concerning the two Anza expeditions.

————. *Coronado on the Turquoise Trail.* Vol. I of Coronado Cuarto Centennial Pubs., 1540-1940. Ed. by George P. Hammond. Albuquerque: Univ. of N.M. Press, 1949.

An account of the origin, course and conclusion of Coronado's expedition, this work complements Hammond and Rey's *Narratives of the Coronado Expedition, 1540-1542,* Vol. II of the same series.

————. "The Early Explorations of Father Garcés on the Pacific Slope." *The Pacific Ocean in History.* Ed. by H. Morse Stephens and Herbert Eugene Bolton. N.Y: The Macmillan Co., 1917.

————. *Rim of Christendom: A Biography of Eusebio Francisco Kino, Pacific Coast Pioneer.* N.Y: The Macmillan Co., 1936.

————, ed. *Spanish Exploration in the Southwest, 1542-1706.* A volume in the Original Narratives of Early American History series, reproduced under the auspices of the Am. Hist. Assoc., J. Franklin Jameson, Gen. Ed. N.Y: Charles Scribner's Sons, 1925.

Brandon, William. *The American Heritage Book of Indians.* Editor in charge, Alvin M. Josephy, Jr. New York: American Heritage Publishing Co., Inc., 1961.

Burrus, Ernest J. *Kino and the Cartography of Northwestern New Spain.* Tucson: Arizona Pioneers' Hist. Soc., 1965.

Calvin, Ross. *Sky Determines: An Interpretation of the Southwest.* Rev. ed. Albuquerque: Univ. of N.M. Press, 1965.

Camp, Charles L. "The Chronicles of George C. Yount." *Cal. Hist. Soc. Qtly.,* II (April 1923), 3-66.

————. "Kit Carson in California." *Cal. Hist. Soc. Qtly.,* I (Oct. 1922), 111-51.

Chittenden, Hiram Martin. *The American Fur Trade of the Far West*. Intro. and notes by Stallo Vinton. 2 vols. N.Y: The Press of the Pioneers, Inc., 1935.

Christiansen, Paige W. "The Presidio and the Borderlands: A Case Study." *Jl. of the West,* VIII (Jan. 1969), 29-37.

Cleland, Robert Glass. *This Reckless Breed of Men: the trappers and fur traders of the Southwest.* N.Y: Alfred A. Knopf, 1950.

Connelley, William Elsey. *Doniphan's Expedition and the Conquest of New Mexico and California*. Kansas City, Mo: Bryant and Douglas Book and Stationery Co., 1907.

Dunne, Peter Masten. "The Expulsion of the Jesuits from New Spain, 1767." *Mid-America,* XIX (Jan. 1937), 3-30.

Egan, Ferol. *The El Dorado Trail: The Story of the Gold Rush Routes across Mexico.* New York: McGraw-Hill Book Co., 1971.

Forbes, Jack D. "Development of the Yuma Route before 1846." *Cal. Hist. Soc. Qtly.,* XLIII (June 1964), 99-118.

Goetzmann, William H. *Exploration and Empire: The Explorer and the Scientist in the Winning of the American West.* N.Y: Alfred A. Knopf, 1966.

Hafen, LeRoy R., ed. *The Mountain Men and the Fur Trade of the Far West: Biographical Sketches of the Participants by Scholars of the Subjects.* 10 vols. Glendale: The Arthur H. Clark Co., 1965-1972.

————, and Hafen, Ann W. *Old Spanish Trail: Santa Fé to Los Angeles.* Vol. I of The Far West and the Rockies Hist. Ser. Glendale: The Arthur H. Clark Co., 1954.
    The volume includes extracts from contemporary records, including diaries of Antonio Armijo and others.

Hallenbeck, Cleve. *The Journey and Route of Alvar Nuñez, Cabeza de Vaca; The Journey and Route of the First European to Cross the Continent of North America, 1534-1536.* Glendale: The Arthur H. Clark Co., 1940.
    The author used the Bandelier translation of Nuñez's narrative in preparing this volume.

Hammond, George P., and Rey, Agapito. *Narratives of the Coronado Expedition, 1540-1542.* Vol. II of Coronado Cuarto Centennial Pubs., 1540-1940. Ed. by George P. Hammond. Albuquerque: Univ. of N.M. Press, 1940.

Hill, Joseph J."Ewing Young in the Fur Trade of the Far Southwest, 1822-1834." *Ore. Hist. Soc. Qtly.,* XXIV (March 1923), 1-35.

————. *The History of Warner's Ranch and Its Environs.* Los Angeles: privately printed, 1927.

————. "New Light on Pattie and the Southwestern Fur Trade." *Southwestern Hist. Qtly.,* XXVI (April 1923), 243-54.

Hodge, Frederick W., and Lewis, Theodore H., eds. *Spanish Explorers in the Southern United States, 1528-1543.* A volume in the Original Narratives of Early American History series, reproduced under the auspices of the Am. Hist. Assoc., J. Franklin Jameson, Gen. Ed. N.Y: Charles Scribner's Sons, 1907.

Hollon, W. Eugene. *The Southwest: Old and New.* N.Y: Alfred A. Knopf, 1961.

Johnston, Francis J. "San Gorgonio Pass: Forgotten Route of the Californios?" *Jl. of the West,* VIII (Jan. 1969), 125-36.

Jones, Rebecca M. "Extracts from the Life Sketch of Nathaniel V. Jones." *Utah Hist. Qtly.,* IV (Jan. 1931), 3-6.

Kroeber, Clifton B., ed. "The Route of James O. Pattie on the Colorado in 1826: A Reappraisal by A. L. Kroeber." *Arizona and the West,* VI (Summer 1964), 110-36.

Lawrence, Eleanor. "Mexican Trade between Santa Fé and Los Angeles, 1830-1848." *Cal. Hist. Soc. Qtly.,* X (March 1931), 27-39.

Linn, Alan. "Corn, the New World's Secret Weapon and the Builder of Its Civilizations." *Smithsonian,* IV (Aug. 1973), 58-65.

Maloney, Alice B. "The Richard Campbell Party of 1827." *Cal. Hist. Soc. Qtly.,* XVIII (Dec. 1939), 347-54.

Marshall, Thomas M. "St. Vrain's Expedition to the Gila in 1826." *The Pacific Ocean in History.* Ed. by H. Morse Stephens and Herbert Eugene Bolton. N.Y: The Macmillan Co., 1917.

Mitchell, Virgil L. "California and the Transformation of the Mountain Men." *Jl. of the West,* IX (July 1970), 413-26.

Morgan, Dale L. *Jedediah Smith and the Opening of the West.* Lincoln: Univ. of Neb. Press, 1964.

————, and Wheat, Carl I. *Jedediah Smith and His Maps of the American West.* San Francisco: Cal. Hist. Soc., 1954.

Roberts, Brigham Henry. *The Mormon Battalion: Its History and Achievements.* Salt Lake City: The Deseret News, 1919.

Simpson, Lesley Byrd. *Many Mexicos.* 4th ed. Berkeley: Univ. of Cal. Press, 1967.

Spicer, Edward H. *Cycles of Conquest: The Impact of Spain, Mexico, and the United States on the Indians of the Southwest, 1533-1960.* Tucson: The Univ. of Ariz. Press, 1962.

Thomas, Alfred Barnaby, ed. and trans. *Forgotten Frontiers: A Study of the Spanish Indian Policy of Don Juan Bautista de Anza, Governor of New Mexico, 1777-1787.* Norman: Univ. of Ok. Press, 1932.

Thrapp, Dan L. *The Conquest of Apacheria.* Norman: Univ. of Ok. Press, 1967.

Villagrá, Gaspar Pérez de. *History of New Mexico.* Trans. by Gilberto Espinosa. Intro. and notes by F. W. Hodge. Vol. iv of Quivira Society Pubs. Los Angeles: The Quivira Soc., 1933.

Weber, David J. "Mexico and the Mountain Men, 1821-1828." *Jl. of the West,* viii (July 1969), 368-78.

————. *The Taos Trappers: The Fur Trade in the Far Southwest, 1540-1846.* Norman: Univ. of Ok. Press, 1971.

Wheat, Carl I. *Mapping the Transmississippi West.* 5 vols. San Francisco: The Inst. of Hist. Cartography, 1957.

Wilson, Iris Higbie. *William Wolfskill, 1798-1866: Frontier Trapper to California Ranchero.* Glendale, Ca: The Arthur H. Clark Co., 1965.

Wood, Raymond F. "Francisco Garcés, Explorer of Southern California." *So. Cal. Qtly.,* li (Sept. 1969), 185-209.

Young, Otis E. *The West of Philip St. George Cooke, 1809-1895.* Glendale: The Arthur H. Clark Co., 1955.

Index

Compiled by Anna Marie and Everett Gordon Hager